# DARWIN, DIVINITY, AND

# THE DANCE OF THE COSMOS

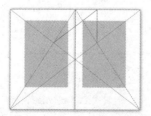
DEPICTION OF THE PROPORTIONS IN THIS BOOK, WHICH HAS BEEN DESIGNED ACCORDING TO THE GOLDEN RATIO.

# DARWIN, DIVINITY, AND THE DANCE OF THE COSMOS

## AN ECOLOGICAL CHRISTIANITY

## BRUCE SANGUIN

CopperHouse

**Permissions:**
Quotations from the Bible are from the New Revised Standard Version of the Bible, copyright 1989 by the Division of Christian Education of the National Council of Churches of Christ in the USA, all rights reserved, used by permission.

The poem "I Was Fashioned in Times Past, in the Beginning," by Susan McCaslin, copyright © Susan McCaslin, used by permission of the author.

Untitled poem by Jere Pramuk (Chapter 1), copyright © Jere Pramuk, used by permission of the author.

Three diagrams from Richard Tarnas, *Cosmos and Psyche: Intimations of a New World View*, New York: Viking, 2006, copyright © Richard Tarnas. Used by permission of the author.

100%
POST-CONSUMER
ANCIENT FOREST
**FRIENDLY** RECYCLED PAPER

Published by CopperHouse
 An imprint of
 Wood Lake Publishing Inc.
9590 Jim Bailey Road,
Kelowna, BC, Canada, V4V 1R2
www.woodlakebooks.com
250.766.2778

Printing 10 9 8 7 6 5 4 3 2
Printed in Canada by
Houghton Boston,
Saskatoon, SK

Editor: Mike Schwartzentruber
Cover and interior design: Verena Velten
Cover photos: © Covey Hochachka / maXx images (front)
                    © Rich Phalin / iStockphoto (spine)
                    © Cameron Mackie / iStockphoto (back)
Proofreader: Dianne Greenslade

CopperHouse is an imprint of Wood Lake Publishing, Inc. Wood Lake Publishing acknowledges the financial support of the Government of Canada, through the Book Publishing Industry Development Program (BPIDP) for its publishing activities. Wood Lake Publishing also acknowledges the financial support of the Province of British Columbia through the Book Publishing Tax Credit.

BNC CERTIFIED | BIBLIOGRAPHIC DATA 2006-07

At Wood Lake Publishing, we practise what we publish, being guided by a concern for fairness, justice, and equal opportunity in all of our relationships with employees and customers. Wood Lake Publishing is an employee-owned company, committed to caring for the environment and all creation. Wood Lake Publishing recycles, reuses, and encourages readers to do the same.
Resources are printed on 100% post-consumer recycled paper and more environmentally friendly groundwood papers (newsprint), whenever possible. A percentage of all profit is donated to charitable organizations.

**Library and Archives Canada Cataloguing in Publication**
Sanguin, Bruce, 1955-
Darwin, divinity, and the dance of the cosmos : an ecological Christianity / Bruce Sanguin.

Includes bibliographical references and index.
ISBN 978-1-55145-545-7

1. Human ecology–Religious aspects–Christianity.
2. Environmental protection–Religious aspects–Christianity.
3. Religion and science.
I. Title.
BT695.5.S24 2007          215          C2007-900485-7

## Dedication

For my father, Gord,
who modelled sustainability before we had a word for it.

# TABLE OF CONTENTS

# GRATITUDES

Reading books has been a staple of my spiritual diet over the last 25 years. Writing them, on the other hand, is new for me. It is a mysterious process. You begin with some scattered thoughts, which have accumulated over the years, and hope that they will be so kind as to assemble themselves into some kind of coherent whole. It's more like witnessing their homecoming than riding herd on them. If I was asked to prove the existence of a hidden wholeness at play in the universe, I would present as evidence a book, any book. I am grateful for the opportunity to have partnered with this Mystery.

It also happens to be more work than I could have imagined. I am graced by friends who lightened the load. Each gave their precious time to read and comment on various drafts of the book. Mary Bartram, my brilliant stepdaughter, took time out from parenting three young children to provide a much-needed perspective from outside the Christian faith. Maureen Jack-Lacroix, earth priestess and founder of Earth Revival, consistently refused to allow me the indulgence of self-diminishment. Susan McCaslin, mystical poet and professor of English, showered this effort from the very start with deep spiritual and literary wisdom. Toni Pieroni, eco-psychologist and therapeutic guide, brought her clear mind and kind heart to the project. Carol Zhong, member of the congregation I serve, helped with the finicky bits of footnoting and bibliography.

I would also like to thank the people at Wood Lake Publishing, a band of unpretentious spiritual pilgrims, whose commitment to their publishing business is deeply personal. Their recognition of me as someone capable of conveying their mission to promote an emerging Christian faith is deeply humbling. The synergies that brought us together speak again of a Mystery at the heart of the universe biased toward meaning and purpose. I would particularly like to thank my editor, Mike Schwartzentruber, who skilfully and compassionately both supported and challenged me. Because of him, the book says more clearly what it is I felt called to say.

Thanks to Canadian Memorial United Church for their wisdom in recognizing this book as an expression of their mission to teach a progressive Christian faith. They have consistently welcomed an ecological interpretation of the sacred story of our faith during my tenure in this congregation.

Finally, I thank my wife, Ann, who, in her prescience, always thought I should write a book. She now knows to be very careful about what she encourages. Ann has suffered gracefully the compulsive focus such an enterprise demands. The book came to live, eat, drink, and sleep with us. Through it all, Ann graciously prepared a room and fresh-cut flowers for our unexpected guest. Thank you, my love.

# PROLOGUE

## Frogs and Our Future

Amphibians are the canary in the coal mine as far as ecological degradation goes. Their disappearance from the planet signals what might be in store for all life forms, including humans. Because their skin is highly permeable, and because they live part of their lives in water and part on land, they are often the first creatures to suffer the effects of compromised ecosystems. Thirty-two percent of the world's 5743 species of frogs are threatened, and 129 have gone extinct since 1980.[1]

Climate change, responsible for the growth of a deadly skin fungus, is the likely cause of their disappearance. J. Alan Pounds, of the Tropical Science Center's Monteverde Cloud Forest, focuses his research on the harlequin frog. Since 1980, almost two-thirds of the 110 species have become extinct. "Disease is the bullet that's killing the frogs," says Pounds. "But climate change is pulling the trigger. Global warming is wreaking havoc on amphibians, and soon will cause staggering losses of biodiversity."[2]

The Kihansi spray toad is a dwarf toad, with adults reaching no more than three-quarters of an inch (1.9 cm) long. It once flourished in a tiny bioregion of Tanzania, at the bottom of a waterfall. The spray from the gorge created a constant temperature and the humid conditions that allowed the mustard-coloured amphibian to thrive. Then the World Bank, along with several other international development agencies, funded a dam project to generate much-needed electricity for the region. A year into construction, an environmental review team noticed and reported the impact that water diversion was having on the toads. The report was ignored, the spray from the waterfall dried up, and the Kihansi spray toad's numbers collapsed. The toads enjoyed a brief resurgence after authorities put a system of sprinklers in place. But then the mysterious above-mentioned fungus decimated the population. As of July 2003, only 40 of these creatures remained.[3]

This same story is being repeated all over our planet, as other-than-human life forms have become mere afterthoughts to our way of life, their extinction merely the cost of doing business. As we colonize more and more of the earth, we are crowding out other life forms, and poisoning the land, air, and water as we go. A story of profound and frightening disconnection from the earth is being enacted globally. From the perspective of an ecological Christianity, species loss is a sacrilege of unspeakable proportions, a loss of a divine mode of presence. In *Beautiful Creatures*, Bruce Cockburn sings a lament for the disappearing animals. The refrain crescendos to a high-pitched, heartbreaking question: "Why?"

# INTRODUCTION

## Renewing Our Minds

As I write this, I glance out my front window upon a virtual Eden. I see a beautiful garden, green grass, flowers, and beyond this view, a glimpse of the ocean, and sails billowing in the wind. Yesterday, the beach was filled with sunbathers, swimmers, Frisbee throwers, and dogs playing fetch. It is a near-Wonderland and I love to see my beautiful city at play.

Only a few blocks from the beach a totem pole of the Burrard Nation towers above the homes. Human faces intermingle with those of the eagle, the wolf, the whale, the raven, and the turtle. It's difficult to discern where the human faces end and the other-than-human faces begin. There is a sense of one being flowing into the other, which we now know is an accurate reflection of reality. Yet the beautiful scene outside my window, and the flowing worldview carved into that totem pole, are threatened at every turn by a deep pathology.

In the last 300 years, during the age of scientific rationalism, human beings have stepped out of the flow of creation. We have extricated ourselves from the story of the life of the planet, and have assumed the position of outside observers, of beings who live *on* the earth, but who are not *of* it. We imagine ourselves to be "in here" looking out at the world "out there." This dualism has enabled us to imagine that the earth belongs to us, when the bio-spiritual truth is that in every way conceivable, we belong to the earth. If we imagine that the earth belongs to us, and if we experience it as separate from us, then it becomes possible to objectify and commodify the earth. It becomes possible to see a forest and think only in terms of linear feet of lumber. It becomes possible to look at an albino moose through the scope of a rifle and see not a sacred creature worthy of our awe but a pair of antlers to hang on a wall, a story to tell our buddies.

In March 2005, the United Nations released its Millennium Ecosystem Assessment. It's the most comprehensive account to date of the state of our ecosystems, compiled after consulting 1400 scientists from 95 countries. Among the findings: two-thirds of our ecosystems are seriously degraded; 90 percent of the world's fish stocks are depleted; and climate change is not something that is *coming*, it is already upon us. The United Nations' Intergovernmental Panel on Climate Change links patterns of rainfall, rising sea levels, forest fires, extreme weather conditions, and even availability of drinking water, with global warming.[1] As I write this, Japan has just announced that it plans to allow an annual whale hunt of two endangered species, the blue whale and the sperm whale, ignoring the voice of the international community. In his book *Waiting for the Macaws*, Terry Glavin predicts that future generations will remember our time as the age of extinction.[2]

Of course, we can hear all of this and hope for a quick technological fix. Or we can delude ourselves into believing that global warming is not happening, even as the ice cap melts, and the polar bears cannibalize each other as food grows more and more scarce.[3] In fact, we can do any number of things that avoid the corporate and personal changes we must make. But, as Freud once said, you can't get out of a problem with the same mind that got you into it. We need planetary minds for a planetary crisis. It is long past time that we step back into the flow of creation.

Over the last 15 years, I have followed with interest the dialogue between the new story of the universe given to us by the sciences of cosmology, biology, chaos theory, and quantum physics; and the Judeo-Christian narrative of the Bible. In the process, I have undergone a conversion of heart and mind, which has issued in both a deepening of my faith and a commitment to be a voice of the earth.

The biblical word for this kind of shift is *metanoia*, a complete reorientation of the heart and the mind. This book is my attempt to share what I have learned. It lays the foundations for this mindshift, away from a perspective that views the earth as a commodity, to a perspective that reveres the earth and all creation as a divine mode of presence. My hope is that it will help you to deepen your own commitment to the healing of the planet.

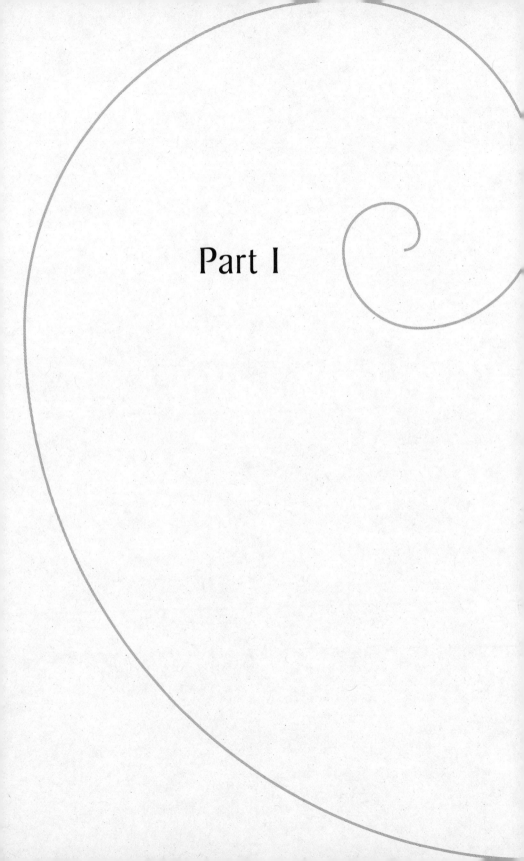

# Part I

# Chapter I

## COMING HOME TO THE COSMOS

Do not remember the former things, or consider things of old.
I am about to do a new thing; now it springs forth,
do you not perceive it?

ISAIAH 43:18–19

You cannot put new wines into old wineskins.

MARK 2:22

ॐ

## I. A Personal Account

Sometime between my second and final year of seminary I was
sent to Milton, Ontario, to do a year-long internship in ministry. On lunch break one day, eating an egg salad sandwich in the
Acorn Café, I read a poem. It was a deceptively simple poem. But
the moment I finished reading it, I was completely transported
into another realm. I don't recall finishing the sandwich. I don't
even remember paying my bill, although I must have because nobody chased after me. It was as though an invisible force lifted
me out of my chair and carried me down Main Street.

Everything happened in slow motion. A man sitting on the
porch in his rocking chair became a source of enormous delight
as I passed by. I do mean "passed by," for the strangest thing
about this experience was that I had no sense of moving my legs,
no sense of my feet touching the ground. Eventually, I ended up

in a farmer's field on the outskirts of town, at dusk, looking out at a field of wheat blowing gently in the wind. It was as though someone had peeled back a layer of reality to reveal the invisible radiance of what lay behind and within all creation. I was suffused with love and overwhelmed by the beauty of what lay before my eyes. My prayer was simple. "God, don't let this end. Let me have it for just a few minutes longer." Ironically, the prayer itself broke the spell.

Here's the poem, which is by Jere Pramuk.[1]

This sunset...
This smile...
This word you are writing...
This pain you are feeling...
The question you are asking...
This omelette you are cooking...

The meaning of life
is the tear of joy
shed at the
sight of
the
well-cooked omelette.

The last line was the kicker for me. I'd been a meaning-freak for years, constantly asking questions like, What is the meaning of life? What am I doing? Where am I going?

The experience that began in the Acorn Café has been foundational for my spirituality. Ever since that moment, whenever I become obsessed with trying to discover the meaning of life in a purely intellectual way, I think of the well-cooked omelette. I open my eyes to the radiant miracle of life. On good days, my intellectual curiosity is supplemented by a condition the mystics call *awe*.

Isaiah, the Jewish prophet, had his own mystical experience "in the year King Uzziah died." A curtain was pulled back on ordinary reality, which causes him to boldly proclaim, "I saw the Lord" (Isaiah 6:1). And then this: "Holy, holy, holy is the Lord of hosts; the whole earth is full of your glory."

It's interesting that although Isaiah finds himself in the presence of angels and seraphs (one order higher than angels according to Dionysius the Areopagite), it's the *whole earth* that he experiences as being "full of God's glory." (In a similar way, in movies such as *Michael* and *City of Angels* the angels always want the assignment that takes them to earth, because they miss sensuality; they miss the sheer pleasure of physicality, and the beauty of the planet.) In any case, in the biblical story, Isaiah is apprehended by awe.

I'm not certain that I saw "the Lord" that day in the Milton wheat field, but I came as close to whatever we mean by *divine* as I had ever come. I suspect the reason the experience came to an end was because I didn't have the capacity to sustain it. No one, the Bible claims, can see the face of God and live (Exodus 33:20). Moses, however, was prepared to take his chances. "Show me your glory," he demands of God. Instead, God places him in a cleft of a rock, and covers him with a divine hand. Moses is allowed to see only God's back. Most of us must settle for glimpses of glory. The biblical tradition affirms that a direct hit would be like looking at the sun without any eye protection. It would fry our eyes in seconds, and scramble our nervous system. If the poem I read expressed any truth at all, it was this: if we could truly see what is before our eyes, day in and day out, the sacred radiance of creation would drop us to our knees and render us speechless. We would know ourselves to be in as much divine presence as we can handle in this earthly realm.

## Awakening

Ten years after my experience in the Acorn Café and wheat field in Milton, my wife, Ann, and I travelled to Narragansett, Rhode Island, for a week-long silent retreat. One afternoon I noticed on the bookshelf a slim volume entitled *The Universe Is a Green Dragon*, by Brian Swimme, a mathematical physicist and cosmologist. Reading the book proved every bit as powerful an experience as my conversion to the Christian faith. Swimme never mentioned God or Spirit. Rather, he talked about the "heart" of the universe, and about what the universe is doing. He wrote about how the universe had taken 14 billion years to arrive at the human being. Through us, the universe had become conscious of itself. I "got it" that I was the universe in human form. I was what the planet was doing, on retreat, in Rhode Island. My identity consisted not so much in being a creature living *on* the earth, but in being a creature *of* the earth. I was a centre of earth consciousness, a particular form of the earth called Bruce.

Brian Swimme's telling of the story was like a sacred initiation into a cosmos I had been living in, but as an alien. I felt like an adopted child who had only now discovered his biological parents as an adult. I discovered that I had cosmological brothers and sisters, and grandparents I never knew. Pieces of my life started to fit together. I discovered things about myself I should have known, but didn't. The earth was my mother, the sun my father. My grandparent was a supernova. We all came from an originating fire; and from a Holy Communion sharing an over-flowing divine abundance from behind, within, above, and below this fire. Our living, in all its dimensions, takes place in the context of the family of the cosmos.

How strange that I didn't know this story of the developing universe as my own. I knew bits of it as told in biology, astronomy, and chemistry classes. But my teachers told it to me as empirical science, not as a sacred story. My education was not an initiation into the mysteries of my cosmic family. It was more like a barrage of isolated facts that I had to learn to pass a test. Walt Whitman captures this experience in his poem *Leaves of Grass*.[2]

> When I hear the learn'd astronomer,
> When the proofs, the figures, were ranged in columns
>     before me
> When I was shown the charts and diagrams, to add,
>     divide, and measure them;
> When I, sitting, heard the astronomer, where he lectured
> with much applause in the lecture room,
> How soon, unaccountable, I became tired and sick;
> Till rising, and gliding out, I wander'd off by myself,
> In the mystical moist night-air, and from time to time,
> look'd up in perfect silence at the stars.

Reducing science to a list of facts has left entire generations to wander off and stare at the stars in an attempt to recapture an innate connection. Actually, I didn't do a lot of star gazing. What was the point? I had learned that the stars were meaningless spheres of gas that gave off light. I couldn't understand why you would want to learn their names. What had they to do with me?

How strange, as well, that in seminary there were no courses on the story of the universe as a sacred story of Spirit's unfolding. Saint Paul's references to a Christ of cosmic proportions were essentially ignored. If Brian Swimme, a mathematical physicist, could talk about the universe having a "heart," why the reluctance on the part of Christian theologians to involve Spirit in the story of its unfolding?

Where *does* the Christ fit into this new story? The typical Christian uses language like "Jesus came into this world" as though he was a guest from another planet visiting on a temporary work visa. Did Jesus really bypass the 14-billion-year evolutionary path, or was his life an integral flowering of this process?

At this same Rhode Island retreat, my spiritual director suggested I reflect prayerfully on the story of Moses and the burning bush. In the story, Moses is tending his father-in-law's sheep near Mount Horeb, when God appears to him in a burning bush (Exodus 3). Moses turns aside and notices that although the bush is on fire, it is not being consumed. It's no coincidence that the storyteller portrays God as an eternal flame. Ancients correctly associated fire and divinity. Just as the Holy manifests in and through the primal Flaring Forth, so out of this desert flame the God of the Hebrews speaks.

God tells Moses to return to Egypt, to confront Pharaoh and demand the release of the Hebrew slaves. Before he will accept this mission, Moses asks to know the name of the one speaking to him. The voice simply says, "I am that I am." This name defines the essence of God, suggesting that conscious awareness is an aspect of the core identity of the Holy. In John's gospel, Jesus is portrayed as the ultimate manifestation of divine consciousness in a series of "I am" sayings: "I am the light... I am the bread... I am the vine..." (John 6:48, 8:12, 15:5).

The story of the developing universe can be understood as a movement toward this capacity for conscious self-reflection in the realm of time and space. And so I began to believe that the universe, from the great Flaring Forth until today, represented an unfolding of Spirit toward the realization of this conscious awareness. The universe, then, was not the empty, mindless, purposeless void that scientific rationalism had taught me. I didn't have to skip over an inert and lifeless universe to get to a God who sat outside of it, on some heavenly throne. I could know God as the Source and Substance of my own conscious awareness. By becoming aware of my awareness, so to speak, I was participating in divinity.

After 14 billion years of evolution, I found myself wandering by the ocean, repeating mantra-like, "I am the Great I Am noticing I Am." Obviously, I contain a mere flicker of the Great I Am within my limited consciousness. But given the affirmation in Genesis that we are made in the image of God, the idea didn't seem so far-fetched. My sense of self expanded exponentially. It was an experience of the sort mystics in every age have described, when we break out of our small selves and catch a glimpse of a much larger and much deeper identity, a unity with the divine.

This mystical moment reinforced an experience I had when I was in grade eight. I remember walking home from school, and, for the first time ever, becoming consciously aware of my being in the universe. This awareness took the form of immense gratitude for how lucky I was simply to *be*, when I could so easily have *not been*. Books tucked under my arm, I was overcome with ecstasy. I got a chance to be! Here I was, on the way home for lunch, not just alive in the universe, but *aware* of being alive. Although I wouldn't have called it so back then, it was a burning-bush moment. The

Great I Am was recognizing itself, in and through a grade eight student on the way home from school.

This early intuition – that I could so easily have "not been" – was confirmed later when I learned that only one-billionth of the original matter that was created in the great Flaring Forth survived this cosmic birth. I am, along with everyone and everything else in the universe, a benefactor of this remnant. Matter, let alone conscious matter, is a very rare commodity. The universe is mostly space. To be precise, cosmologists now know that there are .3 atoms for every cubic metre of space in the universe.[3] Even our bodies are primarily space. Furthermore, the evolutionary process required for this matter to come to life was long and arduous. To get to that grade eight student walking home for lunch, reflecting on the immensities of existence, the universe had to make great sacrifices. To have being, let alone conscious being, is a stunning miracle of cosmic proportions. To understand this is to resonate with the Spirit of the entire universe.

A year after that original silent retreat I took with Ann, I packed up Brian Swimme's video series called *Canticles of the Cosmos* and went on another retreat, this time to a monastery on the shores of Lake Erie, Ontario. For seven days, I watched and rewatched these twelve videos, which describe how the dynamics of the universe are alive and well in the dynamics of our planet, and therefore in humans. And once again, I emerged from the retreat with an expanded sense of identity. I felt connected at a biological and spiritual level with planet Earth and with all its "other-than-human" beings. I was deeply, organically connected to the trees, to the water splashing against the shoreline, to the squirrels running around collecting nuts, and to the birds who sang me into each new day. I knew myself to be biologically and geologically kin, fashioned from the same supernova stardust.

Again I wondered what sort of education, secular and theological, I had received that had made it possible to miss this connection.

These two retreat experiences built upon the mystical experience I had in my internship year in Milton, Ontario. The Spirit was moving in me, encouraging me to explore the sacred dimension of creation within the context of the Christian story of my faith. Ever since then, I have sought opportunities to bring these two stories into dialogue. My desire is to have this dialogue within the faith community of the church. Can we create liturgies, sing hymns, preach sermons, and do mission in a manner that honours both stories? It is time for the church to come home to a radiant universe. This will require some very intentional updating of what it means to be the church, based on a new cosmology and on the new insights of the scientific community.

## 2. The Church's Homecoming

I have discovered, during the last ten years in Vancouver, Canada, a vibrant and dynamic spiritual community composed of New Agers, Buddhists, Sikhs, Jews, Wiccans, and Sufis, to name a few. But without question it is the Christians who are most deeply distrusted and discounted among these spiritually inclined people. A deep suspicion persists that Christianity is anachronistic, that we're not "with the times." Our images and models of God, the way we worship, the songs we sing, our prayers to a satellite God – whom we expect to beam back answers from some location outside the universe – just don't fit for the spiritually inclined.

In other words, it's time for the Christian church to get with the cosmological program. We need new wineskins for the new wine the Holy One is pouring out in the 21st century. There is a new story of creation, which needs to inform our biblical stories of creation. We now know that we live in an evolutionary universe. It follows that evolution is the way the Holy creates in space and in time and in every sphere: material, biological, social, cultural, psychological, and spiritual. This is the new cosmology which simply cannot be contained by old models and images of God, and outmoded ways of being the church.

## Updating Our Faith

We do not yet know what to do with this "new" story of the universe as Christians. While some theologians are just now beginning to take this story seriously, it is conspicuous by its absence in our Sunday morning services. I remember visiting a church in Boston while I was on study leave. By the time the service ended, I realized that I could have been worshipping on the moon; it contained nothing that gave me any clue I was in the city of Boston. The liturgy was devoid of any sense of time or place. In similar fashion, I suspect most people leave church on Sunday mornings without any sense of their spiritual journey taking place within an evolutionary universe, or even on the planet Earth! Too often, there aren't even many clues that we have entered the 21st century. Much of the music we ask people to sing reflects the 17th-, 18th-, and 19th-century worldviews in which they were written. We read Bible passages without helping listeners to hear or understand them in the cosmological, social, and cultural context of the writer. I know doctors and lawyers who still believe that being a Christian means taking the story of creation from Genesis literally. We have at our disposal a new understanding of the universe, but we operate out of an old one. The work of integrating this new story represents a fundamental challenge to our theological and liturgical models. It also represents a rich opportunity to become reacquainted with the Spirit of God moving in and through the very dynamics of the unfolding universe.

If only these cosmological updates were as simple a matter as the ones I can download painlessly on my computer. Every once in a while, an icon pops up, informs me that an update is available, and asks if I'd like to download it at this time. If I want the particular program to function optimally on my computer, I simply click on the agreement to update, wait a few minutes, and presto, I'm ready for whatever cyberspace has to throw at me. I can even set my computer to automatically receive and integrate these updates as I sleep.

There are ways to update our faith, of course, but unfortunately these can't be downloaded directly to our neocortex. Updates in the life of the Christian tend to be far more unsettling. This is because our religious beliefs and practices form the core of our identity. When we identify ourselves with our beliefs, an update can feel like we're being torn apart. Nevertheless, if we want to function optimally as people of the Christian faith, updating is even more critical in the realm of faith than it is with our computers. The predominant virus that slows us down is called "outdated beliefs." Updating, I contend, is a work of God's Spirit in an evolutionary universe.

Take salvation. The word itself means to make *whole*, or to heal. For at least the last 300 years, the church has regarded the planet as a kind of background stage upon which the drama of private salvation has been played out. Most of Christianity continues to be involved in what Thomas Berry calls a "redemption mystique," We are obsessed with our sinfulness and with whether we're "saved."[4] The purpose of Jesus' death, according to this fall/redemption model, was to redeem us from our innate depravity, thus saving our souls for eternal life, in a heavenly realm, somewhere beyond this universe. The vast majority of Christians are so focused on their own "salvation," or on saving others, that they are blind to the deterioration of the very ecosystems that sustain their private dramas. Even in those denominations, like my own, that have moved beyond thinking that God is primarily concerned with the salvation of private souls, we still focus almost exclusively on the human realm of creation. It's time we place the salvation (healing) of the *planet* in the foreground of our mission concerns.

## The Spirit Drives Us into Wilderness

As I reflect on my own life as a Christian, I can trace the work of the Spirit as an urgent push and pull to move beyond the status quo and towards an evolutionary pathway.

I've always been fascinated by the story in the New Testament of how the Spirit "drove" Jesus into the wilderness to be tempted by Satan. *Drove* is a very dynamic verb. For Jesus, taking a rain check wasn't really an option. American writer Wallace Stegner says that "wilderness is the geography of hope." This is true at a couple of levels. At a literal level, planet Earth is running out of wilderness space, as humans appropriate the habitat of other creatures at an alarming rate. Only the recovery of wilderness space will ensure diversity of life forms in the future. At a psychological and spiritual level, wilderness is the psychic space in which transformation occurs. It is the harsh and often chaotic landscape that a soul must inhabit to undergo spiritual evolution. Wilderness is where we'll find hope. For Jesus to evolve into the person God intended him to be, and for Jesus to be able to embrace his mission, it was necessary for him to inhabit both dimensions of wilderness. The wilderness is also where the Spirit is driving us today.

Marcus Borg speaks of two fundamental ways of being Christian in the world.[5] The first he calls the "earlier paradigm" (model), and the second the "emerging paradigm." The former sees no particular need for updates. According to this paradigm, the truth has been revealed once and for all in Jesus Christ. The work of the Spirit is confined to deepening this conviction in the heart of the believer. Dr. Borg does not concern himself with the evolutionary dimensions of the emerging paradigm, but I believe it is a critical update if we are going to function optimally as Christians in the 21st century. The emerging paradigm requires us to evolve. If we are not developing, the universe and the Spirit who animates the universe will simply leave us behind. If the universe is unfolding over time, why would our personal adventure of faith be any different?

I have experienced both ways of being Christian. My life in Christ began as a "born-again." When I was 22 years old, my mother invited me to an evangelical rally. As I heard the evangelist speak of Jesus as the way, the truth, and the life, the meaning-freak in me was hooked. I walked to the front of the church and "received Jesus as my personal Lord and Saviour," to use the language of my evangelical brothers and sisters. I was filled with a love I had never known before. Shortly thereafter began what I now call "the indoctrination." The Bible, I was told, was God's literal, inerrant and infallible word. My job was to get others to believe what I now believed so that they, too, could be saved for eternal life. Those who didn't believe were going to hell. We had the truth. Reason was an enemy, a soldier in Satan's army, used by scientists, philosophers, and infidels to lead people away from Jesus. No need for updates.

I went off to seminary full of "The Truth," but the Spirit didn't waste much time driving me into the wilderness. The first person I met at seminary was my New Testament professor. For a long time I suspected he was one of Satan's soldiers, but, in truth, he was the presence of the Spirit. Dr. Heinz Guenther was kind and gentle; he possessed an enormous heart, a comprehensive intellect, and the patience of a saint. He would turn to me after most classes, point his index finger at his temple, and gently plead, "Think, think."

It took many years for me to get my bearings and to integrate the new information I was receiving from my professors into a more complex and nuanced faith system. In the process of transcending a "born-again" faith system, I left behind a lot of baggage, but I took with me the unmistakable presence of Love, which would sustain me through many more updates.

This is the way of the cosmos, of Spirit, which drives us toward the new thing God is doing through us. The universe evolves through a process of transcending and including those aspects of a system that serve life, and by negating or excluding those aspects that are dead ends. When Jesus taught that we cannot put new wine into old wineskins, he was expressing an implicit evolutionary consciousness. God is never finished with creation. There will always be new wine. Creation is an ongoing dynamic. It happens through all of us, each moment of our lives.

It is the very nature of God to "make all things new." Jesus wasn't interested in destroying his tradition. He didn't emerge on the scene to create a new religion. Rather, he intended to create a new movement born of Spirit. Have we lost this sense of the church being a movement? Do we see ourselves as a community of faith in relationship with a Spirit that drives us into the wilderness to engage in mission in our age? To follow Jesus is to follow not just his first-century teachings, but also his pattern of updating his tradition.

Religious traditions are like cellular structures. Dr. Bruce Lipton has discovered that the "brains" of the cell are not in the nucleus, as was previously believed.[6] The real intelligence is located in the membrane, which both encloses the cell, and, at the same time, interfaces with the environment. Take the nucleus, complete with DNA, out of the cell and the cell will continue to live. Remove the membrane, or as Dr. Lipton calls it, the "membrain," and the cell dies very quickly. DNA stores memories of things that have enabled the organism to thrive in the past. But the membrane picks up signals from the environment, informing the cell about the changes it's going to have to make in order to thrive in the future. The membrane "reads" the environment and "feeds" this information into the cell. The DNA of the church contains the sacred gift of our tradition. Going forward we will need both a healthy DNA and a resilient membrane in order to contain the new wine of God's future.

Membranes enable the cell to maintain its unique identity while also allowing new information from the environment to pass through. Scientists now realize that the information we receive from the outside has the power to override and even change our genetic structure. Biological determinism is part of the old science.[7] Similarly, for a religious life and tradition to remain alive and relevant, its membrane needs to be both porous enough to enable new information to enter and reshape the tradition, and at the same time stable enough to preserve its core identity.

That particular membrane of the Christian church otherwise known as seminary had a lot of difficulty allowing my ecologically informed spirituality through its hallowed walls. In my last year of study, I was asked to give a public account of my faith before a regional court of the church. By this time, thanks to the likes of Matthew Fox, I had begun to appreciate that the planet properly belonged within the realm of theological concern, although it was conspicuous by its absence in the curriculum. I was more interested, even 25 years ago, in a theological model that was creation-centred, not redemption-centred. I stood up and delivered a "green" statement of faith, which referred to the natural world as a sacred manifestation of God's Spirit.[8]

The next morning, I was notified that my faculty advisor wanted to have a word with me. I walked up to his third-floor office, innocently imagining he wanted to congratulate me on the astuteness of my faith statement. I soon discovered, however, that I was being called to the carpet. Some well-meaning soul who had heard my statement had already called to register his concern about what they were teaching me at seminary. The professor sat behind his large oak desk, put his pipe down, and gravely told me that if I continued down this theological road I would be perpetually late for class, because I would have to stop and worship every tree I passed, like the pagans. I recall telling him that if it was a choice between worshipping every tree, and seeing a forest only as a source of toilet paper, I'd be late for class. He was not impressed.

Thomas Kuhn was the first to talk about paradigm shifts in his book *The Structures of Scientific Revolutions*. The word *paradigm* comes from the Greek word *deigma*, which means example. A paradigm is a model on a small scale that we set up beside a large-scale, difficult-to-grasp reality. It is a model of reality consisting of shared assumptions about how the world works, a frame of reference we use to make meaning. When a paradigm shifts, the old frames of reference shift.[9] For example, the era of the Newtonian paradigm, which viewed the cosmos as a machine consisting of parts that fit together neatly, is over. The new science sees the universe as a living organism. The universe is alive and developing. At the quantum level, matter is less a tangible thing than it is a process, than it is wave/particles which seem to have no fixed address. The new physics describes an indeterminate rather than a rigidly deterministic universe that follows fixed laws. The "laws" of nature may be more like cosmic habits. Creation doesn't occur through an external agent acting on a being or a system. Rather, the latent creativity implicit within the system itself "emerges" under the right conditions. In other words, we live in an emergent universe, continually creating out of the apparent chaos of life. We ourselves are centres of emergent creativity.

Saint Paul experienced a paradigm shift after his encounter with the Christ. His way of thinking about God, the meaning of his life, and his worldview were all overturned. He changed from being the captain of the feed-the-Christians-to-the-lions squad to being apostle to the Gentiles. There was a period of ten to 12 years after his Damascus road encounter with the Christ when he disappeared from view to allow the new paradigm to take hold. When he resurfaced, this was his confession and invitation:

> When I was a child, I spoke like a child, I thought like a child, I reasoned like a child; when I became an adult, I put an end to childish ways. For now we see in a mirror dimly, but then we will see face to face. Now I know only in part; then I will know fully, even as I have been fully known. (1 Corinthians 13:11–12)

Paul experienced evolutionary pressure to grow from being a child to being a spiritual adult. The particular form of that evolutionary pressure was the risen Christ. Like Paul, we're meant to continue growing throughout our lifetime. We may see in a glass darkly now, but there will come a time, if we attend to our growth and our relationship with the living Christ, when we will see face to face. This is an evolutionary insight. We move from a childlike stage of faith, driven by dogma and belief, to the stage of spiritual adulthood. Here we enjoy the direct experience common to all mystics. At the end of his harrowing journey, Job is able to affirm, "I had heard of you with the hearing of the ear, but now my eye sees you" (Job 42:5). In an evolutionary paradigm, God never stops revealing Godself to us.

## Earth and Her Creatures as Manifestations of Divine Wisdom

In this new cosmological paradigm, the earth herself is an embodiment of the divine. She is a source of divine wisdom. Her intricate and elegant ecosystems have something to teach us. Rather than exploit her, we can approach the earth as sacred revelation. Creation is a sacred text, along with the Bible and the scriptures of other religious traditions. Her wisdom is immense. For example, scientists are not even close to being able to mimic the process by which an ordinary leaf transforms sunlight into energy. The good news is that they are trying. To quote Janine Benyus, author of *Biomimicry*, "Pond scum may be a synonym for primitive, but the tiny organisms that compose it easily beat the human state of the art when it comes to capturing energy from the sun."[10] Parrots in the Amazon have learned to gather at a particular place at the side of a particular river where there is a particular form of clay. It turns out that this clay contains kaolin, which is not found in the clay just 100 yards down the river. The kaolin binds toxic chemicals that have entered the parrots' bodies. A species of cutter ant wards off infection by coating its body with an antibiotic. We've just "discovered" this antibiotic. They've been using it for 50 million years! In the next chapter, I will trace the history of how we started to believe that humans beings cornered the market on intelligence.[11]

## Beyond Stewardship: Tending the Garden

A corollary to the above involves dethroning humans. In Genesis there are two distinct stories of creation. They come from different periods and convey different worldviews. In the later story, the human ones are given "dominion over" the animals and the wild things. They are charged with the responsibility of subduing nature. I've tried for years to redeem these verbs, to have "dominion" and to "subdue," but the reality is that they are the same words used in Hebrew for conquering a nation. It is time to declare this second creation story unredeemable. Genesis 9:2 has proven to be tragically prophetic: "The fear of you and the dread of you shall be upon every beast of the earth, and upon everything that creeps on the ground, and all the fish of the sea; into your hands they are delivered."

In the first, earlier story of creation, there is more hope. The role of humans is to tend the garden. The act of tending a garden, as any gardener knows, involves loving attention. Frequent strolls through the garden are mandatory, just to check in with what's happening. What's coming up? Which plants are crowding out the others? Is the mint over-reaching? Do the roses like where they're planted? A relationship is established in which the garden silently communicates its needs and desires, to those with ears to hear. Any good gardener knows that there is a genius particular to each piece of land, which determines what will flourish. Unilaterally imposing our will upon the landscape will lead to disappointment. Our best gardeners operate not as masters over the garden, but as one intelligent source of creativity among other centres of creative intelligence, the plants.

Stewardship has been the predominant metaphor in the Christian church to describe our relationship with creation. But it has limited usefulness in the new paradigm. In the stewardship model, we still see ourselves as managers who stand over and above creation, as opposed to being one self-conscious creature embedded in an intricate ecosystem with other creatures. Our task, then, is to find our place in the fit and flow of reality. We must learn to fit in, not manage. If God as immanent Spirit is manifest in the intelligent consciousness of all creation, then what we're involved with is a relationship between different modes of consciousness – divine, plant, animal, and human. It's a communion of subjects, a dance. Precisely because we possess a unique power to shape the future of life on earth, it's imperative that we learn the steps.

We must decide which creation myth will shape our way of being on the planet.. Subduing and dominating is not God's will. We must see creation as a garden and not exclusively as a business opportunity. Still today, we kill whales to grind up their blubber to feed to minks, only to slaughter the minks so we can wear their fur. Only a heart and mind that has been shaped by a creation myth giving us not just permission but a mandate to subdue and dominate creation could enact this kind of terror-for-profit. What forces went into shaping human minds and hearts so that we think and act contrary to our natures? The next chapter will explore our shared history of disenchantment in the modern world.

## What Is "Cosmology"?

Throughout the book I use the word *cosmology* a lot. Recently, I was reminded that it's not exactly a word used in everyday conversation. In the middle of a presentation I was making to my congregation, I noticed a number of eyes glaze over. One brave soul offered, "You lost me at 'cosmology.'"

Cosmology comes in two forms: scientific and cultural.

The science of cosmology refers to the study of the universe as a single, dynamic, and ongoing event. It looks at the large-scale structure of the universe from the great Flaring Forth to the formation of galaxies and our own solar system. Brian Swimme takes it beyond science. He tells the story of this process and structure as a sacred story. This story is not just happening "out there." By appreciating that the dynamics of the large-scale universe are alive and active within each one of us, we gain the psychic energy required to break the spell of other cultural narratives, which tend to narrow and reduce the mystery of life to economic concerns.

A cultural cosmology is the story a culture tells itself about the way reality is structured. It represents commonly held assumptions about the world. Invariably, a culture's cosmology is reflected in its institutions, in the way power is distributed, and in what it gives its energies to creating. For example, if you had been a monk living between 1000 and 1500 CE in Europe, you would have assumed that the universe was a kind of perpetual-motion machine.

John David Ebert, mythology scholar, says it was no accident that during this period there was a proliferation of machines, a virtual explosion of mechanical genius, from mirrors, water mills, sawmills, the spinning wheel, to the treadle loom, eyeglasses, the compass, guns, windmills, cannons, paper, and the printing press.[12] This is functional cosmology. When the universe is thought of as a machine, we become fascinated with machines.

The cosmology that most of us unconsciously were shaped by in our educational systems was scientific rationalism, an outgrowth of Newtonian science. By the time Newton wrote his *Principia*, God was beginning to take a back seat in the affairs of the universe. Johannes Kepler, a scientist who preceded Newton, described his excitement thus: "My vision is to show that the celestial machine is to be likened, not to a divine organism, but rather to clockwork." This clockwork universe required a divine Clockmaker only for occasional rewindings.

In a Newtonian cosmology, reality is thought to be located in the smallest, discrete bits of matter. The universe is made up of these isolated parts that fit together, like a giant machine. When something goes wrong, all you need to do is replace or fix the faulty part. Even today, most of our institutions operate as though we live in a clockwork universe.

For example, when I took my gimpy knee in to see a medical expert, he was not the least bit interested in my tight hamstrings and buttocks, my history of juvenile arthritis, or my theory of how I might be compensating by taking more weight onto my ailing knee. In others words, he was operating unconsciously out of a Newtonian cosmology, in which it was not important to view my knee holistically in terms of the larger system of my body. He "isolated" the problem, looked only at my one knee, took measurements, ordered an MRI, and told me he could operate to replace the faulty part.

One's functional cosmology (the impact of our unconscious worldview on how we live) is reflected in our religious stories about how the cosmos came into being. Historically, there are two basic types of creation stories, both ancient. In the first type, a male God acts as an external agent on the primeval, chaotic forces to impose order. The most ancient story of this type comes from the Babylonian creation myth Enuma Elish, in which Marduk, a male god, slays the female chaos deity, Tiamat. Most biblical scholars believe that the creation story in Genesis is of the same genre, that is, a male god imposing order on a primeval chaos.

The second, earlier creation story begins with Chaos, the yawning void before creation, spontaneously generating an ordered cosmos of deities, beginning with the goddess Gaia, out of whom her husband Ouranos grows like a plant. Recent scientific breakthroughs support the cosmological intuitions of this story. For example, Ralph Abraham's work on chaos theory establishes that a deep order is intrinsic to chaotic systems, and that this order self-organizes under the proper conditions. Order and chaos are flip sides of the same coin.[13] There is no external agent acting on a system to bring order to it. The order emerges from within.

It seems obvious that if our foundational stories feature a male God who imposes order on chaos, identified with the feminine, then these beliefs will find a way into our institutions. They will privilege the male gender, be deeply suspicious of the feminine, and display an aversion to all wild things, including wilderness spaces. Given that the earth is identified as feminine, it is perhaps not surprising that in the last 500 years we have sought to control and subdue her. Cosmological assumptions matter.

The majority of the world's Christians function out of a cosmology in which a male God located outside the universe makes occasional forays into the cosmos to straighten things out. From his extra-cosmic throne, this God controls life on earth by laying down a divine rulebook. He came down from heaven, in Jesus of Nazareth, to "save" us from the chaos-inducing meddlings of Satan. He has a plan for every one of us, which was established from the beginning of time; whatever happens to us is what God planned to have happen, from the very beginning.

Obviously, this doesn't fit with what we actually know about an evolutionary universe in the 21st century. The universe contains genuine novelty and surprise, and an elegant order, which is not imposed, but rather emerges as we trust the divine life within chaos itself. Jesus did indeed function to bring order out of chaos, but not as an external agent beamed down from beyond the universe. Rather, as a child of the universe, Jesus emerged, born of Mary, from the interior, sacred depths of the One God, embodied in the earth. Out of his life, death, and resurrection, a new creation emerges.

# Chapter 2

# THE WEANING FROM WONDER

Forfeit awe and the world becomes a marketplace.

RABBI ABRAHAM HESCHEL

## I. The Disenchantment of the Universe

If you want to gain a sense of the wonder of the world, take a walk with a two-year-old. Do not be in a hurry. I learned this with my own daughter. Every twig and blade of grass was an occasion for her to squat down and take a real good look. Without the same agenda-driven, caffeine-infused urgency of her father, a bug struggling through the forest of grass was an opportunity for relationship. I remember the monk-like, single-minded attention she bestowed upon this creature. Similarly, a piece of coloured glass stopped her in her tracks for a good five minutes, as she turned it over and over in the sun to capture the changing colours. An hour passed and we hadn't progressed even a block. Such is the enchantment of two-year-olds for the natural world.

It takes a good 15 to 20 years for our educational system to wean people from wonder, to demystify and disenchant the universe. This weaning from wonder is a travesty. I remember learning about the life of cells in biology. I had to memorize the various parts of a cell: the nucleus, the organelles, the DNA and RNA, the membrane, and later some of the chemical interactions necessary to produce energy. I learned this stuff because there was "going to be a test." After completing the test, most of the information simply disappeared from my memory. I didn't retain it because it wasn't taught as a source of wonder. A cell was a collection of parts, which worked together like a machine. Furthermore, despite the fact that my own body was made of 50 trillion of these tiny energy fields, I was not helped to make a connection between my own body and its cellular composition. I could go down the list of subjects on the curriculum and tell the same story.

I struggled with math, for example, not because I couldn't learn the formulas, but because none of my teachers could answer my question, "Why do I have to learn math?" No one could tell me. Because I was a "good" boy, I learned the bare minimum. For ancient Greeks, mathematics was revelatory. It was how they accessed invisible forms behind the visible forms of creation. They had a passion for dealing with first principles. Through math, they plumbed the elegance and mystery of the universe. Modern theoretical physics confirms their ancient intuition. The elegance and beauty of a mathematical formula is the primary predictor of whether it will correspond to reality. My grade 12 math teacher first bored me nearly to death, and then threw me out of the class on a regular basis for being restless (for which I am truly grateful).

I chose my undergraduate university because it had the best volleyball team in Canada. The pedagogical methods in the post-secondary system were the same as in high school, except with more information. I received adequate grades, without ever really being interested in any of the subjects. I majored in psychology. The brand in vogue at the time was behavioural psychology. We spent a lot of time proving that B. F. Skinner was right. We could control the behaviour of rats in a laboratory through a system of rewards and punishments. By extension, my professor assured me, human beings could be reduced to the sum total of rewards and punishments received for particular behaviours. He encouraged us to practise our rat-training techniques on our girlfriends. So much for wonder. Our volleyball team, on the other hand, was doing quite well.

A recent study has shown that children are more likely to be able to identify the ten top corporate jingles and brands than name the planets in our solar system. This, perhaps, should not surprise us. Brian Swimme asks where and how we are initiated into the universe. For primal peoples, it happened in caves, through vision quests, and sacred stories told around the campfire. Today, our children are initiated into the universe through television and video games. Ancient chants have been replaced by corporate jingles. By the time a child enters first grade, she has ingested some 30,000 advertisements. Children are being systematically initiated into a worldview of commercialism and capitalism. There's a new 24-hour satellite television station called Baby TV, which targets six-month- to two-year-olds! In other words, from the age of six months, our children are initiated into the culture of television, the medium of choice for advertisers.

Virtually nothing is sacred to advertisers, other than selling products. The industry will appropriate any image in order to initiate our children into the cult of consumerism. The power and mystery of sexuality is exploited to sell every conceivable product, from cars to mattresses to clothing to vacuum cleaners. Previously mysterious and sacred symbols are reduced to mere "hooks" designed to encourage us to buy. These symbols hook us because we retain ancient memories of them. So today, Eternity is a perfume. We don't drive cars; we are transported by Infinitis, Mysteres, and Allures. Our relationship with the planets is reduced to the Mercury or Saturn that carries us to work. Babies sell car tires and toilet paper. Corporations have caught on to our fascination with animals. Lizards, monkeys, sheep, toucans, hippos, and many other species, including those on the verge of extinction, are exploited for their attention-galvanizing power. Literally nothing is sacred in this new religion, into which we are initiating our children.

We are living through a modern-day version of the story of the golden calf in Exodus. In the story, the Hebrew people have escaped the slavery they endured under the Egyptian pharaoh. They find themselves in the desert, starving and looking impatiently for signs that God is with them. In their desperation – while Moses is away, up a mountain receiving some divine instruction – they gather up all the gold and silver they possess and make out of it a golden calf. In the absence of any God they can perceive, they appropriate the symbol of the god of the dominant culture. They remove all their jewellery and cast it into a fire, to be melted and re-formed into an idol.

So today, in a universe devoid of awe and wonder, we are ripe for the picking. Our children and youth, particularly, are susceptible to the allurements of the materialism and commercialism of the dominant culture. Advertising imbues products with the numinous powers of gods and goddesses. It promises that we can participate directly in the good life, through an orgy of consumption. When Moses confronts Aaron, the priest who supervised the forging of the golden calf, Aaron lamely denies responsibility. He tells Moses that he instructed the people to throw their jewellery into the fire, and presto, "out came this calf!" (Genesis 32:24).

We are the Hebrew people, disenchanted with the world into which we have been initiated. Yet we are hard-wired for sacred mystery, the capacity to know that we are accompanied in our journey through this universe by the Spirit of God. We are, therefore, susceptible to golden calves of all shapes and sizes. Only the names, voided of sacred essence, remain. We find ourselves revelling in an orgy of consumption, which is destroying our planet and denying our souls of the deeper meaning and purpose for which we hunger. Marketing geniuses are the high priests of our corporate culture. As contemporary incarnations of Aaron, they deny responsibility for the golden calf of consumerism. After all, they tell us, they are just giving us what we want. And we, the citizenry, also deny responsibility, since our primary civic duty apparently consists of shopping, as President Bush reminded the American people on national television after 9-11. Get thee to Disneyland!

But the calf didn't just pop out of the fire all by itself. This story of the disenchantment of the cosmos was forged within the fire of a particular history. It is to this story we now turn our attention.

## A Story of Disenchantment

For much of what follows in this chapter, I am grateful to historian Richard Tarnas, for his brilliant synthesis of the history of disenchantment in his recent book *Cosmos and Psyche: Intimations of a New World View*.[1]

The modern period, which actually dates back some 500 years, marks the beginning of an era of great liberation for the human species, but also the beginning of a descent into disenchantment.

In 1486, Giovanni Pico della Mirandola called together a meeting of the world's prominent philosophers and presented his work

*Oration on the Dignity of Man*. This work marked a profound cosmological shift, in which humans stopped being passive victims of fate in a universe over which they had very little control, and became creators of their own destiny. In his address, Pico issued what can be regarded as a prophetic utterance. It would usher in a radically new appreciation of the nature of the human being and the purpose of existence. In this excerpt, the "Creator" speaks.

> The nature of all other beings is limited and constrained within the bounds of the Laws prescribed by Us. Thou, constrained by no limits, in accordance with thine own free will, in whose hand We have placed thee, shalt ordain for thyself the limits of thy nature. We have set thee at the world's center that thou mayest from thence more easily observe whatever is in the world. We have made thee neither of heaven nor of the earth, neither mortal nor immortal, so that with freedom of choice and with honor, as though the maker and molder of thyself, thou mayest fashion thyself in whatever shape thou shalt prefer.[2]

Pico anticipated a virtual revolution, which would take place over the course of the next 150 years, when humanity would throw off the shackles of a circumscribed and largely pre-determined fate, to steal with Prometheus the fire of the gods, and use this freedom to "fashion" a self of his own choosing.

In the span of a single generation, Michelangelo, Raphael, and da Vinci would render the new human being in art; Columbus would set sail for the new world; Luther would nail his 95 Theses to the door of the Castle Church in Wittenberg; and Copernicus would develop the scientific proof that the earth revolved around the sun. Copernicus' de-centring of the earth, in particular, would in time shift the centre of power away from the church and toward the scientific establishment. Nature was constrained, but the potential of human beings was declared boundless.[3]

To appreciate just how radical Copernicus' insight into the workings of the cosmos was at the time, think about the last time you went out in the evening to watch the sun "set." Five hundred years later, our language still presumes a pre-Copernican universe, in which the planet is stationary while the sun sets and rises around it. It's what our eyes see. I wrote a song while on vacation with my wife on the shores of Lake Superior, at a remote area called Agawa Bay. It took considerable intellectual effort to write the following stanza in a "cosmically correct" fashion:

Going weirdward on Agawa Bay,
trusting our hearts on a late August day,
watching the sun as the earth slips away,
yeah, we're going weirdward on Agawa Bay.

Copernicus' insight was not appreciated, to say the least, by his contemporaries, or by subsequent generations for that matter. Listen to Martin Luther, father of the Reformation, who is reported to have said,

People gave ear to an upstart astrologer who strove to show that the Earth revolves, not the heavens or the firmament, the Sun and the Moon... This fool wishes to reverse the entire science of astronomy; but the sacred Scripture tells us that Joshua commanded the sun to stand still, and not the Earth.[4]

But the bottle had been uncorked. If the planet orbited the sun, then perhaps other earthly institutions, such as the church, were not as central and immovable as they had appeared. In the beginning of this revolution, those who agreed with Copernicus were convinced that this was a sacred revelation. For millennia there had been a sharp divide between the celestial and terrestrial realms; no human being could hope to understand the complexities of the heavens. But now it seemed as though God's intent was to be known more completely than ever before. Human beings had gained insight into the heavenly realms, and surely this was God's intention. The seeds of optimism in the capacity of the human mind to penetrate the mysteries of the universe were now planted. Pico della Mirandola's prophecy was unfolding. The limitations of previous eras were in the process of being transcended. This new vision of the universe would issue in a new human being.

## Differentiation

With the Copernican revolution, human beings began the process of consciously differentiating (separating) themselves from both nature and God. The universal dynamic of differentiation is captured in the story of Adam and Eve, which describes a primal collusion to eat the forbidden fruit of the tree of the knowledge of good and evil. In the story, the serpent tells Adam and Eve that God's stated reason for obeying the command *not* to eat the fruit is bogus. The real problem, the snake says, is that God will be jealous that the eyes of the humans will be opened; that is, they will consciously be able to distinguish between good and evil. This ability would make them like the gods, evolving beyond rule-bound obedience to an external authority, enjoying the capacity to make decisions about what was good or evil on their own. To become like the gods would mean rising up out of (differentiating) from the rest of creation. Other animals unconsciously obey natural laws laid down by the Creator. But one bite of the apple and humans would start thinking for themselves, and making their own rules.

The problem, in other words, was with the potential downside of differentiation. What's at stake in this myth is the capacity of human beings to make responsible decisions without deference or even reference to an external, divine authority. Their "eyes would be opened." What they would see was a future of their own determining.

This anticipates and describes the modern era's break from the moral authority of external agents, whether that agent is God, the church, or sacred scripture. For example, whatever respect the clergy enjoy these days must be earned. The days are long gone, believe me, when by virtue of the office one holds respect is conferred. This is a distinctive feature of the modern worldview. We will decide for ourselves what is right and what is wrong, what is good and what is bad, thank you very much. All religious traditions, including the Christian, have been suspicious of our human capacity to think for and trust ourselves in the pursuit of the knowledge of good and evil. The story of Adam and Eve is a story of the perilous yet inevitable urge to emerge as freely acting agents. Fully differentiated beings gain the capacity to uniquely manifest the glory of their Creator.

Modernity gave us many gifts. Ken Wilber points out that the shift to the modern worldview enabled the spheres of art, science, and morality to develop along separate lines, without dogmatic interference from the church.[5] Prior to this, religion ruled the roost, with threats of violence and death for anyone who dared express an opinion or an idea not sanctioned by the church. Galileo couldn't report what he discovered looking through his telescope because the three spheres of art, science, and morality were all fused under the authority of the church. Giordano Bruno, a Dominican monk, was burned at the stake, in part for supporting Copernicus' theory. The church's brand of morality and its biblical literalism defined both what science could and could not do. In the modern era, on the other hand, scientists and artists became free to explore non-religious themes; the "good life" could be explored without reference to the scriptures.

The modern era enabled humanity to ask for the first time paradigm-busting questions: Is it reasonable that black people should be slaves, just because of their skin colour? Why can't women vote? Why would we give kings and queens, along with an aristocracy, unfettered powers when they don't represent the people? As a result of this kind of inquiry, slavery was abolished, equality for women was affirmed and promoted, and four major revolutions – the French, English, Russian, and American – were fought on behalf of the universal rights of humankind.

Furthermore, the sciences gave us vaccinations and drugs against all manner of diseases, which increased the quality and longevity of life; and they introduced technological and engineering innovations, which have served us very well. Modernity was the period in which human beings truly gained their freedom to create themselves and their world, precisely by transcending inherited myths and traditions, and by applying their own rational faculties. The freedom humanity gained during the last 500 years of the modern era is a gift of inestimable value.

## The Shadow Side of Modernity

But there is a shadow side. This heady sense of the unlimited potential of humanity sowed the seeds for hubris to surface. As Wilber and others have pointed out, differentiation descended into dissociation. The big three – science, art, and morality – were, by and large, left to develop as completely separate disciplines.[6] Even today, there is very little interdisciplinary cooperation in universities.

Science emerged as king over the "big three," but having no relationship with the arts or with morality, it has operated outside of a binding ethical and aesthetic connection. For example, it has been co-opted by the military-industrial complex and by the pharmaceutical industry. Technological innovation has followed an economic mandate, but the conversation about whether the life of the planet can sustain the new technology still hasn't taken place in any serious way.

In other words, we got carried away with our agency. The myth of Adam and Eve and the warning against eating the apple conveys an image of God worried that differentiation will collapse into dissociation. God wasn't jealous, as the snake suggested – just very, very worried.

## The Tower of Babel as a Story of Dissociation

The biblical story of the tower of Babel perfectly captures the shadow side of differentiation sliding into dissociation. In the story, the people discover a brand new technology – bricks – with which they intend to build cities, and a "tower with its top in the heavens." They desire to "make a name for themselves" (Genesis 11:4).

God gets wind of this project and determines to confound it: "This is only the beginning of what they will do; nothing that they propose to do now will be impossible for them" (Genesis 11:6). God gives them different languages to confuse their communication, making them unable to cooperate in the execution of the project.

We could dismiss this as nothing more than a story about a jealous God wanting to hold back the human race from realizing its potential. However, this ancient story captures the perennial temptation of hubris. The men in the story want to exceed any kind of natural limits. They want the tower to reach into the heavens so that they can usurp the place of the gods. The new technology dissociated them from the rest of creation. The higher the tower, the greater the distance between them and the earth.

The discovery of bricks seems innocuous. But fast forward the technological innovation from bricks to nuclear fission, genetic engineering, stem cell research, or oil sands extraction, and we gain a sense of what's at stake in this biblical story. A series of articles in *The Globe and Mail* has traced the story of how we now live in a virtual chemical soup.[7] PBDEs, the active agent in fire retardant chemicals, found in mattresses, computer shells, CDs, and other hard plastic products too numerous to mention, are being absorbed by the human body.

When absorbed by living things, some of these chemicals act like hormones. For example, in minute amounts, the molecular structure of Bisphenol A (BPA) fits snugly into the receptor cells of the female hormone estrogen. This hormone has been associated with increased risk of breast cancer in women. The scary thing is that this only happens when the concentration is at very minute levels – far below levels which the government has determined to be safe for humans. In mice, the offspring of mothers who received BPA in low enough doses – the effect doesn't happen at higher doses – gave birth to female pups who developed a profusion of buds that grew into milk ducts by the time they became adolescents. In humans the same effect would increase the number of sites where breast cancer may develop. These chemicals have now been associated with rising rates of thyroid cancer as well.[8] This technological innovation went forward without any serious research into the long-term impact of these chemicals.

The dissociation of science from ethics, and of economic interests from nature's limits, is literally killing us. The chemical soup we live in is a result of differentiation breaking down into dissociation.

Technological innovation is not a bad thing. The point is that when science and engineering are dissociated from spirit, morality, and ethics, the important questions don't get asked. What ends are we serving with this technology? What is the cost to the planet, and to human and non-human life forms, and who is benefiting from this technology? For example, we have the technology to build massive dams. But are they ethical? The Aral Sea in Central Asia has shrunk to half its original size because two rivers were dammed. The fishery is non-existent, and 159 species of birds and 38 mammals have disappeared from the river deltas.[9] We have built dams and towers into the heavens, without any sense of connection to the earth.

In the modern era, human beings didn't want to be bogged down by any limitations. We wanted, like Icarus, to fly as close to the sun as possible, unencumbered by planetary baggage. The notion that earth might have a limit to how much abuse she can take was the furthest thing from the minds of industrial barons or politicians looking to be re-elected. The dissociation was, therefore, not only from ethics and spirituality, but also from the earth and the cosmos itself. We wanted no constraints to our agency. Voiding the earth, her creatures, and the encompassing cosmos itself of any intrinsic value or meaning liberated the human creature to be godlike. Here is a diagram from Richard Tarnas, which depicts the radical shift from the premodern or primal worldview (cosmology) to the modern worldview.[10]

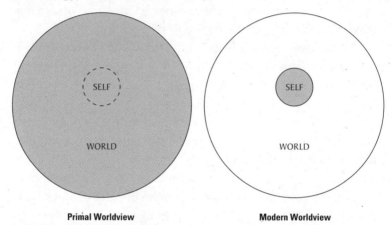

**Primal Worldview**

In the primal worldview, intelligence and soul (the shaded area) pervade all of nature and the cosmos, and a permeable human self directly participates in that larger matrix of meaning and purpose within which it is fully embedded.

**Modern Worldview**

In the modern worldview, all qualities associated with purposeful intelligence and soul are exclusively characteristic of the human subject, which is radically distinct from the objective nonhuman world.

The dotted line around the self in the primal worldview indicates a permeable membrane between the self and the cosmos. Both are infused by a sacred milieu, a cosmos filled with meaning, purpose, and a sense of the sacred permeating all. In the modern worldview, the line around the self is closed; the self alone retains meaning and purpose. The sacred milieu is limited to the self. The paradox of being a centre of meaning in a meaningless universe has haunted modern "man" for the last 200 years. It created the so-called "age of anxiety." The cosmos is clearly externalized, stripped of any intrinsic meaning. Notice that there is no communion possible (or necessary) with the larger cosmos in the modern worldview, and that the subjectivity (interiority) of the cosmos has been removed.

The premodern world enjoyed what has been called a "participation mystique." The cosmos was *en-souled*. The surrounding world of nature and the heavenly realm of the stars were conveyers of meaning and purpose. There was a less defined boundary between external reality and one's internal reality. One's life was a participation in the soul of the world, or, as the Greeks called it, the *anima mundi*. The alignment of the stars and the planets, for example, influenced affairs on earth, both political and personal. Space was not empty and inert. The air was filled with the "spirits of things." When Saint Paul writes about angels, and principalities and powers, he is reflecting a premodern cosmology. Life was a natural communion of beings, visible and invisible.

When Jesus taught his disciples to pray the words "on earth as it is in heaven," he was reflecting a premodern cosmology. The heavenly and earthly realms interpenetrated and influenced each other. Our decisions and actions on earth were believed to be cosmic in scope, registering in the celestial realms. Similarly, the celestial realms suffused and shaped the affairs of earth. The cosmos itself, and not just the human being, was infused with meaning and purpose. Invisible angels and principalities and powers were part of the fabric of people's daily lives.

Modern Christianity, on both the right and the left, has resisted this kind of enchanted universe. The idea that the universe is permeated with invisible, intermediary powers, influencing the shape and direction of history, has been interpreted as unfaithful in modern Protestantism. There is us, and then there is God somewhere over the rainbow, but in between are vast expanses of empty and inert space. But have you noticed that intermediary beings, such as angels, refuse to go away? Bookshelves in New Age stores are filled with them. The Bible is also filled with them. Typically, they come on the scene to announce good news. "Sarah, you're going to celebrate your 91st birthday on the maternity ward!" "Abraham, you are going to be the father of a great nation!" To shepherds, angels announce the good news of the birth of the Christ. Dionysius the Areopagite, a sixth-century monk, provides us with a virtual lexicon of the angelic realms. Saint Thomas Aquinas writes volumes on them. Hildegard of Bingen and other Christian mystics assume the existence of angels from personal experience.

Liberal Christians, seeking credibility within the paradigm of scientific rationalism, are deeply suspicious of invisible angelic beings, nature mysticism, and incidences of sacred coincidence. It's a losing battle, in my experience. Whatever ministers tell their "flocks" about ways we can know God, in my experience people bring with them to church two fundamental sacred experiences. The first is found in nature, perhaps while floating in a canoe down a river, far from the madding crowds. Here people experience what Gerald May calls the "Presence." The second kind of experience is "sacred coincidence." Most people who come to church are keenly aware of the way in which a chance meeting, discovering a book, or even falling ill, led them down a path that eventuated in their spiritual evolution. Many of them, in fact, show up at our churches with a story of sacred coincidence, which they believe is responsible for getting them to church in the first place.

Carl Jung coined the term *synchronicity* to describe these experiences. In a well-known case, a patient was describing a dream to him, about a scarab beetle. At that very moment, a very rare scarab beetle landed on the window ledge of Jung's office. Synchronistic events are those in which an external event inexplicably coincides with an interior psychological state or process. At these moments, the external cosmos appears to be "in sync" within one's interior reality. Spiritually oriented people pay very close attention to these kinds of experiences, perhaps reflecting a longing for a premodern, en-souled cosmos. Synchronistic experiences reassure them that the universe/God is nudging them in the direction of their spiritual evolution, and that their lives are held within the flow of a universe that is evolving in a meaningful and purposeful direction.[11]

Because of a particular conception of the nature of God (in which God occasionally intervenes in history, but otherwise exists outside of natural processes), many clergy, liberal and conservative, tend to dismiss these experiences as flaky, or more dramatically as heretical. Admittedly, as Tarnas points out, we can get carried away, rendering every triviality in our lives with deep purpose and meaning.[12] There is also a danger of spiritual narcissism, in which everything that happens is significant only in relation to one's own reality. But this doesn't tell the whole story.

Seekers within the context of a liberal church soon learn, in my experience, that these experiences of sacred coincidence are not validated in church. They pick up very quickly that church is about values and morals, and learning the Bible stories. These things are important, but a moralistic agenda doesn't typically speak to the hunger for the sacred in the souls of our people. People come to church to validate their experiences of an enchanted or sacred dimension in life. Telling them that the religious life is about being "good," or worse, about being "better," doesn't speak to their spiritual intuition. In other words, in a process I will describe below, the church has participated in what Tarnas calls the "militant de-sacralizing of the world in the service of the human being's exclusive allegiance to the sovereign majesty of the Creator."[13]

As Wilber points out, the rallying cry of the Enlightenment was "No more myths and no more ascent."[14] "No more myths" meant a commitment to scientific inquiry, to the scientific method. It was no longer enough for an authority figure to say that the moon is made of blue cheese. The scientific method was and is simply a way of knowing based on empirical evidence, tested against objective criteria, assessed by a community of the competent, and then repeated to verify the results. As such, it has served humanity well.

To give but one personal example, I often find myself in my yoga class with my Bikram (hot yoga) instructor barking out the benefits of the pain I am experiencing: "You are compressing your joints, and when you release and relax, oxygen-rich blood floods back over the joints, removing toxins and healing your scar tissues." I'm supposed to be focusing, but inside I'm asking, "Have you actually scientifically tested these claims you are so confidently espousing?" It's no longer enough for me, or anyone else, to take an authority's word for it. We want to know that the claims made about reality are empirically valid. No more myths.

"No more ascent" is more problematic. Science limited its inquiry to the realm of matter, the exterior dimension of reality, but declared this to constitute the totality of reality. In doing so, it gave us a flatland world. The ascendant realm of spirit and soul were no longer "really real" because they couldn't be tested by conventional methods.

How does one measure love and compassion, for example? Modern science looks for these interior values in the only realm it knows how to measure, and therefore the only realm it considers valid, the material. So we stimulate the brain (confused with the mind in most scientific models) to find the love centre; or we search for a chemical believed to be responsible for happiness.[15] In the field of genetics, there is great confidence that all human behaviour and all illnesses have a genetic origin. If we just fiddle with the physical stuff in our DNA, we'll discover utopia. Big Pharma is naturally quite interested in getting us to buy into this model of genetic determinism. If the problem is physical, they have the pill to fix it. This worldview, which we have all been initiated into, leaves no room for Spirit. The natural world, voided of Spirit, has no intrinsic value.

## The Postmodern Era

We have now entered into a period that many are calling postmodern. It's a term that gets thrown around a lot and in my experience means many different things to many different people depending on the context, which is pretty much the definition of *postmodern*. All definitions of postmodernism share two basic features, according to Ken Wilber.[16]

First, reality is not totally pre-given. We construct it according to our beliefs, the stories we tell ourselves about the nature of reality, and our stage of development. This is sometimes called *constructionism*.

Second, meaning is context dependent. The meaning I give to an experience depends on the cultures I inhabit. My gender, class, level of psychological and spiritual development, and my educational background, for example, will shape the meaning I give to my world. This is sometimes called *contextualism*. In the process of making meaning, I am obliged to declare "where I'm coming from." In a postmodernist worldview, my meaning, as a white, heterosexual, middle-class, university-educated, prairie-raised, Christian male, cannot be imposed as authoritative for anybody else. No single meaning can prevail as "the truth."

Postmodernism is deeply, and correctly, suspicious of "totalizing" theories, narratives, and myths that do not taken into account the contexts from which they were generated. Michel Foucault and others noticed that those who are in control of these narratives tend to wield a lot of power. They present themselves as the only valid contexts for all other texts. But all of reality is whole/parts; from the sub-atomic to the fields of galaxies to the great religions of our day, everything is a whole in and of itself, but also a part of yet a larger whole. As Wilber says, it's whole/parts all the way up and all the way down.

As a whole, an entity manifests agency and differentiation. It has its own integrity and its own role to execute. As a part, an entity participates in a communion, or an ecology, with other larger wholes. When an entity – be it material, biological, or cultural – refuses to function as part of a larger whole, it is involved in a program of domination. It's my way or the highway. Fundamentalism, be it political, religious, or economic, refuses to assume its partial nature. Coercion replaces cooperation. Postmodernism is helpful in the way it denies the claims of all ideological systems that try to offer more than partial takes on reality.

However, postmodernism has its shadow side, as well; namely its denial of truth itself. If reality is nothing more than perspective and context, then all meaning is an arbitrary construction. This tends to undermine the category of truth as a philosophical or theological category. Postmodernism can end up denying that there is any meaning at all in the cosmos except that which we human beings attribute to it. When an extreme postmodernism is combined with scientific materialism, we end up situated in an incomprehensibly enormous and meaningless universe, travelling through space on a hunk of matter, going nowhere in particular, and left to our own devices to generate some kind of meaning. This meaning is ultimately no more than *our* truth.

The challenge for postmodernist thinking is to acknowledge that the postmodernist worldview itself is a construction. Obviously, postmodernist views are constructed by those who believe that this worldview corresponds more closely to reality, or why take the time to present them. A radical postmodern worldview results in the reality indicated by the diagram below.[17]

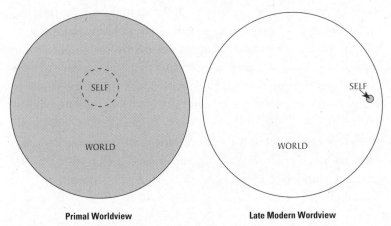

**Primal Worldview**　　　　**Late Modern Wordview**

In the late modern post-Copernican, post-Nietzschean cosmos, the human self exists as an infinitesimal and peripheral island of meaning and spiritual aspiration in a vast and purposeless universe signifying nothing except what the human self creates.

This is not just an academic abstraction. In a Bible study in the first congregation I served, I presented the new story of creation, mentioning the vast number of stars in the universe. One of the women in the group had to leave the room because she was having an anxiety attack. In a subsequent conversation, she talked about feeling appallingly insignificant. How could our lives have any meaning when we were just "specks" of sand in an indifferent universe? It was not merely the expansiveness of the universe that caused her anxiety. It was the materialist cosmology of scientific rationalism combined with a postmodern voiding of ultimate truth from the universe that caused her to leave the room. She felt like an accident of life in an ultimate context of meaninglessness.

Rather than claim that there is no ultimate truth, I think it is more reasonable to affirm that the more contexts and perspectives one is able to consciously bring to bear on an event the closer one is to the truth. The challenge is to avoid making a partial reality the whole enchilada. In this current work, I am attempting to bring to bear a wider cosmological perspective on the Christian faith. In so doing, I am convinced not that I will arrive at "the Truth," but that this added perspective will bring me closer to the truth of the revelation of Jesus, as the Christ, than I would be without it.

As we reconnect Spirit – as immanent all-pervasive Presence – within all of creation, we may rediscover enchantment as the spiritual foundation for an ecological ethic.

## 2. The Church and Disenchantment

The church has played its own role in the history of disenchantment.

There has always been a tradition of sacramental theology, wherein the cosmos was believed to reflect the glory of God. But since the Protestant Reformation, its influence has been minimal. By and large, the church has located God outside the cosmos, as we know it. Theists believe that God intervenes every now and then, speaking to prophets, and, for Christians, incarnating in Jesus, to correct us, teach us, and/or to save us. After these forays, however, it's back to the celestial throne. Deists don't even make space for this much divine intervention. God is like a clockmaker, who every once in a while rewinds the cosmic clock to keep it going, but otherwise leaves it to run itself. The transcendent dimensions of God in most Christian traditions are more emphasized than the immanent dimensions of God. God is unique and separate, "above" the created universe.

In a theistic cosmology, God is portrayed as being almost exclusively concerned with the drama of the human species. Tarnas' insight is helpful here. We alone are made in "His" image, according to our Genesis creation myth. While the non-human forms of life are declared to be "good" in Genesis, they don't participate with humanity in the privileged relationship with God; they don't share God's "image." Just as God is sovereign over humanity, as well as separate and unique, humanity, being made in God's image, is sovereign, separate, and unique in relation to the rest of creation.[18] Our dominant theological models paved the way for the secular domination of creation. The following diagram accurately conveys the typical assumptions of most people sitting in the pews on Sundays.[19]

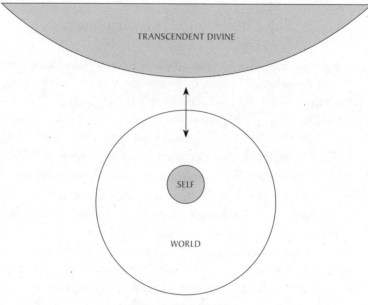

**Western Religious Worldview**

In the Western religious worldview that emerged between the primal and modern, forming a link between them, the human self bears a unique relationship to a transcendent divinity that is separate from and sovereign over the created world: a world that is increasingly perceived as devoid of meaning and purpose other than that associated with the human self.

For the vast majority of evangelical Christians today, the natural world is primarily a backdrop to the unfolding drama of human salvation. We shall see that Saint Paul actually includes creation in the story of salvation, but for the most part this has not been of much interest to Christian theology. For Christians who subscribe to a literal apocalypse, the earth is expendable. That's why James Watt, then Secretary of the Interior under Ronald Reagan, was able to state that it didn't matter if all the trees were cut down on the planet. Christ was coming. The cosmos, including the natural world, is not a subject with inherent value, nor is it a conveyer of purpose and meaning. Certainly it is not, as the great Hindu philosopher Sri Aurobindo affirms, "the garb of Spirit."

I remember writing an essay in seminary about the Gnostic Gospel of Thomas, in which the author writes that we can look under any rock, or a break a piece of wood, and find the Christ. My professor wrote back something to the effect that if we can find Christ in the natural world, why do we need the church? I was dumbfounded. His comment expressed the historical ambivalence of the Christian faith in relation to being able to find God, Christ, or Spirit in nature. One cannot emerge from seminary, even a liberal seminary, without picking up this anxiety.

## Panentheism

Panentheists, as distinct from both theists and deists, affirm that God is in creation, and that creation is in God. The little "en" between "pan" (everywhere) and "theism" (God) makes all the difference. Unlike pantheism, which asserts that God is everything and everything is God, pan*en*theism gives God – and us for that matter – a little more breathing room. Here's the definition from the *Oxford Dictionary*: "The belief that the Being of God includes and penetrates the whole universe, so that every part of it exists in God, but (as against pantheism) that this Being is more than, and is not exhausted by, the universe." In the Christian worldview, creation is not absorbed into God, and God is not absorbed into creation. There's still room for genuine relationship. When my wife and I do pre-marriage counselling, we often come across couples who are so "in love" with each other that they do not actually have a relationship. Their mutual absorption is so complete that they can't see the other as a distinct person. It's sweet, but you know they'll get over it. Only as they gain the capacity to "see each other whole against the sky," to use Rainer Maria Rilke's phrase, and not merely as extensions of each other, will they be able to evolve in their love. Differentiation makes authentic relationship possible. Panentheism affirms that God is not just "up above," but also out ahead, in behind, under, and within; distinct, yet never separate.

In Alice Walker's novel *The Color Purple*, Shug, a bar room singer, plays the role of mentor to a young and naïve Celie. Both are black women, but Shug, anticipating a postmodernist feminism, has deconstructed the white man's version of the Christian faith. She has learned to do her own theology. She has differentiated from the authoritarian structures of the church, while Celie remains obedient. On one occasion, in a conversation about why they go to church, Celie says that it's obvious: she goes to learn about God. Shug responds that anything she ever learned about God she brought *with* her into church. One of the things she learned is that God gets "pissed" when we walk by the colour purple in a field, and don't take notice. For Shug, the natural world is a sacred text, infused by divine radiance. To know God in and through the colour purple, or to see Christ under every rock and every stick, doesn't mean that God *is* purple or that Christ *is* the stick. Rather, God is *in* the colour purple, and *in* the stick, and both the colour purple and the stick are within the one we call God.

# What Good Is a Bear? Or a Frog?

The practical implications of a disenchanted world surround us. In Vancouver we have an annual blessing of the salmon. A group gathers around a reclaimed salmon stream and blesses the hatchlings as they begin their long journey. Some years, these people meet on a busy street corner with cars whizzing by. We are reminded that, below us, there was once a salmon stream, now covered over by layers of concrete, sewers, and wires. In a disenchanted world, a salmon is an "it" and not a "thou," to use Martin Buber's distinction. Our dissociation from the natural world is so complete that we can, without second thought, pave over their natural habitat. It's not only the salmon who have paid a terrible price for this loss of enchantment. Our own souls pay the price. There exists within us a deep grief, waiting to be activated by the cries of the earth. The Spirit groans with sighs too deep for words (Romans 8).

*The Globe and Mail* newspaper carried an article, by Susan Sachs, entitled "An Ursine Battle Brews in the Pyrenees."[20] The French government has implemented a program to reintroduce black bears back into their natural habitat. The bear was once plentiful in the Pyrenees, but has, in modern times, been killed off by farmers and ranchers so that only 15 to 18 now live in the area. The local ranchers are outraged by the initiative to increase the numbers of bears. One of these ranchers summarized the sentiment, not only of the surrounding ranchers, but also of modern humanity: "What good is a bear?" he demanded to know. To pause and actually hear his question is to reflect on the state of our collective souls as we enter the 21st century. What good is any animal that doesn't directly serve our needs?

What good is a tree frog? In Vancouver, the government is building a road right through its natural habitat in preparation for the 2010 Winter Olympics in Whistler, British Columbia. What good is a frog if it gets in the way of wealthy recreational skiers propping up our economy? What good are any of the thousands of animals on the endangered species list? Only a psyche that has been weaned from wonder and initiated into a soulless cosmos can think this way.

## Myth and Mystery

The terms *myth* and *mystery* are often misunderstood. When I use the word *mystery*, you shouldn't think mystery novel. Mystery, in its spiritual meaning, is not the sum total of what we do not know about reality, and which we could discover if we just looked harder. Rather, the term *mystery* refers to the numinous (sacred) dimensions of what we already know and experience. The mystery inherent in a sunset, for example, is not a problem to be solved. It's about the feelings evoked by the beauty of the colours; it's the awareness that what we are witnessing is the slow turning of the earth away from the sun, and that our bodies and minds are preparing to enter into another dimension of consciousness, deep sleep; it's the awareness that we are travelling through deep space in a sacred dance with the orb of light and heat, which is responsible for our capacity to even consciously enjoy the sunset. Even if we are scientists who understand the chemical reactions within the sun, and the precise mathematics of the path of the earth's orbit around the sun, the mystery of the occasion is not reduced. Mystery, then, is the depth dimension of life, which lies beyond rational explanation.

One of the temptations inherent in trying to integrate science and theology is to reduce theology to science, which is an attempt to "solve" a mystery. God is only needed for those aspects of reality we don't yet understand scientifically. This kind of God is known as the "God of the gaps." If we don't have an empirical explanation for something, God fills in the "mysterious" gap. The problem, of course, is that with the next scientific discovery the gap closes. Eventually, the gap narrows and God gets squeezed out. Science can tell us the "whats" and "hows" of life, but is less concerned with and less able to explain the "whys" and "wherefores." Mystery is about entering into the interior depths of reality, both known and unknown.

As for *myth*, there are so many different ways to understand the term that it can be very confusing. Here are three ways of using it.

1.  In popular conversation when someone makes up a story that we know isn't true, we say that it's a myth.

2.  The term myth can be used to describe a set of modern beliefs and assumptions about the way things are, but upon closer inspection are revealed as arbitrary constructions of an elite. For example, sometimes we talk about the "myth" of consumerism, or the "myth" of empire. This use of the word myth is like the first one we discussed, in the sense that it's a story that isn't actually true, only the story is understood and applied on a much larger scale. When it comes to these large cultural myths, most of us are usually shocked the first time we realize that they're not actually true.

3.  Finally, when used in its anthropological sense, a myth is an ancient story that a culture tells itself to capture the essential *mystery* of life. It is a story that is not literally, historically true, but that nevertheless captures a truth about reality. The Judeo-Christian

myth of creation never "happened," for example. But, on the other hand, it is always happening. God didn't literally create the world in six days, and then take a siesta on the seventh day. Adam and Eve didn't literally inhabit a garden, and run into God taking a stroll one afternoon. Nevertheless, the story still expresses profound meanings and insights about the nature of reality for Jews and Christians, which bring a perspective on the search for truth. For example, from the Genesis story of creation, and of Adam and Eve, we can gain the following meanings and insights:

♦ The entire universe was intended into being by the One we call God.

♦ We were meant for relationship with this One.

♦ God delights in all of creation, calling it "very good."

♦ This divine blessing makes the universe fecund.

♦ Our desire to differentiate ourselves from God and the rest of the nature carries with it serious temptations, summarized in traditional theology as "the fall."[21]

One could go on, but the point is that although a myth, understood in this sense, is not factually or historically true, it nevertheless conveys truth.

# Chapter 3

## THE COMMON CREATION STORY
## AS SACRED REVELATION

I, the highest and fiery power, have kindled every living spark
and I have breathed out nothing that can die...
I flame above the beauty of the fields; I shine in the waters;
in the sun, the moon and the stars, I burn.
And by means of the airy wind,
I stir everything into quickness with a certain invisible life
which sustains all...
I, the fiery power, lie hidden in these things and they blaze from me.

HILDEGARD OF BINGEN

Start with an unimaginably dense point of matter smaller than a flea, add 14 billion years, and before our eyes a monarch butterfly wings its migratory way to Mexico.

A supernova explodes in some far-flung corner of the universe. Billions of years later, driving to work, your heart is broken open listening to k.d. lang's cover of Leonard Cohen's song *Hallelujah*.

A tiny planet in the Milky Way galaxy enters into a dance with its sun, and within only a few billion years, a human being sits in wonder as the earth turns away from its solar partner and the sandy arc of beach she's occupying slips into nightfall.

Einstein once suggested that there are only two ways to live our lives – as though everything is a miracle, or as though nothing is. We can tell the story of the universe as dry, scientific prose, or we can tell it as sacred poetry, the mysterious tale of the Holy One entering into the divine dance of creation. We call this sacred narrative the "common" story of creation, not because it's mundane – far from it. It's common in the sense that it is a sacred evolutionary narrative that encompasses *all* beings, human and other-than-human.

When Isaiah saw the Lord high and lifted up, he didn't say, "Holy, holy, holy God, the whole *Bible* is filled with your glory." The shattering insight that came to him was that the whole *earth* was filled with the Holy One's glory. As Christians, we have two sacred texts that tell our sacred story. One is the Bible and the other is the great book of creation itself. This latter story is the context for the sacred text of scripture.

The psalmist affirms Isaiah's witness that creation itself is full of God's glory: "The heavens are telling the glory of God, and the earth proclaims God's handiwork" (Psalm 19). Even though there are no words, and no voice is heard, yet creation tells the story of God throughout all the earth (vv. 3–4). The rising and the setting sun, which the psalmist compares to a bridegroom emerging from his tent to run his course with joy, participates in *"telling the glory of God."*

It is no accident that the psalmist leads with the affirmation of the earth and the heavens as a sacrament of God's radiant presence. For this story is the context of *all* sacred texts, including the Judeo-Christian scriptures. Only after establishing that the whole cosmos tells the glory of God, does the psalmist then launch into an affirmation and celebration of the written witness of God's glory, the Law. The closing verses affirm that by following the precepts of these two stories of God – the one told by creation and the one found in written text – the faithful will stay on the right track. I will follow the psalmist's intuition, setting out in this chapter the scientific story of creation as a sacred, revelatory text.

The story of creation told as sacred narrative does not replace or render obsolete the Judeo-Christian creation myth, or any other creation story of any other spiritual tradition. Myth is one way of knowing our world. Science is simply another way of knowing based not on intuition but on empirical evidence. In fact, it is reasonable to talk about science's version of the creation story as a modern myth. In a thousand years, scientists will read with profound interest, but perhaps amusement, how their earlier colleagues came up with the evidence for their version of the story. Our scientific version of the story is based on a solid and growing body of evidence. Still, it is undoubtedly partial. Evolution in human consciousness means that we will never stop discovering more comprehensive contexts and perspectives from which we do our science. What scientists look for is determined by their assumptions about the nature of reality. In a quantum universe, our assumptions are inevitably entangled with what we "discover" about the world. Therefore, as we turn to the version of creation that science has discovered, we hear it as a story that is as close to how life unfolded as science can presently tell. It represents the consensus view of our best scientists using the tools they currently have at their disposal.

# I. Our Common Story of Creation[1]

Some 13 and a half billion years ago, before time or space existed, the early universe flashed into existence. It's anybody's guess from what medium this flashing or flaring forth emerged. Some call it the All-Nourishing Abyss. Other names given to it include Cosmic Vacuum, Zero Point Energy Field, Fecund Emptiness, a field of Pure Being with no mass or energy, and the Unoriginate Origin. Sri Aurobindo calls it Non-Being or Nothing, as in no thing, but then quickly adds that these are only words. By nothing he means "something beyond the last term to which we can reduce our purest conception..."[2] Calling it the Womb of the Divine ventures into the realm of the spiritual imagination, but it's as good a metaphor as any I've come across.

There's not a scientist in the world who can tell us *why* such a Flaring Forth happened. Again, we're in the realm of theological imagination. So while we're there, let's just say that this was the moment when the Source, the Holy One, began the long (in human terms) journey of manifestation in the realm of time and space. It is, as poet Hafiz put it, "the secret One, slowly growing a body."[3]

This makes the Christian faith incarnational, which means basically that God doesn't have nearly the problem with the flesh-and-blood world of the created cosmos that some Christians display. While we tend to dissociate and privilege Spirit over matter, God apparently is at work in the cosmos knitting them back together, in God's own being! We can distinguish the two realms, but it's a mistake to dissociate them. It is the nature of God's Being to overflow in all dimensions, including the realm of matter.

Dr. Sallie McFague invites us to think about the entire cosmos as the incarnate presence of the divine. She explores the meaning of the created universe as the body of God. Incarnation, Spirit taking material form, is an evolutionary dynamic inherent in the entire unfolding of space and time, and not exclusively in Jesus of Nazareth.[4] Sri Aurobindo, writing from the Hindu tradition in the last century, affirmed that the "physical universe [can be] described as the external body of the Divine Being."[5] Even Plato talked about the natural world being "a visible, sensible God."

## The First Second

For much of what follows in this chapter, I am indebted to the work of Brian Swimme and Thomas Berry contained in their book *The Universe Story*.

It turns out that what happened in the first fraction of a second after the great Flaring Forth may be as important as anything that happened for 10 billion years after it. There's barely enough space on a line of this book for a single-digit number followed by all the zeros required to indicate how hot it was in the first second. It was much too hot for ordinary atomic nuclei to form. Rather, a stream of subatomic particles from neutrinos, to protons, neutrons, electrons and photons poured forth. Some writers refer to this subatomic substance as a kind of cosmic foam. Before you could snap your fingers, the first cosmic law was fixed, the law of expansion. If the universe had expanded one-trillionth of a second faster, those neutrinos, protons, neutrons, and electrons could never have evolved into more complex forms. If it had expanded one-trillionth of a second slower, everything would have simply collapsed back in on itself. We're alive to tell this story because of the precise rate of expansion set in place in the first second of the Flaring Forth.

A word about another feature of this expansion is in order. It came as a revelation to me that we can no longer think about this streaming forth as filling up a pre-existing space, like a whole bunch of guests arriving at your house and filling it up. Prior to the Flaring Forth, there was no house to fill up, there was no universe, no pre-existing empty space. The stream of particles was *creating* space, not to mention time, as it expanded.

This reality so challenges our conventional notion of "space" that when Einstein first looked through the Hooker telescope on top of Mount Wilson and saw for himself what Edwin Hubble had discovered – that the universe was expanding – he was elated. Prior to Hubble's discovery, astronomers had convinced Einstein that his General Theory of Relativity – which stated that the universe must either be expanding or contracting – was wrong; the universe was stable, they said. In a move he later called the greatest blunder of his life, Einstein had changed his equations to accommodate their perceptions. Hubble's discovery proved that he had been correct all along.[6] The universe as a whole was developing. It was going somewhere.

This was news. Darwin had established that evolution was occurring biologically. But now it was irrefutable that the whole universe had been on an evolutionary path before organic life emerged.

## The Triumph of Matter

The next epoch in the story – if a fraction of a second can constitute an epoch! – involved the titanic struggle between matter and anti-matter. Scientists believe that all the subatomic particles cancelled each other out, as they crashed into and annihilated each other. A mere one-billionth of the original matter of the universe survived this clash, passing through the first cosmic eye of the needle and enabling the story to continue.

It's strange how we religious types have historically denigrated matter, given what a rare and precious substance it is in the universe. You can buy space cheap, there's so much of it; but matter is, well, another matter. That matter was even able to form is a cosmic miracle that required cosmic precision in terms of both the rate of expansion and temperature.

## The First Atoms: Seeds of the Star Fields

The third epoch involved the creation of atoms, a stupendous achievement. As the universe expanded and cooled, our remnant atoms gained a window of opportunity to hook up with one another. Hydrogen and helium formed in a remarkable communion event. Prior to this moment, free floating electrons were simply scooped up and carried away by particles of light passing by them. But within the bonded communion of the hydrogen atom, electrons stayed home. The universe, says Swimme, became transparent, as light was now able to pass through a hydrogen atom without destroying the integrity of the atom.[7]

The fourth epoch began with a ripple of gravity, a tiny quantum fluctuation in the fabric of time-space, enabling atoms of hydrogen and helium to cluster together into a trillion huge clouds. After a billion years, these would condense into the galaxies. Scientists think that there are approximately 100 billion galaxies each containing up to 100 trillion stars. I know. It's unimaginable. A friend tried to help me with an analogy. Fill a thimble with sand. If each grain of sand in the thimble represents one star, that's how many stars we can see with the unaided eye. Then fill a wheelbarrow. This is how many stars we can see with all our fancy equipment. Now fill some railway box cars with sand. You'd have to stand for two full weeks, as boxcar after boxcar filed by, to get a sense of the number of stars in the universe.

Our local cluster is Virgo, which has around 1000 galaxies. Our own home galaxy, the Milky Way, is one of them, located on one end of the Virgo cluster. We're approximately two-thirds of the way out towards the edge of Virgo. Home sweet home.

All these galaxies are bonded together in a cosmic dance, spiralling around one another through space. At this point in the story, we're celebrating our one billion year birthday, give or take 100 million years.

## The Supernova Sacrifice

The fifth epoch of "early" creation involved supernovas. A supernova is an exploding star, which briefly outshines its entire host galaxy. The structure of a star is maintained by a fine balance between the powers of gravity and the energy generated in the centre of a star. This energy at the centre of a star comes from the conversion of hydrogen into helium. For very large stars – at least ten times larger than our sun – the hydrogen lasts for about ten million years. When the hydrogen is depleted, this burning can only continue in a shell around the helium core. Gravity then bears down upon the core, increasing the core's temperature. It becomes so hot that the helium is transformed into carbon and oxygen, then into neon, sodium, and magnesium. Eventually, all that's left is iron. Energy conversion becomes impossible. The force of gravity takes over, and the heat becomes so intense that it burns away everything, leaving only neutrons. This super-dense mass of neutrons at the core is about ten kilometres in diameter. If a star has enough mass – 40 times that of our sun – this neutron core will itself collapse in an absolute fashion into a black hole without an explosion.

The smaller stars that do explode – supernovae – release enormous amounts of energy, created by the successive collapses of the core. In the process, a stream of neutrinos is released. As these neutrinos stream away from the core, they interact with the outer layers of the star (which are in the process of collapsing back toward the core). As the neutrinos interact with these outer layers, nuclear fusions begin to occur. In the process, new, heavier elements necessary for the emergence of life are synthesized. These heavier elements get a free ride into interstellar space, on the back of the neutrino stream. You're around to read this book thanks to this stream of neutrinos responsible for both the synthesis of heavy elements and their dispersion throughout the cosmos.

From this supernova explosion, then, all the elements we know about, including the ones essential for life on earth – oxygen, carbon, hydrogen, and nitrogen – flare forth. We are literally made from this stardust. As Barbara Brown Taylor puts it, "the only difference between us and trees or rocks and chickens is the way in which these elements are arranged."[8]

## Interlude: The Narrow Gate

Jesus once said that the "way is narrow which leads to life," and it turns out he was expressing a cosmological truth. On a cosmic scale, you'll remember that, at the very beginning, 99.9 percent of matter didn't make it through the narrow gate, which led to life. Next, countless stars, which took millions of years to form, imploded, then exploded as supernovas, sending new elements required for life hurtling through the next narrow gate. In each epoch, the universe passes through a series of increasingly narrow gates. Like Moses, most of the evolutionary beings in this story (from atoms to stars to the heavy elements) are allowed to reach the shores of the "Promised Land," but are not allowed to cross over into life. Like Moses, they give their life to enable a remnant to cross over the banks of the Jordan to experience and claim the unfolding promise of God. You may wish to pause to give thanks at this point in the story!

The biblical equivalent of this cosmological narrow path is the path of unconventional wisdom, which Jesus taught. When he tells his followers that they must "take up their cross" to follow him, he is expressing a pattern of life embedded in the large scale structure of the cosmos itself. He says that it is a "narrow gate," which leads to life.

To know the evolving story of creation is to comprehend the Spirit's path of wisdom, which requires each being to give its life in the service of the evolutionary arc of the universe. Jesus' death can be imagined as a supernova event, the whole universe collapsing back in on itself after 14 billion years of evolution, in a cataclysmic act of violence. Yet from this destruction new life streams forth, as we, Jesus' followers, embrace this path of sacrifice and align ourselves with the evolutionary thrust of the universe.

The Promised Land, cosmologically speaking, can be thought of as the planet itself coming to life. Prior to the Hebrew people, there were cosmic nomadic beings – neutrinos, elements, galaxies, and stars – that made the treacherous journey through the wilderness of unfurling space, propelled by an implicit promise that the journey was not in vain. Life on earth represents the land of milk and honey on a cosmic scale.

To reduce the scope of this cosmic promise to a particular piece of land, and then to be willing to kill for it, is to have lost our cosmological bearings. When Jesus affirmed that the kingdom of God dwells within, he was challenging his listeners to expand their consciousness beyond identification with geography, ethnicity, and belief systems. He knew that peace would be impossible if people identified with and idolized these things.

## A Commercial Break

I interrupt this narrative to bring you breaking news of cosmological import. It just dropped through my mailbox. A glossy advertising brochure tells me, "When You're in a Perfect Moment, Time Stands Still." Underneath is an image of a new luxury car, a handsome vehicle to be sure. The letter is personally addressed to me.

Dear Bruce Sanguin,

Some people are content to let life's perfect moments just happen. While others actively pursue them… what exactly are the elements that make up this perfect moment? They begin with the heart of the 2007 ES 350, the new 3.5 Litre, 272 Horsepower V6 engine…

Here I was, associating the perfect moment with the great Flaring Forth, the triumph of matter over anti-matter, the precise rate of expansion of the universe, the setting of the four fundamental laws (gravity, weak and strong nuclear forces, and electromagnetism), the moment when hydrogen and helium emerged, and the way in which these first atoms seeded the cosmos for the harvest of galaxies. I had been thinking about a supernova moment, when a star imploded so that the elements necessary for the emergence of life on earth might emerge. These, I thought, were the perfect moments, manifestations of Spirit. It turns out that all I had to do was make an appointment to see a salesman about a new car. The perfect moment awaited me behind the wheel of this sacred vehicle.

These advertisers do not spend good money for naught. Marketing works, and it works precisely because we've lost our connection to the sacred dimension of our creation story. We are, in fact, activated by this advertising. Our innate yearning for a numinous dimension is being exploited and connected to a product. I am being asked to believe that a 272 horsepower engine is the central element in the conversation around perfection. The 24-inch brochure features another caption: "Feel the Rush!" If we're not feeling the "rush" of the way in which the Spirit creates in and through this evolving story of creation, we'll feel it any way we can. It is ludicrous to compare the engine of a car with what's "under the hood" of the cosmos. Yet we get hooked. In the absence of a sacred narrative, these powers have a way of getting confused.

Now, where were we...?

# Our Galactic Goldilocks

The sixth epoch, which occurred approximately five billion years ago, was the age when our solar system came into being, from the seed elements of a supernova. It was formed from what had been a "parent nebula," composed of swirling particles and gases. One portion of this parent nebula condensed under the influence of gravity. The temperature increased at the core, igniting the thermonuclear reaction of our "Protosun."

Other bits of matter spun off from this parent nebula and began to form individual units, which took their orbit around our sun. These became the planets of our solar system, including earth.

Five billion years ago, earth situated itself at exactly the right distance from the sun for life to eventually emerge. Everything you see around you, from the cup of steaming tea you might be drinking to the chair you're sitting in, to the thought you just had, is the result of the one-billionth of the sun's energy reaching the earth. You are a solar event! The heat you're giving off is the heat of the sun.

It turns out that earth is the geological equivalent of the story of Goldilocks – not too hot and not too cold, not too big and not too small. The cosmic porridge was "just right." Jupiter, on the other hand, simply had too much mass to evolve beyond a gaseous state. The force of gravity exerted because of its mass meant that it never developed permanent geological formations. The interior radioactivity couldn't solidify. The mass of Mars was too small. There wasn't even enough mass to keep the fires within burning, so it turned to rock, without enough electromagnetic energy to bring it to life. It got as far as red boulders, and no further. Earth was the right size and the right distance from the sun for the evolutionary force of the universe to continue its journey.

# Life Emerges

The seventh epoch of the universe story holds the emergence of life on our planet. Earth took a pounding in its early years. For several hundred million years, it was bombarded by meteors with such intensity that its surface was literally boiling because of the friction. When the pounding tapered off, the temperature dropped, which enabled rocks to solidify instead of melting and sinking into the core. Then came the lightning. Imagine the worst lightning storm at your summer cottage and multiply it by a million. Have it last a few million years. You get the idea. It was this lightning flashing incessantly over the waters of the earth that sparked life into being.

To say "life came into being" on the planet is to understate the profundity of this stunning moment. There is, hidden within the fabric of the cosmos, a bias toward increasing complexity and organization. This bias is driven by what Swimme refers to as a fundamental "ethic" of the universe, manifest in three interrelated dynamics. The first is communion. The universe is a single, dynamic event, in which attraction at all levels plays a pivotal role. For example, hydrogen and helium seem to be hard-wired to enter into a dance with one another. If there was no intrinsic attraction, things would simply fly apart. The second dynamic is differentiation. Within this communion, each and every emergent being is different from the rest, leading to the breathtaking diversity we see around us. "To be is to be a unique manifestation of existence."[9] The third dynamic inherent in all creation is *autopoiesis*. Another word for this is self-renewal. Each being simply "knows" from the inside the next step to take in order to be a player in the ongoing evolution of life. There is, in other words, an interior dimension to all of life, which enables all beings to manifest or express their unique identity. Taken together, these three dynamics suggest a universal ethic biased toward life. They constitute a hidden pattern in the heart of the universe.[10]

When surrounding conditions are sufficiently intense and there is enough free energy present, these hidden patterns are activated. This is just the way it is. It is a fundamental condition of the universe. This capacity speaks to a deep mystery, and, for those of us who are spiritually inclined, it suggests the presence of a Creative Power at the heart of the universe.

The particular form of life that was sparked into being by the millions of years of lightning was bacteria. The fancy name for bacteria is *prokaryote*. It just means they don't have a nucleus. Their descendants, the *eukaryotes*, out of which the plants and animals emerge, are nucleated cells. If you had forgotten this from biology class, join the club.

Swimme and Berry describe the emergence of these early life forms using the language of myth.[11] Aries, the astrological sign signifying the spring equinox, is the name they gave to the prokaryotes, which emerged four billion years ago and which lived for two billion years. During that time they lay the foundation for the evolution of successive, more complex forms of life, including, eventually, humans.

Promethio (named after Promethius, the Greek mythological figure who stole fire to help humanity) figured out how to capture sunlight and turn it into food, through photosynthesis. In this ability, he was the progenitor of future generations of plants – eukaryotes – who would exploit this photosynthetic capacity of their prokaryotic ancestors. Before this little guy got going, the atmosphere of the earth would have killed us in a heartbeat. But Promethio learned how to convert carbon dioxide into energy. In the process, it released oxygen into the atmosphere, fixing it at the current level of 21 percent. If this level was 22 percent, we'd all go up in flames; if it was a little lower, life as we know it could not have evolved. It's one of those exquisite coincidences that doesn't necessarily prove the existence of a Supreme Intelligence in the universe, but certainly hints at it. Personally, I don't have much problem imagining Spirit working with bacteria to establish ideal oxygen levels for future life.

It's a little more complicated than this, however. The reduction in carbon dioxide levels and the increase in oxygen levels worked out just fine for us, but at the time it was virtually apocalyptic. Oxygen poisoned the atmosphere. It precipitated the first Ice Age. Carbon dioxide is a greenhouse gas, locking in heat. When its levels were reduced by the $CO_2$-eating bacteria, the planet cooled. Actually, oxygen turns out to be somewhat of a nasty molecule. It destroyed cell membranes, tore electrons from stable molecules, and created free radicals. Today we're told to eat blueberries and to drink red wine to try to moderate the influence of these destructive free radicals in our own bodies.

Fortunately a new bacterium, Prospero, the name given to the magician in Shakespeare's play *The Tempest*, arrived on the scene. Prospero, an aerobic bacteria, was able to use the new oxygen in the atmosphere. Just as Promethio was the ancestor of the plant kingdom, because of his capacity for photosynthesis, so Prospero was the progenitor or ancestor of the animal kingdom, because of his ability to breathe oxygen. This was an astounding achievement.

These two bacteria – Promethio and Prospero – disrupted the early conditions of earth. Together they created a dynamic disequilibrium, which destroyed previous life forms but simultaneously enabled more complex and elegant forms of life to emerge.

Next to arrive on the scene were the eukaryotes, beginning with Viking. Listen to Brian Swimme: "The eukaryotic cell, the first radically new creation within the oxygenated Gaian system, is the single greatest transformation in the entire history of Earth, overshadowed in significance only by the emergence of life itself."[12] Who knew!?

Viking had a serpent-like tail, which it used to chase down Aries, the prokaryotes (the bacteria without a nucleus). It was a hostile takeover in the beginning, thus the name Viking. Viking used the host cell's memory to manufacture its own proteins and nucleic acids. This new symbiotic being eventually swallowed, but didn't digest, a photosynthetic bacterium, and the second kingdom – the nucleated eukaryotes – were born.

We are now able to date the emergence of these eukaryotes to 2.45 billion years ago. Scientists recently found them preserved in little globules of oil discovered in rocks in a sandstone outcropping in Elliot Lake in Northern Ontario, Canada. "These are our ultimate ancestors," said University of Washington geologist Roger Buick. He added, "This is a big deal!"[13]

If you're beginning to wonder why you should care about any of this, it might help to know that you wouldn't work without these little guys. They continue, in modified form, to be part of your own body. Lynn Margulis, a cellular biologist, presents evidence that Viking's whip-like tail went on to become other things in our bodies, like the tail of sperm; the cilia, which line the esophagus; and perhaps even the dendrites in our nerves.[14] Recently, scientists have discovered that descendants of our primal bacterial cousins constitute 90 percent of our cellular structure; only 10 percent of our cells are distinctly human. The myth of the rugged individualist simply doesn't hold up in the new cosmology. We each have around three pounds of these little guys in our bodies doing all kinds of things that we wouldn't otherwise know how to do, from making vitamins not found in our diet (including B vitamins), to creating enzymes that break down plant fibres so we can digest them, to breaking down other cancer-causing plant chemicals.

One further character deserves mention. After three billion years, Kronos got the notion to swallow other creatures whole – this is known as heterotrophy. Up until this point, cells had learned to eat the sun, other chemically rich molecules, and the decayed bodies of other cells, but this was a whole new ball game! The predator-prey dynamic kicked into gear and with it, the ecological dynamic we know today. It now became necessary to pay close attention, to live in an intimate, co-evolutionary relationship with other beings. Predators began to evolve according to the demands its prey exerted upon it, and vice versa. Now, all of life would develop, not autonomously, but rather in community.

The story thus far represents the successful triumph of the evolutionary process over four major crises: the emergence of matter over anti-matter in the first millisecond of life, which eventually allowed hydrogen and helium atoms to develop; the forging of the heavy elements necessary for life out of apocalyptic supernovas; the hammering of the earth by comets and lightning over a period of hundreds of millions of years, which lead to the rise of Aries, or bacteria; and then the oxygen crisis, which threatened to end the story in disaster. We have built into the fabric of our being a resiliency, which we can draw upon in this great work of repairing the planet. In other words, what we're facing today in terms of a planetary crisis is not new. We've been here before and have survived.

With the triumph over these crises, the foundation for the emergence of the rest of life was laid: first came the marine invertebrates, then plants ventured forth out of the seas, then fish with bones, amphibians who could swing both ways, reptiles, mammals, birds, primates; and finally the upright ones, including homo sapiens.

## Conscious Self-Reflection

The eighth epoch of the creation story involves the emergence of conscious self-reflection in the human race. The point is not that other forms of life do not have consciousness. In fact, many credible scientists affirm that all living forms participate in consciousness to varying degrees. But humans gained the capacity to be aware that we are aware. The universe stood up and gazed out upon itself with the arrival of humanity.

We are the presence of the universe in a form capable of understanding that there is a single thread connecting all creation, from the tiniest atom to the largest galaxy, and including all forms of organic and inorganic life. The elements of our bodies are linked to the elements that came out of a supernova. Every cell on earth consists of the same 50 organic molecules. Every creature on earth derives its energy from the same sun; plants and animals do the work of converting it into energy usable by human beings, but every act of eating is an act of solar communion. Every being shares the same four nucleotides and the same 20 amino acids to help us with protein formation; we all carry the memories of our ancestors in a double helix formation, in DNA or in RNA. The 50 trillion cells that comprise our bodies form a community of elegant cooperation, producing the proteins necessary to sustain life, and allowing the exchange of information with our environment, enabling us to adjust to changes.[15] If human beings spent as much time thinking about what connects us as what separates us (belief systems, lines on a map, ethnic backgrounds, divisions of class and race, and gender), we might come to our senses before it's too late.

This kind of meditation is a cosmological prayer, and with just a little thought in the direction of our common creation story, the cosmos would appear to us as it actually is – a teeming, vital miracle. More than this, for Christians it is a self-communication of the Holy One in and through this story, which is now ours to tell. Our unity with all creation is not a romantic abstraction. It is the most real thing about us. We are kin with skunks, gazelles, red-wing blackbirds, salamanders, and walruses. Along with the mountains and the rivers, they all share the same stardust with us. Ultimately, we are all fascinating reconfigurations of the orig- inating fireball. We are children of the One who fired it all into being and who is our one Source.

Imagine giving this evolutionary story, told as sacred nar- rative, a central place in our educational and spiritual curricula. Imagine it being told as a numinous, sacred tale, encompassing all beings. Each culture, religious and secular, would retain its own distinctive identity and yet become aware of a profound uni- ty underlying our diversity. Unity through differentiation is the way of the universe. The uniqueness of all beings is what enables us to play our distinctive roles in sustaining the ecological web in which we live and move and have our being. This sacred story of creation has the potential to be the basis for a powerful new ecumenism. All religions share this common story. As we learn it and tell it to our children, we will find our way back home.

Susan McCaslin, poet and English professor, tells the creation story as sacred narrative in poetic form.

~ *I Was Fashioned in Times Past, in the Beginning* ~

Think ballerina stars
then throw them back to a point.

Think sea –
then meld it to the stars,

let it swallow the moon and the sun,
let it shimmer as it devolves to mire

and a small sucking sound, a single cell
perfect in its finite way.

Think earth, springs, mountains, hill,
pockets of incensed air, pine needles erect

whirring in a vortex-white dwarf.
Then in that utter silence

long before past was what you call past
imagine me, leafless, twigless,

pregnant with myself,
pregnant within creative spirit,

single before the fecund blast
danced out of the unformed

into what you see – blue camas, manzanitas,
blue-eyed Marys, sea-blush,

lavender shooting stars, coral root, orchids –
a thousand islands floating across time.[16]

## 2. Signs of Re-enchantment

My third ear is always listening for stories that indicate that our species is on the verge of rediscovering an enchanted universe. I came across an article in *The New York Times* News Service, from the art culture, which captured my attention.[17] The auction house of Bonham in New York sold a chunk of a meteorite believed to have originated from an asteroid belt between Mars and Jupiter, for the tidy price of $93,000 US. Somebody had the bright idea of mounting it on a pole, and turning it into an art piece. Now, either this reflects a world in which some people, with way too much money, have gone mad, or it expresses an ancient intuition that the heavenly realms are enchanted. Modern scientific consensus is that those comets that pummelled the young earth for a few million years carried with them trace elements of organic life. This art piece is either nothing more than a 355-pound chunk of iron, or it is a sacred artifact, a cosmic icon, connecting us to the origins of life on earth, and to the heavens.

In art circles, they're calling these works of art "aesthetic meteorites." People are buying them not for their scientific value, but because of their intrinsic beauty. In the same auction, a two-gram piece of the moon brought $4,250, a space rock found in Africa with a naturally formed hole went for $42,000, and another smaller meteorite with naturally occurring gemstones fetched $11,950. The curator of the museum said, "For me, aesthetic meteorites are the closest thing to being able to behold that which is in the heavens."

## Evidence of the Big Bang

The Big Bang, or the great Flaring Forth as I have chosen to refer to it, has emerged as the best explanation of how our universe began. There are detractors, but scientific evidence is solid and growing. Brian Swimme presents the evidence as threefold.[18]

The first piece of evidence occurred when Edwin Hubble confirmed Einstein's prediction that the universe was expanding. When Hubble looked through the Hooker telescope he saw that the other galaxies were moving away from our own galaxy, the Milky Way, and that the farther away they were, the faster they were moving; in fact twice as fast. If you reverse this process of expansion, ultimately you end up at an initial point – what cosmologists call a singularity.

Second, scientists realized that there should be some evidence around for the Big Bang, in the form of background cosmic radiation. A couple of scientists, Penzias and Wilson, in 1965, were working on a completely different project, but kept picking up this annoying interference. At first they thought that roosting pigeons might be messing up their satellite signals with their droppings. They scraped a considerable amount of this "interference" from their equipment, but the hiss persisted. The temperature of the hiss at 2.7 degrees Kelvin (2.7 degrees above absolute zero) was consistent with what cosmologists hypothesized the background radiation from the Big Bang would be.

They had inadvertently discovered the best proof for the Big Bang, and won a Nobel Prize for their efforts.

Finally, the amount of hydrogen, lithium, and helium we actually find in the universe is consistent with what scientists have concluded would be the case in the Big Bang scenario.

# Chapter 4

## EVOLUTION AS DIVINE UNFOLDING

The affirmation of a divine life upon earth and an immortal sense
in mortal existence can have no base unless we recognize not only
eternal Spirit as the inhabitant of this bodily mansion, the wearer
of this mutable robe, but accept Matter of which it is made, as
a fit and noble material out of which He weaves constantly His
garbs, builds recurrently the unending series of His mansions.

– SRI AUROBINDO, LIFE DIVINE

In 1859, with the publication of *On the Origin of Species*, Charles
Darwin confirmed scientifically what the Idealist school of philosophy had intuited a century before. Life on earth developed
through an evolutionary process.

> I have a grand body of facts and I think I can draw some
> sound conclusions. The general conclusion at which I
> have slowly been driven... is that species are mutable
> and that allied species are co-descendants of common
> stocks.[1]

This idea that all life descended from common stock, which
evolved into all the diversity we see around us, was so radical
that Darwin sat on it for almost 20 years. In fact, Darwin was
intentionally coy about whether to include the human being as
derivative of that common stock. He only hinted at it at the end
of *The Origin of Species*. His wife, a devout Christian, was deeply

concerned about the salvation of her dear husband's soul. Indeed, the pain his theory caused her may have been one of the reasons he delayed so long in publishing the book.[2]

Apparently, the idea that human beings are part of this evolutionary process is still a fairly radical idea. The Gallup organization put the following statement to over 1000 Americans in November 2004: "God created human beings pretty much in their present form at one time within the last 10,000 years or so." A full 45 percent of respondents agreed. That's 100 million people walking around with no sense that we have any biological connection to the rest of creation! One wonders how this impacts lifestyle choices and environmental policy-making.

Darwin's penchant for collecting massive amounts of data before publishing came to an end with the arrival of a package he received in the mail from a young amateur naturalist. Alfred Russel Wallace was virtually unknown in scientific circles, but put in his innings on remote islands in Indonesia. The manuscript within the package was entitled *The World of Life: A Manifestation of Creative Power, Directive Mind and Ultimate Purpose*. Darwin felt sickened as he read words he himself could have penned. Wallace had nailed the theory of natural selection, independently from Darwin, and what was worse, had beat the venerated scientist to the publishing punch.

The theory of natural selection was actually more radical than evolutionary theories, which existed prior to Darwin. Darwin's own grandfather stumbled onto the idea, writing that, "All warm-blooded animals have arisen from one living filament."[3] He had no proof. His grandson, on the other hand, had gobs of it.

Natural selection described the "how" of evolution in the biological realm, and it wasn't via a divine Creator who lay down a blueprint. Neither was it the so-called "essentialist" position, which posited that there were four or five essential and unchanging types of animals, within which there was variation, but that variation didn't result in the emergence of whole new species. On the contrary, Darwin presented natural selection as a purposeless dynamic, driven by chance and random variations within species. Some variations were better suited for survival, and so were selected by nature. Others didn't cut the mustard. Over vast amounts of time, these slight variations and adaptations could result in what Darwin called "transmutation," the emergence of a new species.

Darwin's argument was based on the practice of breeding, employed by humans in botany and farming. Just as domestic breeders fashioned different varieties of pigeons from one species of wild dove, so nature selected certain variations within species in each new generation. In other words, a natural breeding process equivalent to the artificial breeding used by farmers occurred in nature. Darwin, however, couldn't say what accounted for these variations.

It took an Augustinian monk, Gregor Mendel, shortly after the publication of *On the Origins of Species*, to point in the direction of a solution. Mendel spent eight years conducting cross-breeding experiments with the common garden pea. He tracked the inheritance traits in flower colour, leaf characteristics, seed shape, concluding that some traits are dominant, others recessive. When a dominant trait is crossed with a recessive trait, the dominant one wins out. But the recessive trait hangs around until it's mixed with another recessive trait, and then it emerges.

A German zoologist, August Weisman, working around the same time as Mendel, came up with the theory that molecular material located in the nuclei of cells was responsible for the passing on of hereditary traits.[4] He also posited the theory that chromosomes get tangled up with each other, break down and recombine. In sexual reproduction, this results in all manner of possible combinations, ensuring that there is variety passed on from generation to generation – genetic mutation.

With those discoveries, Darwin's puzzle of what accounts for variations among species was essentially solved. The mutation and recombination of genetic material within species over vast amounts of time is a very effective survival mechanism. (It also accounts for diversity and novelty.) Nature "selects" the variations best suited for survival within a particular ecology.

Fifty years ago, Francis Crick, an English biologist, won the Nobel Prize for co-discovering the structure of the DNA molecule. Nature is very efficient. Rather than start over with each new species, it makes use of the accumulated evolutionary memory and wisdom of the universe stored in genes. Ever since Crick's discovery, the central dogma of science has been what he called "the primacy of DNA," more commonly known as biological and genetic determinism. At first, this idea was expressed in relation to physical characteristics. But more recently this belief has been extended to include psychological and emotional traits as well. The doctrine of biological and genetic determinism has led many people to believe that we are passive victims of an indifferent nature.

## Survival of the Fittest?

Most of us have been taught that evolution is devoid of any Spirit or sacred mystery. The struggle to survive within an indifferent and hostile universe is the engine that drives all of creation, including the human. This is the essence of the doctrine of the survival of the fittest, which is assumed to be nature's way. The "fittest" are those with the biggest teeth, strongest muscles, and the most testosterone – in the human species, that means the male warriors. This doctrine (and it is no more than a doctrine) logically leads to what is known as social Darwinism. Those at the top of the heap, in terms of social class, privilege, and status, deserve to be "kings of the castle," because they are the "fittest." The "dirty rascals" at the bottom make a good labour pool.

The problem with the survival of the fittest as a theory is not that it totally misses the mark. It is apparent that struggle is part of the evolutionary story. Necessity may indeed be the mother of invention. But what began as a *descriptive* metaphor has become a *prescriptive* metaphor for humans. Nature, voided of any grace or cooperative capacities, becomes the norm for human interactions. Based on this model of nature, competition becomes a virtue in and of itself so that, now, ruthlessness in business is seen as natural. Nations compete for pre-eminence and influence. North Korea notices that other nations listen to those who have nuclear weapons. Those with the biggest guns win. This is just the way it is; this is what you have to do and have to survive in the "real world."

Biologist Brian Goodwin has noted the similarity between the doctrine of survival of the fittest in biology, and the doctrine of original sin in theology.[5] Just as organisms leave copies of themselves in the form of selfish genes, so humans reproduce, passing on an inherent selfishness to their offspring. Just as the inherent selfishness of organisms is reflected in their competitive interaction with one another, so humans are fated to a life of conflict and perpetual toil (Genesis 1). (Paradoxically, though, human beings may transcend this inherent selfishness by developing moral fibre through education.) Theologically, only an intervention by God saves humanity from itself, redeeming our sinful nature.

Both models reflect a belief that an innate selfishness is at work within the universe, which is fundamentally hostile; and that this innate tendency to selfishness requires education and/or divine intervention to overcome.

Thank goodness ever increasing numbers of people are repulsed by this model. What a miserable story to tell ourselves, not to mention our children! It's a dog-eat-dog world out there. Only God and some serious moral training can counteract the sinful nature of both humans and creation. Furthermore, our lives have been determined by blind physical forces acting in and through passive bundles of nerves and chemicals. Nature, including human nature, is void of any interior value.

But other theorists, such as biologist Charles Birch, believe that all organisms enjoy an inner life, a feeling dimension.[6] Brian Swimme calls this quality of being "subjectivity."

Biologist Elisabet Sahtouris notes that in their early adolescent stage, our primal kin, the bacteria, evolved from a survivalist to a cooperative ethic. They learned to feed each other, not fight each other. At some point, Sahtouris argues, it is likely that single-cell bacteria proliferated to such an extent that they were competing with each other for survival, so they learned to team up in the service of ongoing life.[7] Cellular biologist, Lynn Margulis, has finally convinced the scientific community that this dynamic, which she calls *symbiogenesis* – bacteria and cells actually cooperating with each other, not competing, to produce an entirely new life form – plays a larger role than random mutation in evolution. It is now standard text book material.[8]

As humans, we are at a stage in our development when we are likewise proliferating to such an extent that we imagine ourselves to be competing for scarce resources. We need to take a lesson from bacteria and learn to cooperate. We are, after all, unique expressions of the universe; or, to put it theologically, we are expressions of the Oneness we call God. At this point in our history, the ethic of *the survival of the most loving* is what will enable us to serve the evolutionary purposes of the universe.

In other words, the survival of the fittest and genetic determinism are only two aspects of a more nuanced story. Robert Sapolsky, professor of neurology at Stanford University, wrote an article entitled "A Natural History of Peace," for *Harper's Magazine*.[9] In the article, Sapolsky points out that the bonobo species of chimpanzee are female dominated. They get along very well, thank you very much, using copious amounts of sex (in pairs, in groups, and between genders) to keep the peace.

It's an interesting exercise to contrast these chimpanzees with baboons. Most male baboons die as a result of violence. Half of the male aggression is directed at innocent bystanders, primarily female. But, as it turns out, it's not necessarily the genes of the *aggressors* that get passed on. In fact, it may be that social conditions override a genetic tendency toward violence. Ingenious female baboons find ways to sneak off from the alpha male spouse-abusers to mate with those who are adept at social grooming, child-rearing, and building affiliative relationships. Can we call these guys "sensitive new age chimps" (SNACs)?

There is plenty of evidence emerging that suggests that *biology is not destiny* in the world of primates. Sapolsky shares his own story of working, during the early 1980s, with savannah baboons. Two groups of baboons, Forest Troop and Garbage Dump Troop, became combative over the food that a tourist lodge threw out each morning. Soon after these morning melees began, both troops caught tuberculosis from contaminated meat. Garbage Dump Troop lost most of its members, and Forest Troop lost all of its fighters who showed up at the dump. This meant that the ratio of female to males in Forest Troop doubled. More significantly, the remaining males, who weren't part of the aggressive garbage dump brigade, were more affiliative. The resulting changes in the social milieu were dramatic and lasting.

Forest Troop morphed into the peaceniks of the baboon world. Females began to trust that they weren't going to be attacked, and therefore exhibited more loving behaviour toward the remaining males. A virtuous cycle led to some remarkable shifts in the culture. Typically, to guard against inbreeding, young male baboons leave their birth troop to mature elsewhere, returning only years later. Normally it takes years for a returning male to reintegrate, as females ignore them and other males beat them up. But within the new culture of Forest Troop, these young males returned to a drastically altered experience. They didn't know what hit them! They found themselves uncharacteristically inundated with female attention. Within 18 days, females presented themselves sexually to these new males, whereas in "normal" troops this takes 63 days. And they started grooming the new males after 20 days, whereas the norm is 78 days. Today, over 20 years later, this "alternative" baboon culture persists in Forest Troop. Sapolsky concludes, "It appears that this troop's remarkable culture is not passed on genetically, but rather *emerges*, facilitated by the actions of the resident members."[10]

## Epigenetics

The new science of epigenetics ("beyond genes") is undermining strict genetic determinism. An experiment with mice has shown that DNA has been overrated as the determinant of behaviour. Agouti mice are known to produce obese offspring due to an abnormal gene. In the experiment, one group of mice was given vitamins known to be high in methyl-rich chemicals. These chemicals counteract the genetic defect, enabling the gene to "read" signals from the environment, which the defect prevented it from doing. The other group was denied these vitamins. The offspring of the group fed the methyl-rich vitamins were born with the flawed gene, yet were normal, lean, mice. The control group's offspring were obese.[11] In their book *Epigenetic Inheritance and Evolution: The Lamarckian Dimension,* the authors conclude, "In recent years, molecular biology has shown that the genome is far more fluid and responsive to the environment than we previously supposed. It has also shown that information can be transmitted to descendants in ways other than through the base sequence of DNA."[12]

## Self-Organization

For example, complexity scientists have discovered a remarkable quality intrinsic to all dynamic systems, including living organisms. When a dynamic system moves towards chaos and disequilibrium, the system seems to have the innate capacity to reorganize itself at a more complex level. It evolves to become more of itself, transcending, yet including, the former structure in its new expression. This is called self-organization or emergence, and it happens all the way up the evolutionary line: particles evolve into atoms; stressed bacteria evolve into cells; and so on. It even extends to cultural evolution, including the formation of the World Wide Web.[13]

## Nature Versus Nurture Versus Conscious Awareness

In humans there is one more factor that materialist science tends to ignore. The argument is often presented in terms of nature versus nurture. "Naturists" believe that we are determined by blind forces of nature and by genetic material. "Nurturists," on the other hand, believe that cultural factors, such as education, modelling, good parenting and religious education, are more determinative of behaviour. But in humans there is a third factor: *consciousness*. Conscious awareness gives humans the capacity to override both nature and nurture, both biological and cultural influences. The reason we have underestimated the power of conscious awareness is that science has taught us that it comes out of our grey matter. If this is true, then consciousness is nothing more than a biological phenomenon, serving the ultimate goal of survival.

But consciousness doesn't come *out* of the brain. It comes *through* the brain. The brain is a physical instrument, an exquisite information processor, which receives, interprets, and transmits signals from the body and from the environment. We live and move and have our being in a vast, unified field of consciousness or intelligence. Evolution, understood as a spiritual dynamic, is the story of how various life forms manifest this consciousness.

Look how far we've come from understanding evolution as nothing more than random genetic mutations being selected by nature for survival. Epigenetics tells us that organisms have the capacity to switch genes on and off in response to environmental signals, by passing information from the environment through the cell membrane. We've seen that symbiogenesis – the capacity of cells and organisms to cooperate altruistically – must be added to the mix. Complexity theorists are now telling us that dynamic systems simply enjoy an innate capacity to re-create themselves in response to environmental signals. Finally, we've discovered that humans can consciously evolve, changing limiting belief systems, which impede our evolution. Notice the movement – the evolution of evolution – away from mere physicalistic assumptions and towards increased mystery, a deep innate intelligence or wisdom, a mysterious life force biased in the direction of what we might call "the spiritual."

## Evolution as Spiritual Dynamic

Using theological language, God is in the evolutionary process and the evolutionary process is in God. Genesis affirms that humans are made "in God's image." This means that each of us is a unique reflection of God. I would extend this theological affirmation to all forms of creation. The evolutionary aim of the universe seems to be in the direction of an increasing capacity to consciously reflect this image.

## "Emergence" and the Importance of Time

According to Thomas Berry, the universe has been involved in "a sequence of irreversible transformations," a fact largely unappreciated until the last few decades.[14] The great Flaring Forth or Big Bang, which gave birth to the universe, will never occur again; supernovas, which led to the production of the "heavy" elements necessary for life on planet earth, will not be repeated; the age of the earliest prokaryote bacteria, which fixed the earth's oxygen level at 21 percent, is over.

In the human realm of cultural evolution, certain historical movements signalled the arrival of new modes of consciousness, which cannot be removed. For example, the feminist revolution has meant that the treatment of women in all cultures will inevitably be measured against the standard of equality. There is no going back. Patriarchal regimes and institutions may resist feminism, but now that it has emerged into human consciousness, it can never be "undone." In and through the medium of time, the universe has been and continues to be involved in a sequence of transformations, each of which is foundational for the emergence of the next transformation. This is the basic evolutionary principle.

The ancients dwelled primarily within the realm of spatial, not temporal, consciousness. The march of time as we understand it hadn't entered their awareness. They considered the cosmos to be static. They believed that the mountains, rivers, plants, and animals had been plopped down in their existing form right from the beginning. The cosmos endlessly repeated its seasonal cycles. When the writer of Ecclesiastes penned the famous line "for everything there is a season, a time for peace and a time for war" (Ecclesiastes 3:1–8), he did so out of the common belief in an endlessly repeating cycle of life. There is peace, and then there is war. The cycle happens over and over again. Without an evolutionary perspective, we associate fatalism with God. The way things are is the way God must have made them.

But introduce a temporal dimension, and this fatalistic view of life loses support. It becomes conceivable that "the time for war" may indeed one day pass, when an irreversible transformation of consciousness in the service of peace has occurred. War is not an historical inevitability. Neither is ecological degradation.

The writer of Ecclesiastes notwithstanding, the Jews were the first to introduce this understanding. Their God, they claimed, journeyed with them *through* a historical process. History was the arena in which their God acted, through them, to redeem the world. (This idea is not found in Eastern philosophies, which view time as cyclical and repetitive.)

The story of evolution, wherein more fundamental beings create the conditions necessary for successive and more complex forms of life to emerge, requires this kind of understanding of the centrality of time.

The church's Eucharistic prayers typically include the line, "In the fullness of time, Jesus was born." From an evolutionary perspective, the timing was not solely determined by a God who stands outside the universe, checking "His" Rolex. It was neither arbitrary nor was it a unilateral intervention. The "fullness of time" is a shorthand way of indicating that the foundational cosmological structures had been adequately laid: no galaxies, no solar system; no solar system, no earth; no biological life forms, no Jesus. Furthermore, the social and political milieu of Roman imperialism played an instrumental role in shaping the mind and heart of Jesus towards being a social prophet and a spiritual mystic. Finally, Jesus' own willingness to be a vessel of the Spirit was integral to the fullness of time. In an evolutionary model, "the fullness of time" does not refer to a unilateral decision made by a Cosmic CEO. Rather, Jesus of Nazareth "emerges" out of the interplay of these internal pressures and external conditions. The idea of *emergence* is a central pillar of the new science and systems theory.

Ervin Laszlo, philosopher, systems theorist, author of 74 books in the field, and nominee for the Nobel Peace Prize, has written a definitive text on evolution. In it, he sums up the idea of emergence:

One kind of evolution prepares the ground for the next. Out of the conditions created by evolution in the physical realm emerge the conditions that permit biological evolution to take off. And out of the conditions that permit biological evolution come the conditions that allow human beings, and many other species, to evolve certain forms of organization.[15]

This basic idea came clear to me in my hot yoga (Bikram yoga) class. Each class is an ordeal, as it's conducted in a 110°F (43°C) room. My body, after years of abuse as a jock, required strong medicine. One of the poses, called "Head to Knee," is particularly challenging. The knee in question belongs to a leg which you stick out at a 90-degree angle, parallel to the floor, while standing on the other leg. You interlock your fingers around the foot of the outstretched leg. Both legs are "lamppost straight," which means those like me, with piano wires for hamstrings, experience an unimaginable amount of pain. But it's not over. You then place your forehead on the knee of the outstretched leg, and leave it there for the better part of a minute. *Some* people do this. For others, it involves a progression, whereby the foundation of the posture is built over time. A lot of time, in my case.

You build the foundation by standing on one leg until you can do it without crashing into your yoga neighbour. Next, you lift your other leg and place your interlocked fingers under the foot. When you can do this, and keep the standing leg perfectly straight without wobbling, then you can start to kick out your raised leg. Remember to breathe, or you *will* pass out. Finally, when both the standing leg and the outstretched leg are perfectly straight, you are allowed to try to bend forward to touch your forehead to the knee of your raised leg.

The teachers, blessedly, are in no rush for us to arrive at the final expression of this posture. They tell us that we must first build the requisite strength at each stage. It takes some students six months just to stand on one leg. If we cheat, we only cheat ourselves. (We also risk injury.) It takes time to build capability. It is, in other words, an evolutionary process. I've been going to Bikram yoga classes for over a year, and I'm just starting to kick my leg out, without wobbling.

"Head to Knee" is only one of 26 postures we repeat in each class. The goal? Certainly it's more than simply stretching out the body. Ultimately, the purpose is to heal the spine. Why? The entire nervous system passes through the spine, and connects with the brain. Our neural network, including our brain, is our physical antennae and transformer for the Spirit. A healthy spine issues in a healthy mind and spirit. Bikram says that if we heal our spine, the gods will come chasing after us. The series of 26 postures is designed to move the practitioner sequentially toward the goal of increasing his or her capacity to reflect, receive, and transmit Spirit – which is what evolution is all about.

From the moment of the Flaring Forth to the emergence of self-conscious, upright beings, the universe has been building the foundations or the capacities of the cosmos to reflect, receive, and transmit Spirit in different realms or levels. These levels are given different names by various theorists. Ervin Laszlo calls them material, biological, and historical. Eric Jantsch uses cosmic, biological, and sociocultural. Ken Wilber likes physiosphere (matter), biosphere (life), and noosphere (mind). It's possible to further refine these levels into matter, life, consciousness, soul, and spirit.

But whatever we call these realms, it's important to note that evolution isn't limited to Darwin's realm of the biological.[16] Each realm is a manifestation of the incarnating Spirit. Spirit emerges not *out of* but rather *through* the foundational structures at each level. Thomas Berry and Brian Swimme believe that the evolutionary direction of the universe is toward increased consciousness. Teilhard de Chardin believed it was toward what he called the "divinization of humanity." Others, such as Alfred North Whitehead, think the evolutionary thrust is toward increased beauty and diversity.

# The Great Chain of Being

The levels of being (material, biological, cultural, and spiritual) constitute what historically have been called The Great Chain of Being. Every major religion has had its proponents of The Great Chain. Arthur Lovejoy's research into this philosophy demonstrated that there are three essential components involved.[17]

1.  All phenomena and all events – from matter to minerals, from plants and animals to people – are manifestations of Spirit, which overflows its goodness and beauty into all forms.

2.  Since all levels or realms originate in Spirit, and are manifestations of Spirit, there are no gaps between them and no "unbridgeable dualisms." All the levels overlap and intertwine, the connecting braid being Spirit.

3.  While there are no absolute gaps, there are gradations and distinct emergent qualities with each successive level. Slugs don't do theoretical mathematics. Humans do. Okay, some humans do. I struggled with grade 12 math, but that doesn't make me a slug. (Are you listening, Mr. McKay?)

I would add a fourth component, which is that each being at each level is absolutely necessary and intrinsically valuable. That is, beings in each realm have value, separate and apart from their usefulness to other beings. Each being on each level is a full manifestation of Spirit, but there are different capacities, according to where a being is on the evolutionary scale.

So we could say that the Spirit has been involved with a 14-billion-year yoga practice. She has patiently and cooperatively laid down the foundations of existence as we know and experience it today, from the four basic energy fields, to atoms and molecules; to galaxies, supernovas, the heavy elements, and our sun; to the geological dynamics of the planet, the emergence of life from bacteria, and the arrival of humanity. I'll never complain about my slow progress in yoga again!

Now, what I've just done by stopping at humanity makes it seem as though we are the final and absolute expression of the cosmic posture, both legs lamppost straight, with forehead resting on the cosmic knee! This is, of course, absurd. I witnessed an "über-yogi" do the head-to-knee posture with no hands! I would have thought it impossible.

In other words, just when we think we've arrived at the ultimate, someone breaks through to another level. Humanity, through conscious intention, is able to cooperate with the Spirit of the evolutionary process and take it to another level. We lay down the foundations for a more spiritually evolved form of life to emerge. This is what we're involved in; it constitutes the glory and the dignity of the human life. We can choose to give our lives to serve this evolutionary thrust. This is what gives us joy. It is what our life in Christ is intended to be about.

Critics of the Great Chain fear that it leaves us with a kind of social Darwinism whereby the privileged believe that they necessarily occupy the highest rung on the evolutionary ladder. Nazis believed that they were more evolved than Jews, gypsies, and gays. They believed that they were *born* to occupy a higher rung. This notion plays itself out in caste systems throughout the world. People with this worldview make no distinction between *dominator hierarchies* and *growth hierarchies*. Dominator hierarchies are violently imposed upon other groups and then coercively sustained. Growth hierarchies are truly natural. Atoms cluster into molecules, molecules into cells, cells into organs, etc., in the service of increasing complexity, beauty, and consciousness. Each successive level has an increased holistic capacity.

Rather than the Great Chain of Being, some people prefer to use the term the Great Nest of Being. This image captures the sense in which each successive level develops out of, and envelopes, the previous level. Imagine those Russian dolls, which are nested one inside the other. The more evolved a being or system is, the greater its nesting capacity. The nest of self-reflexive human consciousness enjoys the capacity to hold all previous levels.

Again, this doesn't make humans "better than" other forms of life. The Spirit is the ultimate context. It is the largest nest, but is also fully present in each and every "doll" or form of existence. Arthur Koestler calls these nests holarchies, rather than hierarchies.[18]

## Diversity and Beauty

Cosmologist Brandon Carter was the first to suggest what has come to be known as the "anthropic principle."[19] This principle states that human beings are what the universe was aiming at from the beginning – in other words, the universe appears be "designed" with the goal of generating and sustaining observers. To get to us, the cosmic dynamics had to be precisely calibrated just as we find them to be. The universe, in other words, had been expecting us. There is a strong version of the theory and a weaker one. The strong version tends to favour a designer God. The weak version notes the finely calibrated nature of the universe, but doesn't posit a purpose to it all.

Is there a middle ground? Is there a way to preserve both purpose and novelty, freedom in creation and divine involvement? A variation of the anthropic principle, much more attractive in my opinion, is the "strong aesthetic principle."[20] The universe *does* have direction and purpose, evidenced in the human being certainly, but not exclusively. The "aim" of the universe is seen throughout all of creation, in the form of beauty. Beauty, in a cosmological context, includes our common notions of beauty, but also much more. Alfred North Whitehead talks about it as "a harmony of contrasts," or the "ordering of novelty."[21] As John Haught points out in his book *God after Darwin*, without contrast (chaos), there is only the monotony of sheer order. Without order, there is only chaos. The universe's unfolding involves the intricate interplay of these two poles at every level of being. Beauty is a "delicate synthesis of unity and complexity, stability and motion, form and dynamics."[22] The capacity for conscious self-reflection in the human being is one, but only one, expression of this delicate synthesis, which the universe displays. This also means that, at any given moment in time, disharmony may predominate, but, in the wide sweep of the evolutionary process, it will always be gathered up in the service of beauty.

If beauty, understood in this broad sense, is the aim of the universe (the strong aesthetic principle), then diversity needs to be understood as a primary expression of beauty, and also, therefore, as one of the primary values of Spirit in an evolutionary universe.

Thomas Aquinas, a 13th-century theologian, spent some time reflecting on the mystery of diversity in creation. Why is there so much of it? The answer he came up with was that diversity is the only way creation can come even close to reflecting the fullness of God's goodness, beauty, and truth. In other words, God's "will" is to maximize beauty and diversity. The loss of diversity, represented most starkly by extinction, is a loss of divine radiance from the earth.

The loss of diversity in the intellectual realm is no less profane. So while fundamentalists and world leaders may enjoy high IQs, to the extent that they are unwilling to embrace and promote diversity in the human and non-human realm, they exhibit a low level of *evolutionary intelligence*. A person with Down's syndrome may, through their loving presence and unique way of being in the world, manifest God's intention to a greater degree than more intellectually gifted human beings. Spirit loves diversity, for only through diversity is the beauty of the divine manifest.

Sin, understood from within this paradigm, is the refusal to participate in, or the active resistance to, this universal dynamic. Original sin simply indicates that we're born into cultures that resist this divine impulse to beauty and diversity. The extinction of species is a manifestation of this kind of sin, a symptom of the current human propensity to monopolize the earth. To follow the Christ is to turn from these cultures of monotony and monopoly.

## The God of Evolution

In keeping with the scientific bias of the day, Darwin eventually jettisoned any notion of a God, let alone one that might be involved in the process of evolution. But, as one reads about his struggle with faith, it becomes clear that the God Darwin ultimately rejected was a very constricting and restricting God. On the one hand, standing in a Brazilian rainforest in 1832, Darwin wrote, "I was led by feelings... to the firm conviction of the existence of God, and of the immortality of the soul." But then, only a few years later, having realized that the gospel accounts could not be harmonized, and that they were not eyewitness reports on the life of Jesus, he concluded, "I gradually came to not believe in Christianity as divine revelation." He also could not abide the doctrine that non-Christians were hell-bound. Later in life, watching his beloved ten-year-old daughter, Annie, succumb painfully to a mysterious disease, his turn away from religious belief and spirituality became complete.[23]

But who was the God Darwin rejected, and what constituted the Christianity he could no longer abide? Clearly, Darwin rejected a designer God, who was in absolute control of the universe; in other words, the God of supernatural theism. This God intervenes at certain points in history, but is inexplicably restrained at other times, such as during the painful death of an innocent child. This God punishes unbelievers with eternal banishment, and rewards believers with eternal peace. The only valid source of revelation, according to this version of the Christian faith, is the Bible, considered to be inerrant and infallible.

This continues to be the God and the "Christian faith" most atheists and agnostics reject, in my experience. It is also the God, and the Christian faith, rejected by progressive Christians. When evolutionary theory is pitted against this controlling monarch-in-the-sky, people are forced to choose. And to be honest, if those were my only choices, I'd also toss God. This kind of God simply doesn't and can't fit into an evolutionary universe that unfolds with any kind of dignity. He'd hog the agenda and dominate the whole affair.

How, then, are we to understand an evolutionary God? This God would need to be immanent in the process of evolution, not as a controlling presence but as the cosmic urge to self-transcendence. This God would be the hidden wholeness, the non-coercive intelligence nudging hydrogen and helium molecules to organize into galaxies; galaxies to birth solar systems; and cells to cluster together in formations of increasing elegance, beauty, and diversity.

At the same time, this God would continually make room for the freedom of creatures to determine their own destiny. In Philippians, Christ is known as the one who does not count equality with God a thing to be grasped. Rather, he empties himself, taking the form of a servant (Philippians 2:6–11). When Paul thought about Christ crucified, he came to understand something very important about God, something absolutely countercultural. Unlike the monarchical models, in which kings rule with absolute power, on the cross Christ emptied himself of power as domination, and rather exercised power as humility. In the context of an evolutionary universe, this means that God makes room for all levels of creation to unfold with dignity and integrity. There is no divine blueprint predetermining this unfolding process. Rather, because of this self-emptying character of God (known as the kenotic principle), there is room for genuine novelty and surprise.

## The Universe and Evolution as Sacred Story

One reason we haven't heard much about Alfred Russel Wallace – the amateur naturalist who, independently of Darwin, arrived at the theory of natural selection – is that he left room for God, a death sentence for "serious" scientists. In the *Quarterly Review*, April 1869, Wallace broke with Darwin, concluding that evolution is more than simply the result of the blind processes of natural selection. He was one of the first to articulate the strong anthropic principle, without naming it as such. He thought evolution was guided by an "over-ruling Intelligence," which had "watched over the action of natural laws, so directing variations and so determining their accumulation," to arrive at the human being.

Beginning with Darwin's insight into biological evolution, it became increasingly clear that human beings are latecomers on this planet. As such, we are seamlessly connected to and given life by all the life-forms that preceded us. Following Darwin, cosmologists discovered that this was true on a cosmic scale. Human beings developed out of a great procession of life, which began with the great Flaring Forth 14 billion years ago, and which continued to evolve, more recently in cosmological terms, into single cell amoebas and eventually into the great apes of the African plain.

While some Christians find the idea that we "come from the apes" offensive, our greatest hope for planetary survival may lie precisely in making this connection. We can literally re-member ourselves; we can locate ourselves as *members*, not as *rulers*, of a great procession of life.

The universe is a developing reality, best understood as a sacred story. As we learn to read our common creation story as a sacred text, it becomes possible to recover a felt sense that the planet and indeed the entire cosmos is enchanted. The Christian faith has yet to make a concerted effort to convey this enchanted reality within its theological models, its liturgical life, and its way of being the church in the world. If Spirit is not involved in this evolving story of the universe coming to life and to consciousness, then Spirit is not involved with reality as we know it to be. On the other hand, if Spirit is integral to the developing story of the universe, and if its Presence renders the universe "full of glory" (Isaiah 6:6), then it is incumbent upon Christians to imagine their lives within an evolutionary paradigm.

The story of the universe, the story of evolution, is our story. It is not just happening "out there." It is happening *to* us and *through* us, as well as all around us. We call it a story because we now know it had a beginning, it has a middle, and it's going some-where. There is a developing plot line, which we're now capable of reading as a sacred text having everything to do with us. Our very bodies and minds are concentrated amalgams of this evo-lutionary process. The large-scale dynamics of the universe are not lost on us; rather, they are active in us as we consciously em-brace our evolutionary journey. Our physical bodies are a virtual ecology of systems and beings, who laid down the foundational structures for our emergence. Every organ in our body has been passed down to us by another planetary "being." Furthermore, it is all shot-through with Spirit. As Elizabeth Barret Browning has written:

> Earth's crammed with heaven
> And every common bush, afire with God
> But only he who sees, takes off his shoes.

## An Evolutionary Covenant

To believe that all creation manifests the presence of Spirit in an evolving universe is to cultivate the sensibility necessary for a deep ecological ethic and practice. The destruction of the earth, the degradation of her biosystems, and the disappearance of spe-cies is a choice for death in the kingdom of life. But we are called to further the evolutionary unfolding of Spirit.

The Jewish and Christian people live out their lives in the con-text of a covenant relationship with their God. These covenants evolved over time. God made new covenants with Noah, Abra-ham and Sarah, Moses and Miriam, Jeremiah, and for Christians, through Jesus of Nazareth. In the 21st century, it is time to enter into an evolutionary covenant with our God. It might be stated, using God's voice, as follows:

*I will be your God, if you will be my people. I have come to you in many forms, and will continue to be present to you in radiant diversity and beauty. My people will never stop growing, because I manifest anew each moment. If you remain open to my presence in new discoveries, and continue to evolve – loving diversity, growing in mind, heart, and body, and loving wisdom – I will be your God. Learn from other creatures the sacred intelligence of the universe. These creatures are your kin. I will be with you in the tumult of change, giving you the courage, the power, and the wisdom to endure and to celebrate transformation.*

## Evolution versus Intelligent Design

Currently, a debate is raging between so-called evolutionists and intelligent designers. The advocates of intelligent design tend to be over-represented by the Christian right. There's a soft position and a hard-line position among this camp. The hard-line position begins not with scientific method but with a dogmatic belief in the Bible as the literal word of God. If Genesis says creation happened in six days and then God took a rest, then that's the way it happened. The universe is not a developing reality. With a wave of a magic wand and a word from the great Jehovah, it all got plunked down about 6000 years ago, and has remained essentially unchanged until today. The softer version of intelligent design is less dogmatic, but still promotes the idea that God had it all figured out right from the get-go, and that creation is just unfolding according to a divine blueprint.

At the other extreme are the evolutionists, over-represented by secular humanists and materialistic scientists. They are justifiably suspicious of religious convictions that blind believers to scientific evidence. They *do* see the universe as a developing reality, but are sceptical about Spirit being involved in the process. If it's all unfolding according to some kind of divine blueprint, laid down at the beginning of time, where's the dignity in that? Where's the capacity for novelty and surprise, which seems to be a genuine feature of evolution. They take blind chance over divine blueprint any day of the week.

Fortunately, there is a middle position. According to the theology described earlier, God continually empties God-self to make space for the universe to unfold in surprising and novel ways. There is a bias in an evolutionary theology toward beauty and diversity in all realms. The universe is winding itself up according to these inherent values. Yet the precise forms and the intricate ecology of relationships between systems at all levels are indeterminate. Creation enjoys a certain freedom. We would expect that if this freedom is genuine, it will sometimes issue in evolutionary dead ends, and in what we call in the human realm "evil." There is a cost to freedom.

All creation is drawn, by the inherent promise of beauty and diversity, to fulfill its potential. The life force, what the Greeks called Eros, is the agency of Spirit at loose in the universe, non-coercively nudging all life forms in the direction of their fullest potential. This subtle push and pull is a divine power encouraging all forms of creation in the direction of divinity. So it's not a case of intelligent design or evolution. It's design for evolution by a respectful Intelligence.

# Part 2

# Chapter 5

# BIBLE STORIES IN A COSMIC CONTEXT

The metaphorical approach [to reading the Bible] enables us to
see and affirm meanings that go beyond the particularity of what
the texts meant in their ancient setting. It is a large umbrella,
encompassing a range of disciplines. What everything beneath
the umbrella has in common is a way of reading the Bible that
moves beyond the historical meanings of texts.

MARCUS BORG[1]

The evolutionary universe is a sacred text revealing God's purposes, intentions, and very being. Christians have another sacred
text, of course: the Bible, that library of books that is the witness of
God's people to their relationship with God throughout history.

In the congregation I serve, the person reading scripture ends
by saying, "This is the witness of God's people." In an evolutionary paradigm, to say that the Bible is a "witness" of the people is
to acknowledge that the original scribes could not help but reflect
the social, political, psychological, and spiritual worldview of
their day. In other words, scripture, like nature, reflects an evolutionary dynamic. At times, the writing soars and seems to reflect the very essence of Spirit. At other times, the writing reflects
an "us against them" mentality, which is less inspiring, to put it
mildly. Occasionally, a single story reflects both.

For example, in a beautiful passage, Elijah the prophet is running from the authorities and finds himself in a cave, where he discovers God not in the wind or in the fire, but in a "still, small voice (1 Kings 19:12). Yet his reverie is tempered by the context of the story. The reason he's on the run is that he has just slaughtered 400 of Baal's prophets. The author tells this story approvingly, as a narrative that establishes God's superiority over the gods of the bad guys. It could have been written by Osama bin Laden, Jerry Falwell, or George Bush.

I teach an intensive 34-week Bible study during which we read most of the Bible. I can say that the participants, almost without exception, go through a phase of being deeply disappointed by what they find in scripture, and by what they *don't* find. The violence enacted by God's people, and condoned in places by their God, is the first turnoff. Those looking for pearls of wisdom to help them through a difficult time in their life don't fare much better. What they find is a story of frail human beings who attempt to live in a covenant relationship with their God, and who for the most part, fall short. Then, they get back up on their feet and try it again, by the grace and compassion of their God.

In other words, what these students of the Bible discover is the story of their own struggle to be faithful to their understanding of God. They find a story of a people journeying through history, evolving in their understanding of God's nature and intent. This represents both less and more than what they thought they were getting into when they signed up. It's less in the sense that if they expected the voice of God to speak to them, unmediated by the circumstances of flesh-and-guts human beings, they are out of luck. But it's also more, in the sense that their own journey is affirmed, and their shifting and evolving understanding of God is validated. To a person, those who hang in there for the 34 weeks encounter the mystery of divine Presence mediated through the biblical story.

Many of my students would prefer to skip over the "Old" Testament and get right to the New Testament. Certainly, it contains less violence and the violence that *does* exist is presented as contrary to God's purposes. It is also natural for a Christian to want to get to what Jesus has to say, and to what the early church says about Jesus. However, given that Jesus was Jewish, it's impossible to read the New Testament without understanding the Old Testament. In his teachings, Jesus assumed that his listeners knew the stories from the Hebrew Bible, our Old Testament. His parables and all his teachings are "riffs" on themes found in what was his Bible – the Torah and the prophets. Furthermore, when it came time for subsequent generations to write down what he said, they invariably interpreted his life through the narratives and themes running through their own scriptures. The accounts of Jesus' life, the gospels, are also interpretations, then. Again, they reflect the worldviews, psychology, and social arrangements of first- and second-century Palestine. We don't get anything pure and unfiltered. We end up with a version of Jesus' life, death, and resurrection, as seen through the eyes of Mark, Matthew, Luke, and John, each writing for their own particular community.

This raises the issue of the "authority" of scripture. If it's all a matter of interpretation, if the original events were first interpreted by the *writers* of scripture, and then those writings are again interpreted by us 2000 years later, what does this mean for the search for "truth"? To get anywhere near to "truth" in a postmodern worldview requires a capacity and willingness to bring as many contexts and perspectives to the subject as possible. To put it bluntly, there's no other way to the truth other than through the lens of interpretation. It's not that there is no truth, but rather finding it takes a little digging. So again, how is the Bible authoritative?

## The Bible: A View from Below

Scripture's authority lies partly in the fact that it offers a unique view of history, that is, from the perspective of the victim, not the victor. The Bible contains triumphalistic claims, to be sure, but the Jewish people got the short end of the stick as far as history is concerned. And yet, through it all, we find the paradoxical claim that the God of the universe is with them, and working through them, for the redemption of humanity!

The "truth" of scripture, then, is what some scholars call "oppositional" as opposed to "propositional" truth. In other words, the stories are told in opposition to the dominant culture, by a people oppressed. The Bible is a collection of stories told by those who view the accepted order or dominant culture from below, but who nevertheless see the power of the Divine at work in and through their own story. This unique interpretive perspective is one of the most important gifts of the scriptural witness.

Jesus himself offered us a view from below. Because he identified with the poor and the marginalized, he saw history differently than the Roman conquerors. The empire Caesar reigned over – its values and norms, its hierarchical class system, the meaning it assigned to wealth, and how it exercised power – all of this was challenged and undermined by the "kingdom" Jesus proclaimed. As John Dominic Crossan and other scholars have pointed out, this was no accident. The Holy One was siding with the losers. Not until the poor were lifted up out of the dust, and the wealthy were brought down a notch or two, would anything approximating a reign of God be realized (Luke 1:52). Caesar and his minions were ultimately opposed to this interpretation of the direction of history. Crucifixion was their way of expressing their opposition.

Given our present ecological crisis, I find it helpful to use the same interpretive lens when reading the sacred text of creation. We need to follow the intuition of the biblical prophets, and of Jesus himself, that God has a preferential option for the poor of the earth, for the victim. In the 21st century, the list of victims is long, and includes all of our non-human relations: the plants, the animals, and the biosystems that are under siege. We need to widen our circle of compassion, so that we recognize these beings as integral to the full manifestation of God's glory on earth.

Vancouver, Canada, is currently preparing for the 2010 Winter Olympics. To help visitors get up to Whistler Mountain, where the skiing events will take place, the province is expanding a highway that runs through an environmentally sensitive area called Eagleridge Bluffs. Recently, a birder spotted a Cassin's vireo, a migratory bird, nesting in an arbutus tree in an area slated to be cleared. At best, and this is unlikely, a court order may be issued restricting construction in the area of the tree for the duration of the nesting season. The provincial government will fight the possibility of this delay.[2]

Interpreting history through the lens of the Cassin's vireo is consistent with the biblical tradition, which takes the perspective of the marginalized and discounted. To do so is to engage in an act of Christian discipleship.

One measure of how closely we reflect the heart of the Creator is how we treat the forgotten and marginalized in our midst. Creating zoos to make sure animals don't go extinct, while we decimate their habitat, is a symptom of our profound dissociation from the earth. We've gone about our business, literally, for the last 300 years with precious little concern for the wild ones. We consider them "separate" from us, and their demise the acceptable cost of doing business, a necessity to keep our economic engine running smoothly. In truth, within our increasingly urban context, we're not even aware that that cost is being paid.

The authority of scripture is also found in three or four overarching narratives, called metanarratives, which got it right. These narratives tell us something essential and true about the nature of God, and about the plight of humanity and what's required to fix it. They also tell us, I would argue, something essential and true about plight of all non-human life forms, and what's required to fix it.

These stories, which our tradition has gathered, told, and retold over the millennia, refer to a loving and compassionate Presence. This Presence has been personally experienced and testified to in the stories of scripture. We trust this to be true because subsequent generations have had similar experiences of the Presence. We trust as well that in the arc of these sacred narratives – which show the evolutionary emergence of Spirit into the consciousness of these communities through time, and which show their struggle to be God's people – our ancestors have something essential to teach us about God. In other words, through it all, they got the big picture right, even if some of the details are a product not of inspiration but of historical and cultural conditioning. In what follows, I engage in a dialogue between the sacred story of the evolutionary universe, and the sacred story of scripture.

# The Great Narratives of the Judeo-Christian Faith

Marcus Borg identifies three primary stories, or metanarratives, in the Christian scriptures, each of which tell us something essential and true about the nature of God.[3] I would add a fourth story. What follows is a brief summary of these stories, and then a dialogue between these narratives, the common creation story, and related scientific insights. These narratives are

1.  The story of the Exodus: The God of freedom.
2.  The story of the Exile: The God of homecoming.
3.  The story of the Temple: The God of sacrifice.
4.  The story of call and response: The God of allurement.

## The Story of the Exodus: The God of Freedom

A paradigmatic tale for Jews, and subsequently for Christians, the story of the Exodus begins with enslavement of the Hebrew people by Egyptian pharaohs (kings). In the story, the Egyptian pharaoh, fearing that the Hebrew slaves have become too numerous and thus pose a threat, issues an edict stating that all male Hebrew babies must be killed. When Moses is born, he is saved from this awful fate by what amounts to the first feminist conspiracy. Shiphrah and Puah (two Hebrew midwives), Moses' mother, and his sister, Miriam, outsmart the Egyptians and save him from death by placing him in a reed basket and hiding him by the river's edge. Shortly thereafter he is discovered by the Egyptian princess, who rescues him and raises him as her own.

Years later, the adult Moses witnesses an Egyptian prince abusing a Hebrew slave. He kills the Egyptian and heads for the hills. There, he encounters a burning bush and hears the call of God telling him to return to Egypt to confront the pharaoh with God's command, "Let my people go." After a series of confrontations with the pharaoh, which result in various plagues and natural catastrophes, the pharaoh relents and the Hebrew people make a dramatic break for it (Exodus 1:6 – 2:10).

Taken as a whole, this first metanarrative is one of liberation from oppression.

## Cosmological Participation in God's Purposes

There is not much historic evidence to support the story of the Exodus. The most we can say is that something occurred in the history of the Jews that conveyed to them that the God they worshipped was offended by injustice and was deeply involved in liberation.

The first thing I notice about this story is that creation itself participates in both the awakening of Moses, and in the judgment of the system of oppression. The burning bush is the natural medium through which God speaks to Moses. It's interesting that the way the story is told, God requires Moses to notice the radiance of the bush before issuing the call (Exodus 3:3–4). The radiance of the Holy in and through nature doesn't speak to any of us until we decide, with Moses, "to turn and look at this great sight." Our capacity to notice this radiance is compromised by the history of disenchantment that has shaped our age. But as we grow in our capacity for awe, we may, like Moses, know ourselves to be standing on holy ground (Exodus 3:5).

Later in the story, a series of natural disasters and plagues convey God's judgment to the pharaoh. The Nile, a river symbolizing fertility for the Egyptians, is turned to blood. Then come frogs, gnats, flies, cattle plagues, boils, and ultimately hail. Each of these plagues represent naturally occurring disasters in Egyptian history, but through the eyes of faith they are interpreted as nature expressing God's yearning that God's people be set free. This is not the only place in scripture where we see the cosmos participate in God's purposes. For the prophets, the earth both celebrated God's purposes and expressed God's judgment on unjust behaviour committed by the people of God. Thus trees clap (Isaiah 55:12) and sing (Psalm 96:12), the heavens proclaim (Psalm 19:1), deserts rejoice and blossom (Isaiah 35:1–2), the valleys and the meadows sing for joy (Psalm 65:13), and stones may cry out in response to the gracious activity of the Holy One (Luke 3:8); justice abides in a wilderness and righteousness in a fruitful field (Isaiah 32:15–16). On the other hand, the land (earth) experiences fear and goes silent before God's judgment (Psalm 76:8–9), the land vomits out the people in response to injustice and unfaithfulness (Leviticus 18:25), the land mourns and all who live on it languish, with the animals and birds – "even the fish are perishing" (Hosea 4:3). Perhaps the most vivid expression of the cosmos reflecting the sin of humans is found in Isaiah 24:4–5: "The earth dries up and withers, the world languishes and withers, the heavens languish together with the earth. The earth lies polluted under its inhabitants; for they have transgressed laws, violated statutes and broken the everlasting covenant."

This may be nothing more than the anthropomorphizing of nature (attributing human characteristics to the natural world). Or it may reflect a deeper premodern sensitivity to the biospiritual connection between the humanity and the earth. In a panentheistic worldview, creation is in God, and God is in creation. From this perspective, we shouldn't think about creation's participation in celebration and judgment as the action of an external God manipulating nature for God's purposes.

Rather, a sacred immanent Presence holistically manifests and is reflected *in* the relative states of health of all of the earth's systems: biological, social and cultural, and spiritual. It is a basic premise of evolutionary theology that Spirit is the connecting thread and ground of all realms. In this light, we would expect that injustice would impact all realms simultaneously; that is, that all realms would express, through their own capacities, the presence of this injustice.

We don't typically make such connections because we've been immersed in a worldview that absolutely separates the realm of the human from the realm of the non-human. What we do in the human realm is disconnected from the non-human biological realm. The increased incidence and intensity of tsunamis, hurricanes, and droughts, understood within an emergent panentheistic theology, are not *literally* the divine judgment of an angry God. Rather, they are natural manifestations of a sacred, evolutionary process being thwarted by the wilful ignorance of humans. In this sense, and in this sense only, ecological catastrophes can be interpreted as a judgment upon humanity. They may be seen as both a natural warning that our ethic of domination has dire consequences, and as the call of God to end the oppression we're enacting upon the planet.

We have placed ourselves in the role of pharaohs upon the earth. The earth herself may be the new Moses. The "firmament" proclaims not just God's "handiwork," but also our failure to fit in with earth's biosystems. As the psalmist says, "day to day pours forth speech," although there is no speech and there are no words (Psalm 19). The mode of communication is depleted fish stocks, massive rates of extinction, melting glaciers, toxic whale blubber, and increased incidence of asthma from pollution. Using her own voice, creation is groaning to be set free (Romans 8:22).

Zoos are the animal equivalent of slavery. There are good zoos to be sure, which have as their mission the reintegration of threatened species into the wilderness. But overall, zoos reflect a sad capitulation to the seeming inevitability of the extinction of species due to the appropriation of natural habitat by human beings. As the Hebrew slaves were gradually dehumanized by the Egyptians, kept only for their value as human labour, so animals in zoos are kept for their utilitarian value, to entertain human beings. The novel *Ishmael*, by Daniel Quinn,[4] presents the world through the eyes of a wise silverback gorilla, who teaches a human being. Ishmael calls human beings the "takers." The path of "the takers" has resulted in a world in which the only hope for a magnificent gorilla is in a zoo.

The pain we feel at the loss of wild animals and of wilderness spaces represents a participation in the heart of a God who yearns for all beings to enjoy freedom. Beginning with the Exodus story of liberation, and reading the God of this story back into the story of the cosmos, it becomes possible to imagine the entire 14-billion-year history of the universe as a movement toward increasing freedom. The whole universe unfolds according to this urge to freedom. Liberation is the direction we're headed, a freedom the Spirit already enjoys and yearns to manifest throughout creation.

Freedom, in other words, is part and parcel of the unfolding universe. When the universe arrived at human beings, this dynamic of freedom became a central problem in the story. Greed, the lust to dominate, and a fear of death took hold in the self-conscious ones. God's self-emptying made room for our self-aggrandizement. God made room for us to choose the path of domination. God's self-emptying allowed for this abuse of freedom, but God did not and does not remain passive. God's offence at injustice registers in creation, in the exhortations of social prophets, and in the sensitivities of those who have not lost their spiritual connection to God, neighbour, and the planet.

For the Christian to be free *in* Christ also implies being free *for* Christ. The spiritual discipline of growing in freedom from attachments involves being liberated *for* something. Moses was saved by a feminist conspiracy for something other than retirement to a gated community and golf. He heads for the hills, but his call to be liberator follows him. The same liberating dynamic that was present in those women as the urge to subvert oppressive systems was bred in the bones of Moses.

When Jesus stood up to read his mission statement in the synagogue, he chose a text from Isaiah.

> The Spirit of the Lord is upon me,
> S/he has anointed me to proclaim release to the captives…
> and to let the oppressed go free. (Luke 4:18–19)

With the arrival of human beings on the evolutionary scene, the ultimate expression of freedom becomes one of justice-making. Justice is the conscious intention to ensure that all beings have an opportunity to participate in the freedom God intends, and to speak out on behalf of this freedom. That same Spirit moving through cosmic evolutionary processes to arrive at Jesus anoints each one of us to express our freedom by helping to liberate others. For life to continue on this planet we must live into God's image within us by employing the same kenotic, or self-emptying, dynamic of our Creator. It is now a cosmological imperative that we empty ourselves, to make room for the freedom of other species to flourish. This means reducing our planetary footprint, increasing wilderness habitat, and reducing our carbon emissions, which lead to global warming.

## All Creation Longs for Freedom

St. Paul was concerned that all creation be included in God's redemptive and creative purposes. He writes that "creation itself will be set free... to obtain the glorious freedom of the children of God" (Romans 8:21).

Boo the grizzly bear displays the natural instinct for liberation. After his mother was shot by hunters in the interior of British Columbia, he was taken into captivity and placed in an elaborate mountain zoo. One night Boo waited until his keepers went home, then dug a four-foot tunnel under the fence and escaped, following the scent of a young female. For 19 days he eluded the search party, before he was tranquilized and brought back to the enclosure. Forty-eight hours later, Boo once again waited patiently until the evening shift had gone home, and then made another dramatic escape. This one was truly exceptional. He broke down a 400-pound steel door specifically designed to prevent another escape, broke through two electrified fences, which he somehow managed to deactivate, and then scaled a 13-foot wall. "He did the impossible," said Michael Dalzell, spokesman for the Kicking Horse Mountain Resort.[5] Boo caught a whiff of a female. Which only goes to prove that you can take Boo out of the wild, but you can't take the wild out of Boo. Yet his keepers are seriously considering neutering him, once they catch up with him. Run, Boo, run!

# The Story of the Exile: The God of Homecoming

In 597 BCE, the Babylonian empire laid siege to Jerusalem. The Babylonians destroyed the Temple and carried away the brightest and the best of the Jewish people to a distant land. This trauma became a paradigmatic narrative for the Jewish people. They knew what it was like to live as strangers in a strange land, to live in a profound state of alienation; and they knew that this was wrong. "By the rivers of Babylon we sat down and wept" (Psalm 137:1). The experience of exile created a crisis of faith for many of the Jewish people. How could God allow this to happen? Many found the answer in Israel's own unfaithfulness, which, they reasoned, must have triggered God's judgment in the form of the Babylonian invasion and forced exile. We don't need to endorse this kind of theology, in which God rewards the good and punishes the bad, to empathize with a people trying to make sense of their profound alienation.

The story doesn't end with the people's captivity in Babylon, however. When the Persian Empire defeats Babylonia, the emperor Cyrus allows the Jewish exiles to return home to rebuild their Temple.

In the actions of Cyrus, the Jews believed that God was at work in history overcoming alienation and exile. When Christians applied this story to Jesus, they saw him as the one who lights our collective path home to God. Jesus is the power of God working to overcome alienation in humanity. Jesus tells parables that centre around the theme of exile and return: a shepherd seeks out a lost sheep; a woman seeks a lost coin; a man throws a banquet, to which the lost and lonely are invited. Jesus gains a reputation for being a drunkard and a sinner precisely because he associates with the most alienated people in the society of his day. Clearly, Jesus understood his own mission within the context of the narrative of exile and homecoming.

Within the context of this metanarrative, sin represents a state of alienation. We find ourselves out of relationship with self, God, neighbour, and the earth. We are lost and longing to find our way back home. A scene from the popular film *E.T.: The Extraterrestrial* plays on this theme. E.T., a creature from another planet, points a long, green finger in the direction of the stars, and, with a tear forming in his eye, voices one word: "Home." The reason the scene brings tears to *our* eyes (okay, to my eyes) is that we know what E.T. is going through.

Einstein once said that he wanted to know the answer to a single question: "Is the universe a friendly place or not?" Is it our home? Do we really belong? In chapter 2, I traced the story of the 500 years of the modern period, during which scientific rationalism concluded that we do *not* actually belong. We are the result of a cosmic fluke: a meaningless process of genetic mutation, the random collision of atoms, and natural selection. Since we're here we might as well enjoy the ride, but only faint-hearted romantics could imagine that we actually belong. Radical versions of postmodernism contributed to this disenchanted view of our place in the cosmos. There is no intrinsic meaning or purpose to the tale of life as told by a disenchanted postmodernism. In fact, we are told that it's merely a story we tell ourselves to curb our fear. The only meaning that exists in a soulless universe is the meaning we attribute to it. This is, in itself, a story of course. It's a story of disenchantment, and we have traced how this story has left us vulnerable to the false gods of modern commerce, politics, and religion. The psalmist's lament is our own: "How can we sing the Lord's song in a foreign land?" (Psalm 137:4).

Matthew Fox tells the story of a friend who was addressing an aboriginal audience in Australia. His lecture was being translated into their native language. He moved into a section of his presentation concerned with loneliness. Suddenly he noticed that the translator was not speaking, but was huddled with some other members of his tribe. When the translator emerged, he told the lecturer that they had no word for loneliness in their language. What about missing family members who have died, he inquired? The translator said that when they look up at the stars, they don't see stars. They see the campfires of their ancestors. These people had a cosmological story, which told them that their hearts were made for this universe, and this universe for their hearts.

Both sacred stories, the story of the evolving universe and the story told by our scriptures, are invitations to come home to the heart of God. As we realize that we have hearts made for the universe, we will also realize that we aren't the only ones who belong. We may choose to bring with us the flying, the crawling, the swimming, and the walking four-legged ones. They, too, were made for this planet.

## Extinction as a Story of Exile

> God created every living creature and every winged bird and saw that it was good. God blessed them saying, "Be fruitful and multiply and fill the waters in the seas and let birds multiply upon the earth." (Genesis 1:21–22)

Subsequent generations may look back on our age as the period of extinction, when biological diversity itself was wiped out. Legendary biologist E. O. Wilson notes the stark statistics: if habitat conversion continues at present rates, half the species on the planet will be gone by the end of our century. Climate change alone will wipe out one-quarter of the species. The rate of extinction has increased 100-fold since the arrival of human beings. That number is expected to increase 1000 times in the next three decades. "If this rise continues unabated, the cost to humanity, in wealth, environmental security, and quality of life, will be catastrophic."[6] We are entering what he calls the Eremozoic Era – The Age of Loneliness.

Wilson helps us to remember the causes of extinction by using the acronym HIPPO, the order of the letters corresponding with their rank in terms of destructiveness.[7]

H habitat loss
I invasive species
P pollution (including global warming)
P human overpopulation (a root cause of the first three)
O overharvesting (hunting, fishing, gathering)

In an article entitled "India's Vanishing Tiger," Umarah Jamali tells the story of how the Royal Bengal tiger's numbers have been vastly overestimated. An independent audit revealed that there are only one-quarter of the number remaining in a national park in India than was first estimated; 64 tigers remain, not the 249 that park wardens claimed. Poaching is the main culprit, and the government hasn't prioritized law enforcement to curb this atrocity. A single tiger skin brings $20,000, while a tiger's penis, used in a traditional treatment for impotence, brings $28,000 a kilogram. In countries such as India and Pakistan, which have 80 percent of the world's tigers, but where half the population lives in extreme poverty, poachers willingly risk being caught. The connection between poverty and the extinction of species is undeniable. Poor people cut down forests, the natural habitat of tigers, for fuel. If killing a tiger puts food on the table, who are we to judge? We need to make the connection between social justice and ecological disaster.[8]

Terry Glavin devotes a chapter of his book *Waiting for the Macaws and Other Stories from the Age of Extinctions* to telling the story of the extinction of birds. One-fifth of all birds that existed 20,000 years ago are now extinct, mainly because of humans. The Great Auk, for example, was slaughtered to extinction for its flesh, its oil, and for its feathers and skins. The passenger pigeon was once so numerous that hunters refused to listen to the warnings of eccentric conservationists. By the beginning of the 20th century, they were gone. Glavin, a native of Vancouver, grieves the passing of the mynah bird from our city. These were little black birds, who, when tamed, could be taught to repeat words. "In February 2003, the last pair of mynah birds disappeared. One of them was hit by a car at 2nd Avenue and Columbia. The last mynah kept a faithful vigil beside its dead mate, until it too was run over, two weeks later. And then there were none."[9]

A team of marine scientists have recently completed the most comprehensive research to date on the state of the 7800 species of seafood available today.[10] They have concluded that if we continue to fish at the same rate for the next 50 years as we have for the past 50 years, 100 percent of these species will be collapsed. With each lost species, the quality of the water itself is compromised. At some point, the water will be unable to sustain fish. The silver lining in this story is that, if given half a chance, species that have dwindled to 10 percent of their original populations are able to stage remarkable comebacks. An area called Georges Bank Marine Protected Area, located off the coast of New England, was once almost totally fished out. Today the haddock and scallop are flourishing. There is still time.

But first we must break the spell of the narrative of the disenchanted cosmos. If these animals are divine modes of presence, then extinction is not only biocide, the death of life, it is also deicide, the death of Spirit, a 21st-century crucifixion of planetary proportions. The destruction of these creatures is made possible because we lack the sensibility and sensitivity to see them as manifestations of Spirit. The story of extinction is a story of exile on an absolute scale – oblivion.

## Homecoming: God's Covenant

The Bible's answer to Einstein's question concerning whether the universe is friendly is unequivocal. The God of this universe chooses to be in intimate relationship with *all* of creation, human and other-than-human. This commitment is sealed in a series of covenants, with Noah, Abraham and Sarah, Moses and Miriam, Jeremiah, and Jesus of Nazareth. In the covenant with Noah, God laments his decision to destroy creation in a flood. God sets a rainbow in the sky not for our benefit, but to remind himself of the travesty of destroying creation (Genesis 9:13). This covenant, and the ones that follow, are built upon a foundation of love. God's love for us demands that we treat our neighbours with justice. This covenantal requirement is extended beyond the human realm in the Sabbath practice of allowing beasts of burden to rest, and in a quirky folk legend from Numbers concerning Balaam's donkey.

In the story, Balaam's donkey sees an angel blocking the road and so refuses to pass by. Balaam is unable to see the angel and beats his donkey. The donkey protests, "What have I done to you, that you have struck me three times? Am I not your donkey, which you have ridden all your life? Am I in the habit of treating you this way?" The angel scolds Balaam, telling him that the donkey saved his life (Numbers 22:21–35). Balaam's donkey speaks for all animals. What have they done to us to deserve the treatment we have meted out to them?

Bill Lishman, at 67, is listening to the cry of Balaam's donkey. He is leading a flock of whooping cranes out of the exile of captivity to find their way back home. Forty years ago the bird was on the verge of extinction. Its population stands at 500 thanks to programs such as Operation Migration.[11] After successfully training Canada geese to follow his ultralight airplane on their migratory paths, Lishman turned to the whooping crane. These birds, raised in captivity, needed to be taught by humans their migratory route. They learned to accept white ultralights and humans dressed in white costumes with artificial beaks, as maternal figures. Every year, an entourage of ultralights leads these enormous birds from Wisconsin to Florida, landing in the fields of cooperative farmers along the way, so that both humans and cranes can rest and feed. Hopefully such stories can inspire many more people to take up the Christ-like vocation of guiding other creatures from the verge of oblivion back home.

## The Story of the Temple: The God of Sacrifice

A third metanarrative found within sacred scripture is the story of the Temple, with its sacrificial practice. The most profound writer on the history and meaning of religious sacrifice today is René Girard.[12] He traces how the blood sacrifice of human beings was employed as a remedy against the potential escalation of violence in early human communities. Girard's theory is just that, a theory, but it is compelling nonetheless. Early communities noticed that when violence resulted in someone being killed, the murder caused a temporary cessation of violence. It created a "holy hush" as both sides gathered around the corpse. Noticing the power of a murder to create a temporary cessation of hostilities, early tribes ritually re-enacted this violence through an annual sacrifice of a human being. Blood sacrifice had a redemptive function in that it controlled the potential for escalating violence. Girard calls this the "myth of redemptive violence."

The early Hebrew community had to make a decision about sacrifice. When Abraham journeyed in the Sinai desert, he discovered that the surrounding cultures engaged in human sacrifice. The story of God calling him to sacrifice his son, Isaac, may represent a turning point in Jewish history. When Yahweh relents from this demand, providing a ewe to substitute for Isaac, it may represent the point in history when the Jewish people turned away from human sacrifice. From that point on, animals would substitute for humans, but blood sacrifice remained a holy obligation. Its explicit connection with controlling violence was transmuted into other functions, such as purification, atonement for sin, and pleasing God.

The altar of the Temple was located in the holy of holies, the inner sanctum where only priests could enter to perform the solemn duty of slaughtering all manner of animals. It was serious business. If they happened to miss a step in the process, their own blood became the substitute sacrifice (Exodus 28:35–38).

The solemn precision with which the ritual had to be executed suggests an unconscious association with the original meaning of the sacrifice, the taking of a life as a means of controlling escalating violence. Get it wrong, and all hell could literally break out.[13]

The practice of Temple sacrifice continued through to the end of the Second Temple period, some 30 years after Jesus' death.

John Dominic Crossan believes that it was Jesus' action of over-turning the tables of the money-changers and the vendors selling animals for sacrifice that led to his crucifixion. He was symboli-cally destroying the entire institution of Temple sacrifice.[14] Read-ing this incident through the lens of our modern-day willingness to sacrifice entire species at the altar of human "progress," Jesus' actions may be interpreted as a defence of all victims of sacrificial violence, including animals.

It is one of the greatest ironies of history that the predomi-nant meaning of Jesus' death on a cross in our age is precisely the one he most opposed. Like Jewish prophets 600 years before him, Jesus railed against the priestly meaning of religious sac-rifice. Speaking for God, the earlier prophets thundered judg-ment upon the priests: "For I desire steadfast love, not sacrifice of animals, the knowledge of God, rather than burnt offerings" (Hosea 6:6). Caiaphas, the High Priest who turned Jesus over to the Romans to be executed, asks, "Is it not better that one man be sacrificed than a whole nation?" He was setting Jesus up as a sac-rificial offering, a scapegoat offered to prevent further violence. The authorities hoped that spilling Jesus' blood would deter his followers from instigating any future possible uprisings against the state.

Girard contends that the story of Easter undermines and sub-verts the myth of redemptive violence. State violence didn't work. Jesus' followers experienced his presence with them following the crucifixion. A movement of non-violent followers emerged to take up Jesus' mission. While Jesus and the gospel stories subvert the myth of redemptive violence, it nevertheless continues to be the predominant interpretation of Jesus' death.

The most prevalent atonement theory of Jesus' death pre-sumes a God who plans to have his own son tortured and executed instead of us. It presents us with an image of God as child abuser. I was told, as a born-again Christian, that God, being just, had no choice but to judge sin harshly. Sinners had to die. Sin had to be taken care of once and for all. But God lets us off the hook by sacrificing his only son. God loves us so much that God gives God's only son to die on our behalf. We are saved by the blood of Jesus. We've heard it all before. Jesus had to be sacrificed so that we could be forgiven.

Notice, however, what Jesus does with sin while he's alive. He forgives it. Then he tells the forgiven person to straighten up. The crucifixion was a straightforward execution. Jesus didn't die *for* our sin. He died *because* of it.

According to the gospel story, at the moment of Jesus' death the curtain of the holy of holies is torn in two. It is an apocalyptic moment. The true meaning of apocalypse is to reveal what has been concealed. The holy of holies, the symbolic centre of the myth of redemptive violence, where the blood of the innocent was spilled as the sacrifice God required, is exposed as nothing more than smoke and mirrors. The whole cosmos participates in this unveiling. The sun stands still and the sky darkens. The myth of redemptive violence is undermined, leaving space for a more cosmologically oriented understanding of sacrifice to take its place.[15]


## Recovering Sacrifice as Sacred Story

It's tempting to simply stop talking about sacrifice in the progressive church, because of its associations with blood atonement. But sacrifice is a cosmological dynamic of the universe itself. By setting the gospel story within the context of the evolving universe, we may reclaim sacrifice, including Jesus' own self-donation, as integral to the Christian story. Sacrifice has two aspects: one is to make sacred or to hallow, and the other involves what we are prepared to offer of ourselves in doing so.

O. Henry writes the tale of a watchmaker and his wife. They are very poor, but rich in their love for each other. The watchmaker's most prized possession is a watch given to him by his father. He cannot wear it, however, because he can't afford a fob for it. His wife's most prized possession is her beautiful hair, long and thick and radiant. She covets a special comb, so that she might gather it up, and care for her hair properly. At Christmas one year, they both plan to give to the other their heart's desire. He sells his watch to purchase the comb, and she cuts her hair and sells it to buy him the watch fob. In doing so, they hallowed their love. They made it sacred, above even their most prized possessions.

At first glance there seems to be nothing in the universe story that approximates this kind of self-giving love. But even in the earlier stages of our evolutionary story, the foundations for this kind of sacrifice were being established. To give the most obvious example, everything we see around us, our families, the food we're preparing, the thoughts we have are made possible because of the sun's light and heat. The sun burns four million tons of hydrogen every second in the service of life. The sun dies and is reborn in a caribou, in the smile of a toddler, and in the passionate embrace of lovers. Plants capture the light of the sun, and for millions of years human beings have been feasting on converted solar energy, in wheat and corn, and in the animals that feast on these. Every meal we ingest is solar sacrifice.

This is relatively new information for human beings, and not many of us have been helped to integrate what Copernicus discovered 500 years ago, that the sun is the life-giving centre of our beings. This is the cosmological model of sacrifice, giving one's whole being in the service of the evolving wonder of life. It is no wonder that the ancient Egyptians worshipped the sun as a god who gave life.

Even before the sun, the great unfolding involved sacrifice. In chapter 3, I discussed the great moments in the story of the evolving universe as the cosmic equivalent of the "narrow gate" Jesus talked about. Ninety-nine percent of all matter didn't make it beyond the first few moments of creation. Stars that took 10 million years to form exploded, and out this death the heavy elements necessary for life on earth emerged. The story of life on earth is the story of early life forms offering wisdom, memory, and even physical shape to successive forms of life. We enjoy the shape we have – two legs, two arms, a torso, a head with eyes and mouth and ears – precisely because earlier animals found these shapes to be most effective for negotiating their environment.

I'm not suggesting that any of this happened through conscious intention. Rather, self-donation in the direction of life is a latent evolutionary dynamic in the universe story. Like supernovas and our own sun, we are hard-wired to give ourselves in the service of life. In this cosmological sense, we can understand Jesus' life and death within a sacrificial context.

## Gaia's Gift of Self-Regulation

Genetic scientist Richard Dawkins begs to differ. He writes about the selfish gene. Genes are basically survival machines seeking to increase their gene pool by every and any means. Everything we see around us is the result of every form of life acting in accordance with this impulse. This extends to the human species, so that we should expect others to lie, cheat, and generally manage their relationships in such a manner that serves their chances of survival.[16]

Unquestionably, life wants to reproduce itself and engages in this task ferociously. But it is equally possible to view life through the lens of sacrifice. The Gaian life system, that mind-boggling system whereby the planet regulates itself, has managed to keep earth fit for life for one-third of the lifespan of the universe. Despite the sun throwing off 25 percent more heat today than it did when the planet first formed, Gaia has kept the temperature relatively constant.

James Lovelock, originator of the Gaia hypothesis, does not even pretend to understand the complexities involved. But his work is now becoming mainstream science. Lovelock doesn't think of Gaia as a living being with conscious intent. But I'm not a scientist, and whereas scientists will go to great lengths to keep Spirit out of the equation, my agenda is the opposite. From my perspective, the Gaian system participates in the evolutionary intentions of Spirit, in the service of life. She weaves together an intricate web of life, in such a way that each being and each system offers itself in the service of more abundant life and greater diversity. She gives herself to the sacred purpose of regulating the biosystems of the planet. Gaia is our model, in this sense, for the sacrifice humans need to make in the 21st century. At this point in the history of our planet, acting in our own self-interest may, paradoxically, mean acting sacrificially. Refusing to relinquish our present mode of living upon the earth will ultimately kill us. Perhaps the selfish gene is being recoded to incorporate sacrificial living in the service of life.

When Jesus teaches us to pray the words, "Hallowed be your name," he is teaching us to reorient our lives around that which is truly worth making sacred. Sin can be defined as making sacred that which is not worthy of hallowing. The Bible calls this idolatry.

Idolatry, by the way, is inevitable as we pass through evolutionary stages of our own development. As a spiritual exercise, look at your life and ask what you are making sacred. This will vary according to your psychological stage, your spiritual awareness, your cultural worldview, and the social arrangements you find yourself in. A teenager might hallow peer acceptance. S/he will make whatever sacrifices are required to meet this need, even if it means loss of integrity. A young man, steeped in the story of empire, will hallow the flag and be willing to make the "ultimate" sacrifice, even if the cause is less than noble. An entrepreneur may hallow the security, status, or freedom conferred by the accumulation of great wealth, and be willing to sacrifice love in order to achieve it. A clergyperson may hallow the image of being a holy person, and sacrifice his or her authentic self, replete with shadow, to live into the image. What these situations call for is not harsh judgment, but compassion toward ourselves and others. What we need is genuine discernment, and a willingness to allow the evolutionary Spirit to nudge us in the direction of our next stage of development. What we hallow determines what we will sacrifice for it.

Hallowing the earth and its diversity of life forms is a spiritual discipline we must embrace with our heart, soul, and mind in the 21st century. Currently, we hallow laissez-faire economics, and sacrifice the planet on its altar. Recognizing the planet as a manifestation of Spirit, and therefore also its sacred character, is the first step toward relinquishing whatever gets in the way of our hallowing. As part of this discipline, we will ask ourselves whether our lifestyles are aligned with this hallowing. Do we buy local produce, or do we eat vegetables trucked in from across the country, adding to the carbon levels of the atmosphere? Do the cars we drive honour the sacred nature of the planet? Do we invest in companies who try to reduce their ecological footprint? Do we use household products that are toxic? Do we play on a golf course certified by the Audubon Society? Does our work, our vocation, contribute to the "Great Work" of repairing the planet, or at least not impede her recovery?

## Servanthood

Jesus seemed to take every opportunity to hammer home a message about servanthood. Walking down a road one day, two of Jesus' disciples, John and James, hatch a plan. They notice that Jesus is growing in popularity, and think that the movement just might have legs. They see an opportunity to position themselves as prominent players in the new organization, and take action. "Wouldn't it be great, Jesus, if we were your right- and left-hand men?" (Mark 10:35–45). They are hallowing status, and are willing to sacrifice their equality with the other disciples to assume a dominant role.

It's clearly a teaching moment. "The Gentiles," Jesus tells them, "do things that way, but not you. They 'lord' it over others, but you serve." In Jesus' cosmology, the rulers of the world are servants as well, but they serve the Prince of Darkness, who promises that if we will just hallow him, we can get others to serve *us*. His ethic is domination. He is also known as the Father of Lies, in John's gospel. Jesus went a few rounds with this fellow, in the wilderness, before beginning his own ministry. He consciously refused to hallow status and worldly wealth. He chose carefully whom he would serve. In this, he only asks us to do what he has already done.

To be a servant of God is to repent of the ethic of domination. John and James were going down the road of serving the wrong guy, in the model of empire, not in the model of the kingdom of God. They were reading off the wrong script. Caesar's script to be precise. It's the imperial story, which has its own conventional take on prosperity, security, and meaning.[17] But Jesus turned this script, this story, upside down. If John and James want to be first, they should be last and servant of all. If they want to follow him, then they must take up their cross. The spiritual life is not about what we *accumulate*, but rather about what we *allocate*. It's about divestment, a stripping down of ego, not a fortifying of it.

Caesar, following an ethic of domination, requires that we sacrifice others to get what we want. Jesus, following an ethic of compassion, calls us to make a sacrifice of our own lives for the sake of others. For 300 years we have been serving the ethic of domination, sacrificing the animals and plants, the rivers and oceans, and the very air we breathe. We have lost sight of the fact that in doing so we have placed our own lives on the altar of destruction. As we give ourselves over to the flourishing of other life forms, we ourselves will be revived. This is the paradoxical wisdom of self-donation and servanthood. We find our lives by losing them in the hallowing of what is truly sacred.


## The Story of Call and Response: The God of Allurement

When I was in junior high school, on Sunday afternoons, I would find an excuse to leave the football or baseball game I was play-ing with my buddies, make my way home, and turn on the TV at 3:00. A program called *The Firing Line* aired at this time. The host was a man named William F. Buckley Junior, whom I later discovered to be a staunch Republican, and an ultraconservative philosopher. But I didn't leave the football game because of his politics or philosophy. I loved to listen to him speak, the way he carefully formed his words, and then strung them together in such a spellbinding way to make meaning. If someone caught me watching the program and asked me what I was doing, I would have gone mute. I didn't have a clue.

I understand now that William F. Buckley Junior was a source for me of what Brian Swimme calls "allurement." In his presence, a mysterious power, beyond and beneath my conscious awareness, and transcending my capacity to name it at the time, called to me. It was as though this is what I was intended for. In a mysterious way, his presence reminded me of what my life was to be about. I would fall in love with words, written and spoken. It would matter to me how words were used to make meaning.

I suspect that most of us have had this kind of experience, but there is no way in our culture to talk about those experiences. In my case, it was my own little secret. By grace, I was able to listen to my own life, and be led to my vocation – a word translated from the Latin word for call.

Call and response is a central story, a metanarrative, in scripture.

In the Old Testament, Abraham and Sarah heard a call to leave urban culture, load up the U-haul, and head out into the wilderness. All that sustained them, as the passing years mocked their decision, was God's promise that, if they took the first step, God would make of them a great nation.

Joseph discerns his call through dreams. He ended up in a pit, left for dead by his jealous brothers who didn't appreciate their little brother's gift.

Moses heard the call coming from a burning bush. Responding to that call would mean exchanging his royal robes for a fugitive's rags, and putting up with the ingratitude of a liberated people, but there was no denying it.

Young Samuel heard his song in the middle of the night, mistaking it at first for the voice of his mentor, Eli.

In the New Testament, the birth narratives depict an enchanted universe alluring a host of characters to embrace the mystery of Jesus' birth. Stars, angels, and dreams join in a conspiracy of good news, calling the human participants to believe what God is doing through them. Zachariah and Elizabeth are called by an angel to believe that their son, John, will prepare the way for the Messiah. Mary and Joseph are told by angels to trust that they are being called to bear this holy child. The shepherds hear the song of the angels. A star in the east lights a path to the birthplace of a new creation. Magi, trained in the art and science of astrology, realize that something is up. For them, the call to pack up the camels with panniers full of gold, frankincense, and myrrh, and to head out across the desert, originates from the heavenly bodies. The whole universe is a source of allurement, drawing all creation toward the birth of the Christ.

Each of the gospels tells the story of the call of Jesus to the disciples. They drop everything to follow him. In his presence, everything their lives had previously been about pales in comparison. Jesus is a source of allurement for the first disciples, and has been for millions of people for the last 2000 years.

Allurement appears to be a fundamental dynamic of an evolutionary universe, calling all beings and all systems to realize their destiny. Most New Testament scholars think that the portrayal of the disciples suddenly dropping their lives like a bad habit and following Jesus is an exaggeration. I'm not convinced. Jesus was for them like the sun is to the earth. He lit them up, and awakened them to their purpose. My own experience is that when this happens, there's not much that can stop a person. In response to Jesus' alluring presence, those he heals and teaches turn their lives around and follow him.

I wrote, in the first chapter, about my experience of reading Brian Swimme's *The Universe Is a Green Dragon*. That little book changed my life. Actually, it was the presence of the man who wrote it that awakened me to the mysteries of the universe. To be in Brian's presence is to be in the presence of the universe story, embodied in human form. As a mathematical physicist, he concerned himself with gravity, the field that binds all things together. Whereas for Newton it was the fall of an apple that caused him to become fascinated by gravity, for Swimme it was a rock. Once, on a fishing trip, while waiting for his father, he held a rock up and dropped it to the ground, over and over again. He realized that he could write out the mathematical equation that described the dynamics of gravity, but he couldn't say *why* the rock fell to the ground. He found himself on holy ground, fascinated by the pull of a mysterious, invisible power.

Why did the first primal particles enter into a dance and become hydrogen atoms? Why did hydrogen atoms organize themselves into stars? Start with a black field of hydrogen atoms. These atoms become attracted to each other and suddenly a switch is turned on. The result is a magnificent light show called a star. A star is the life evoked by the attraction of hydrogen atoms to one another. One of those stars, our sun, enters into a dance with a planet. The planet becomes fascinated by the star and spends a billion years with it, in a relationship that Swimme characterizes as adoration. There is something about the star that has the capacity to awaken this planet, and the planet gives this source of allurement its undivided "attention." When it figures out how to make a chlorophyll molecule, the love affair really begins. Through photosynthesis, the earth discovers how to convert the sun's light into the energy required for the procession of life to emerge. This is why it found the sun's presence so alluring. The sun had the capacity to awaken the latent potential of the planet to come to life.[18]

We live and move and have our being in this field of attraction, which in cosmological terms is called gravity. But we can call it love. Love, in this sense, is the alluring dynamic of the universe calling us to realize our fullest potential. It is pure mystery, a fundamental force, which cannot be explained. It's just there for us to participate in. If you could snap your fingers and remove this field from the universe, the stars would fly apart; the earth would disappear into a black void; the guitar you've been learning to play would hold no interest; Bach would be bland; you would not be inclined to sacrifice your life for your children, for you would stop caring for them; all love-making would cease; the salmon would stop running upstream to lay their eggs. You get the idea. Saint Paul intuited this field of attraction and named it Christ, the divine, cosmic being, "in whom all things are held together" (Colossians 1:17).

In primal or indigenous cultures, adults intuit the distinctive allurements of their children. Matthew Fox tells the story of a tribe that spontaneously sings a song at the birth of a child. This song captures the child's unique identity and destiny. As she passes through the various stages of her life, the tribe gathers and sings her birth song. It is the song of allurement, drawing their latent potential forth. If she becomes ill or acts in an anti-social manner, the tribe will gather around and sing this song, to call her back to her original sacred self.

The universe has a song for each of us. When we hear it sung, it unlocks a deep intuition of what we were intended for in this life. For those with ears to hear, this song is sung from every corner of our experience. To deny this song is to fall ill, in body, mind, and spirit. It is to be out of relationship with self, with God, and with our very lives.

The song that culture sings, however, is a siren song. It plays much louder than our birth song. It hollers at us from the media, from billboards, and from our educational institutions: "Get an education, make sure it leads to a good job, make money, live the good life." But a job is not a vocation. Silence is the mast to which we must bind ourselves, or the siren song of consumerism, celebrity, insufficiency, and empire will be too powerful to resist. I watched William F. Buckley Junior by myself, in our little sun room, witnessed only by the silent presence of my father's plants. I was able to indulge completely in the allurement my soul was undergoing. It is only through silence that we can turn our ear to the strains of our sacred vocation.

In this chapter, I have begun a dialogue between two sacred narratives: the narrative of nature and the narrative of the Bible. By exploring these four metanarratives through a cosmological lens, we discover that scripture does indeed speak to our ecological crisis.

We turn now to the central figure of the Christian church, Jesus of Nazareth, to continue this dialogue between his teachings and the universe story as sacred narrative.

## Scriptural Evolution and the Old and New Testaments

At the beginning of this chapter, I proposed that scripture, like the story of the universe, reflects an evolutionary dynamic; the evolution, over time, of the spirituality, psychology, and worldviews of the various writers is reflected in their writings.

I want to be clear about what I do *not* mean by this. I do not mean that the New Testament is uniformly superior, more enlightened, or a more highly evolved collection of writings than the First Testament, the Hebrew scriptures.

In fact, if you read John's gospel – the last gospel to be written – you'll find the core theology that supported Hitler's anti-Semitic and anti-Judaistic beliefs. When I say that the scriptural witness is evolutionary, I mean that it invariably reflects the stage of spiritual consciousness of both the writer and the community for whom s/he is writing. John's cultural worldview is "mythic" (Habermas), his psychological stage reflects an "us" psyche rather than an "all-of-us" psyche (Wilber), and a "conventional" stage of spirituality (Fowler). If we have evolved to higher stages of development in these various spheres (psychological, cultural worldview, and spiritual) it causes us to recoil when we read offensive passages – even if they are found in scripture.

John's writing inevitably reflects his stage of development.[19]

We can say, then, that the more accurately the gospels reflect the heart and mind of Jesus of Nazareth – and, as we've seen, they don't necessarily do this – the closer they are to reflecting the most evolved aspects of Judaism. (Remember, there's nothing in the New Testament that you won't find somewhere in the Hebrew scriptures, including Jesus' admonition to love your enemies.) Jesus reflected the most highly evolved features of his own (Jewish) tradition. At least that's what we claim as Christians. There are, no doubt, Jews who wouldn't agree with this statement. That's fine. But what we *cannot* claim, in a postmodern worldview, is that the Christian religion, including the New Testament, is more highly evolved, or is a better window onto God than Judaism. We may make the claim that it works for *us*, but not that it is more "true" than Judaism.

It would serve us well to continue in dialogue with our "mother" faith so that we might learn what God is revealing to our Jewish friends today, even as we share our experience of what the Holy is revealing us.

# Chapter 6

## JESUS' TEACHINGS:
## AN ECOLOGICAL PERSPECTIVE

When Christ comes to one of his faithful it is not simply in
order to commune with him as an individual; …when, through
the mouth of the priest, he says *Hoc est corpus meum* [this
is my body], these words extend beyond the morsel of bread
over which they are said: they give birth to the whole mystical
body of Christ. The effect of the priestly act extends beyond the
consecrated host to the cosmos itself…the entire realm of matter
is slowly but irresistibly affected by this great consecration.

PIERRE TEILHARD DE CHARDIN

Jesus didn't have to contend with global warming, overpopulation, the extinction of species, or the toxic soup in which we
live. As a Jewish mystic and social prophet, his ministry was a
response to the concrete realities of his day and age: the imposed
transition from an agricultural village culture to the imperial
system of the Roman Empire. Caesar's empire introduced a new
urbanism; a new economic system; an egregious tax burden; and
foreign ownership of land, with its accompanying displacement
of people from their ancestral lands. The result was widespread
poverty, social displacement, and physical disease. The religious
leaders of the day were dealing with the temptation to accommodate the imperial worldview. Jesus was contending with a
popular expectation that God would act soon and decisively to

restore Israel's independence and rid the land of these imperial intruders. The focus of his ministry was on alleviating human suffering, not on the plight of the earth herself.

If Jesus was conducting his ministry in today's world, I believe his circle of concern would include the ecological crisis facing our planet. Ecological degradation results from the same dynamic that causes injustice in the human realm. We are out of relationship with God, self, neighbour, and the planet. Our biblical narrative confirms that we are in bondage to a way of life that is destroying our planet; we are addicted to unsustainable patterns of consumption. If Jesus is to be relevant to us today, we need to interpret his teaching through an ecological lens.

To do so follows in the tradition of feminist and Central American theologians in recent years. When women and the peasants of Central America began to read and interpret the gospels through the lens of their experiences of oppression, the text came alive with new meanings. Same parable, unexpected wisdom. Specific insights, which were not even seen without the advantage of the new lens, emerged from the biblical stories. And so Mary sings the same Magnificat (Luke 1:46–55) that has been sung for 2000 years in great cathedrals, and suddenly she's recognized as a subversive feminine presence, not as queen of the imperial status quo. Jesus announces that the Spirit of the Lord is upon him to proclaim good news to the poor and release to the captives (Luke 4:1–8), and through the lens of Central American peasants, it's no longer the milquetoast "spiritual" metaphor it has been to wealthy North Americans. If you're a peasant, when the Bible speaks about the poor it's talking about physical poverty, not spiritual impoverishment.

What happens, then, if we read the teachings of Jesus through a cosmological lens? What new meanings emerge when Gaia is the interpretive lens through which we look at these teachings? Perhaps the "old, old story" may offer up fresh perspectives that can help us to rediscover awe and to find our way back home as planetary citizens.

## The Greening of Jesus

Whatever ambivalence the church has felt historically about recognizing creation as a mode of divine presence, that ambivalence or reticence didn't originate with Jesus. Jesus was a bit of an earthnik. He looked around at the natural world and saw God everywhere. Matthew Fox points out that it was Augustine, writing in the fourth century, who was responsible for splitting nature off from grace.[1] For Augustine, nature, including human nature, was grace-less. Grace belonged to the spiritual realm, which was located above and beyond the natural world, and which was mediated exclusively by the church and her priests. Meister Eckhart, a 14th-century mystic, tried to correct this theological mistake. He said simply, "Nature is grace."

Jesus would have agreed. Jesus saw what Fox calls a "natural grace" everywhere he looked. He paid careful attention to nature as a way of discerning and conveying the presence and activity of God.

Thus, for Jesus, mustard seeds are a symbol of the kingdom of God (Luke 13:18–19). Fig trees bearing fruit are a sign that God is near (Mark 13:28–29). A gardener adding manure to a struggling tree becomes a metaphor of God's patient love and mercy (Luke 13:6–9). A farmer pruning back vine branches that bear no fruit signals God's intention that we thrive (John 15). The growth of a seed is a metaphor of the grace of God (Luke 8:5). Lost sheep reflect the alienation of humans (Matthew 9:36). Wind is a metaphor for Spirit (John 3:8). Jesus invites us to take a lesson in life from the lilies and the ravens (Matthew 6:26–28).

It's likely that Jesus spent most of his time, day and night, outside. "Foxes have dens, birds have nests, but the son of man has nowhere to lay his head" (Matthew 8:20). He was acquainted with the stars in a way most modern urbanites cannot comprehend because of light pollution. He compared the kingdom of God to treasure buried in a field (Matthew 13:44). It was like a fine pearl discovered in an ocean (Matthew 13:45). Jesus intuitively knew how various landscapes conveyed different modes of divine presence. When he needed to find a "thin place," transparent to Spirit, he ascended mountains (Mark 9:2). When he needed help to discern his call, he retreated to the desert to fast (Matthew 4:1). When it was time for him to be reborn, he naturally headed for the waters of the Jordan to be baptized by John (Matthew 3:16). Jesus understood nature to be a source of grace.

When he predicted calamity, all creation participated. "There will be signs in the sun, the moon, the stars...the nations will be confused by the roaring of the sea and the waves" (Luke 21:25). According to Jesus, even the mountains will respond to the will of the faithful (Matthew 21:21). If the crowds are silent, the very stones will cry out in recognition of his holy purpose (Luke 19:40). For Jesus, all of creation mediated holy Presence.


## The Kin-dom of God

Because it was absolutely central to his spirituality, it's not possible to understand Jesus' teaching without coming to terms with the metaphor of the kingdom of God.

Like many things, it's easier to say what the kingdom *isn't* than to say what it is. First, you won't find the kingdom on a map, and you won't find it in the "Great Beyond." It's neither the country of the good and the faithful, nor the place they go in the next life to receive their reward. Both these misunderstandings have been the cause of too much violence, both physical and ideological.

The kingdom-of-God metaphor has come under criticism in recent years for being patriarchal and imperialistic. I agreed, until I read John Dominic Crossan's take on the kingdom. He sees it as an intentionally subversive metaphor. It's what the world would look like if God, not Caesar, reigned. The realization of the kingdom would involve shifting from an ethic of domination, Caesar's rule, to an ethic of mutuality, God's rule. In other words, the kingdom of God is an oppositional metaphor. It gets at the truth of things by intentionally setting itself up alongside the dominant cultural metaphor of the day, and by shocking listeners out of their allegiance to it.

We shouldn't be too quick to rid ourselves of this metaphor. Imperialistic worldviews and institutions are never far away, and, in recent years, a neo-conservative political elite in the United States has not been shy about promoting a new imperialism.

Yet, within the context of the ecological crisis we face, there are good reasons to evolve the metaphor slightly. Keeping its original subversive intent in mind, let us drop the "g" in kingdom, leaving us with kin-dom of God. Why?

The metaphor of kin-dom is a family metaphor. To be kin is to belong, no questions asked. In an evolutionary universe, I'm interested in kin as a metaphor that includes *"all of us,"* not just "us." From this perspective, kin is not just about our tribe, our nation, our family, our religion, or even our species. Kin suggests the radical belonging of *all* our relations, human and other-than-human.

Viewed holistically, from the perspective of the universe story, kin-dom breaks down false boundaries that separate and alienate. When the first astronauts saw earth from space, they were struck by the lack of visible national borders. The earth shone brightly, just one beautiful blue-green jewel in a sea of darkness. They recognized earth as one sacred community of life.

This is more than romantic fantasy. It is a spiritual truth, grounded in empirical science. We have traced our cosmological kinship already. We have also seen that we participate as one component of a Gaian system intent upon keeping the conditions on earth fit for life. The ocean's waters and our blood contain very similar levels of salt. In our mother's womb, we recapitulate the evolutionary process; each stage in the embryo's life re-enacts the work and wisdom of life forms at every step of our evolutionary path. Each of us is knit together out of the wisdom of the bacteria, plants, and animals that came before us. Our very bodies are composites of our kin, who have given us life. To be fascinated by this reality is to enter into the kin-dom of God.

> I praise you, O God, for I am fearfully and wonderfully
> made. Wonderful are your works; that I know very well.
> I was made in secret, intricately woven in the depths of
> the earth. (Psalm 139:14–15)

In this sense, the kin-dom of God is no less radical than the kingdom of God as metaphor. To dwell upon our cosmological reality is to subvert the dominant stories and metaphors we live by. An ethic of domination is a hellish thing to embody when we know we are kin. The extinction of species represents a loss of family members. The conversion of Amazon rainforest into pasture for cattle and farmland for soy crops is tantamount to taking a knife to our own lungs. Our biosystems evolved to serve the needs of Gaia, including, but not limited to the needs of human beings. The jungles of the earth play a specific role in the kin-dom of God. They were never intended to be converted into hamburgers.

## The Mustard Seed
### (Luke 13:18–19)

Jesus said that the kin-dom of God is like a mustard seed. Early interpretations of this parable, found in the New Testament, missed the point. It's not that this tiny seed grows up and becomes a tree, providing shelter for the birds. (They become shrubs, in fact.) Crossan points out that the mustard plant was considered a noxious weed. It was invasive, planting itself where it wasn't welcome, making life difficult for the farmers. As the Roman Empire appropriated ancestral lands, replacing the subsistence crops of the local farmers with export crops to make foreign landowners wealthy, the little mustard seed takes on new subversive meaning. Jesus was advocating that his followers be a contaminant of these fields. As a movement, the church is a kin-dom of "nuisances and nobodies" infiltrating the dominant culture with an alternative ethic.[2]

Take the seeds of kinship, the ethic of earth's unity and mutuality, and cast them upon the carefully cultivated fields of the dominators. Be a nuisance weed; plant your ideals alongside the ideals of Caesar. Today, Jesus might tell us to live simply, buy locally, allocate wealth in the service of the kin-dom, rather than accumulate it for personal gain. Consume consciously, using only those products that don't harm Gaia. Be a voice for the other-than-human ones. Be annoying when necessary, sprouting up unexpectedly at meetings to speak a word that might not be welcome, reminding your kin that sustainable retreat, not sustainable development, is the order of the day.[3] A member of the congregation I serve makes a point of politely approaching the drivers of idling cars and asking them if they've thought about how they are contributing to global warming. He's an annoying mustard seed.

## The Kin-dom as Priceless Treasure
### Matthew 13:44–45

Jesus teaches that the kin-dom is like a priceless treasure. A man finds treasure buried in his field, and goes and sells all of his goods in order to buy the field. A merchant discovers a pearl, and in his joy goes and sells all of his earthly goods in order to buy this single pearl. Those who discover the treasure have found something of absolute and ultimate value. Selling their possessions to acquire it is a no-brainer.

Jesus doesn't tell us anything about the pearl or the treasure hidden in the field. But, looked at from within his own Jewish tradition, there is strong support for the idea that he had spiritual wisdom in mind. (We will explore this further in the next chapter.) In Job, Wisdom (Sophia) is the hidden treasure whose location is known to God alone (Job 28). Only those who have a capacity for awe – what the biblical writers name as fear – are able to discover Wisdom (28:28). She is hidden from the eyes of the wise – those who think they are smart – and revealed to those with humble hearts. She is priceless. (She can't even be bought with MasterCard!) All other possessions are pale substitutes, even the finest jewels (vs. 17).

Jesus, as Wisdom's child (Matthew 11:19), reveals the way to her. The kin-dom of God is the spiritual awareness that Sophia/ Wisdom is the hidden wholeness, the very presence of the divine, at work and at play in the heart of all creation. The path of humility reveals her presence everywhere and in every thing. The universe and the planet earth is infused with her glorious presence, making all things whole, for those with eyes to see and ears to hear.

The farmer found this treasure in a field, as I did that day in my own wheat field in Milton, Ontario. The pearl merchant discovered it in the ocean. A mountain climber will discover the treasure in a mountain meadow. Beach-walkers will find the treasure hidden there. Sip a latté on a busy street in an urban café, and there it is. Once you enter the kin-dom, the treasure of this Sophia-infused creation is ubiquitous. The farmer and the merchant allocate all of their existing wealth for the sake of this treasure. Like the farmer and the pearl merchant, what will we relinquish to possess the treasure of living wisely upon the earth? The beginning of wisdom is the awareness that the whole living earth is a divine manifestation of Sophia. The ethical imperative implicit in this awareness is to be willing to exchange our life-styles for the repair of the planet.

## Human Ones as Harvesters of Grace
Mark 4:26–28

Jesus says that the kin-dom of God is like someone who scatters seed on the ground, goes to bed, and wakes up to discover that the seed has sprouted, "but he does not know how. The earth produces of itself, first the stalk, then the head, then the full head. But when the grain is ripe, at once he goes out with his sickle, because the harvest is ripe."

Jesus would have received top marks in any biology class today. In this parable, he describes what scientists call self-organization. We have finally confirmed what farmers have known for 10,000 years; the planet knows what she's doing, and so does a seed. Throw them together, add time, and presto, you've got wheat. In an emergent universe, there are no external forces causing an organism to do its thing; the latent tendency of the wheat plant exists within the seed. The farmer in the parable of the kindom *"does not know"* how this happens, and neither do our scientists. All the fancy names might give us some sense of control, but they don't lessen the mystery.

Earth's capacity to "produce of itself," through a universal intelligence, requires us to acknowledge that we exist in a state of grace. It's not our gig. As previously mentioned, there are a lot of brainless organisms on earth that exhibit astounding intelligence. Seeds are just one of those. Algae figured out how to eat carbon dioxide and release oxygen. Without this intelligent being acting on our behalf, the temperature of the earth would rise beyond what we could endure. In other words, slime-mould still puzzles our brainiest scientists.

But we refuse to take our place in grace. We "help" nature along by making petroleum-based chemical fertilizers and pesticides to increase crop yields. Wes Jackson, Director of the Land Institute, says that we grow our food in oil, not soil. Farmers have become dependent upon the "protection ring" of the petrochemical industry. Once farmers entered the vicious cycle, there was no clear exit strategy. Yet there is no credible evidence that the use of these products increases harvest yields. Since 1945, pesticide use has risen 3300 percent, but overall crop loss to pests has not gone down. Insects, with their puny brains, annually outsmart our brightest chemists. So despite pounding U.S. crops with 2.2 billion pounds of pesticides annually, crop losses have increased 20 percent. The soil is less productive as a result. Farmers compensate by pouring 20 million tons of fertilizer on them annually, an average of 160 pounds for every person in the U.S.[4] This further destroys the soil, in a vicious cycle of "crops and robbers." The net result? Chemicals destroy the soil, leach out into the rivers, and end up – where else? – in our bodies.

We don't need to improve upon nature. We are born into a planetary biosystem that has already done the work on our behalf. And so, after 14 billion years of the universe working it out, we arrive on the scene, and like the farmer in Jesus' parable take out our sickle. We reap a harvest of pure grace. Day in and day out, we are harvesters of grace. Flowers adorning the table; food on our plates; bodies to taste, digest, assimilate, make new proteins, and, on a good morning, eliminate. This is what the kindom of God is like, says Jesus – pure grace, handed to us on a silver platter. All that's asked of us is a little appreciation, and a lot less attitude. We can't begin to "get it" rationally any more than the farmer understood how the earth produced of itself, and the plant grew up. We weren't meant to "get it" with our heads. We were meant to receive it with our hearts. God is gracious.


## Ordeal as Evolutionary Passage

Barbara Brown Taylor tells a story about her husband, who befriended a local First Nations band. He was invited to participate in a Sun Dance festival. This festival involves ritual sweat lodges, ecstatic dance, chanting, and vision quests. It is a sacred ordeal, which one embarks upon with the goal of preparing oneself to be more open to the Great Spirit. After the week was over, Barbara Brown Taylor delivered some food for the celebrants. When she spotted her husband, she almost didn't recognize him. He looked haggard, as though he had aged, but his eyes were on fire. Her husband's first words to her were, "Your church is too easy."[5]

Jesus teaches his disciples that they must take up their cross if they are going to follow him. If they want to find their life, they must be willing to lose it. Jesus' choice to use the cross as a symbol of ordeal got their attention. It was a particularly nasty way to die. Rome used it as their favourite way to deter anyone who had a notion about taking on the empire. Jesus certainly didn't mean that all his disciples would end up crucified. But each and every one of them would be required to undergo a psychological and spiritual death.

This spiritual principle has its cosmological correlate in the great Flaring Forth, and in the march of evolution itself. It took the ordeal of a supernova explosion to synthesize and spread the heavy elements necessary for life as we know it. Earth was pummelled by meteors and lightning storms for millions of years, which further prepared the conditions for the emergence of life. The cost the universe has paid to arrive at self-conscious human beings has been significant. Evolution proceeds as the latent potentialities of each organism are activated by both internal and environmental pressures. When the pressure is sufficient, new adaptations emerge, which give rise to new forms. Each time this occurs, an earlier form of life must first let go, to make room for the novel and more complex form to emerge. This evolutionary pressure is built into the fabric of the universe.

When John the Baptist told the crowds that Jesus would baptize them with "the Holy Spirit and with fire" (Luke 3), he affirmed that to be in the Christ's presence was to enter the fire of creation. Christ was a concentrated manifestation of the great Flaring Forth, of the supernovas, and of the lightning that flashed to bring forth life on the planet – each of which ushered in a new evolutionary stage of the universe. To be baptized by the fire of the Christ is to undergo an ordeal of transformation as we enter and create the new age.

Humans are the ones who may consciously choose this re-formation. Christians must at some point "undergo" Christ. Being "born from above" (John 3:7) is the conscious willingness to allow Spirit to move in us in a way that Spirit moves in all creation "from below," that is, through instinctual processes. We are also the only species with the freedom to refuse to cooperate with the evolutionary Spirit. A rich young man becomes sad and walks away from Jesus when he is told that he must loosen his grip on his money in order to enter life (Mark 10:17–22). Attachment to wealth is the most common impediment to entering the kin-dom of God, according to Jesus.

Taking up the cross in an ecological age means exiting the culture of convenience. The term "vampire loads" refers to the draw on our energy grid caused by TV satellite receivers, and other electronic equipment, left on all day. We leave them on because if we turn them off the next time we watch TV it will take the receiver a good 30 minutes to download the programs. Pressing a button is such a small gesture it's embarrassing that it feels like a sacrifice. But imagine 200 million of these devices sucking energy 24 hours a day. And this doesn't include all the computers that are left on all day. The power being drawn by our gadgets when we aren't actually using them has to come from somewhere – nuclear energy stations, coal-fire energy plants, hydroelectric generators – all of which release heat-trapping carbon-dioxide into the environment. Those who have the mind and heart of Christ in this age make the connection between our addiction to convenience and global warming.

And it is an addiction. Breaking it will not be easy. We have been raised to believe that it is both a right, and a symbol of progress, to have what we want, when we want it. In the realm of personal transportation, reducing the amount we drive means slowing down and adjusting our schedules to the pace at which we can walk or take public transit. In a culture in which multitasking is a virtue and productivity the highest value, slowing down is a subversive act – an ordeal of inconvenience.

Indigenous cultures require young men and women to embark on a vision quest, which typically involves spending time apart fasting, and in intense prayer. These cultures recognize that there are aspects of our egoic personality that need to be dissolved in order for Spirit to emerge. Sweat lodges were designed for precisely this purpose. In the sweat lodge, heat burns away impurities of the heart and habits of the mind, allowing the person to get honest with him- or herself, and the community. These rituals represent a symbolic re-entering of the originating fire. Evolution, at all levels, including the spiritual, requires sufficient heat to forge the "new thing" God is doing.

I'm not sure that the typical confirmation class, or sprinkling water on an infant's forehead, quite compares. Soft-pedalling the high cost of following Christ for the sake of increasing the number of bums in the pews implicitly legitimizes the dominant myths of our culture. Besides, it's not what young people – and many older ones as well – want. Extreme sports, in which people put life and limb on the line, represent a re-enactment of primal ordeals of initiation, in the absence of any cultural equivalent today.

Barbara Brown Taylor's husband is right. Church is too easy. We've domesticated the wild Spirit of the evolutionary universe. Annie Dillard once said that our ushers should pass out signal flares and hard hats along with the Sunday bulletin. If church is as it should be, the Spirit will be at work, reconstructing the souls in attendance. Signs should be posted in the narthex: "Watch for Falling Egos!" The choice to come to church is a choice to enter into the evolutionary pressure created by being in the presence of the risen Christ. Church *should* be uncomfortable. We should be sweating it out a little. We're entering a reconfigured, liturgical form of the fireball.

The liturgy is a crucible to hold the wild stirrings of Spirit. Crossing the threshold of the sanctuary should be a risky affair. The hymns, the prayers, and the preaching invoke our ancestors, all the saints, including the wild prophets such as Isaiah and Jeremiah. Hosea and Amos are present, thundering the truth to the power structures who desire to freeze the evolutionary process in the service of their personal security. John the Baptist is present, locust juice dribbling down his beard, with one eye out for hypocrites, and the other for the secret police, who've heard that subversive things are going on. Word's out that these crazy Christians are engaged in subversive activities, such as walking to church, consuming consciously, replacing stained glass with photovoltaic windows to convert the sun's light into energy, and making plans to go off the energy grid!

Every fall sockeye salmon make an epic journey up the Fraser River to the spawning grounds of the Adams River in British Columbia. En route at least half will either be caught in fishing nets or will succumb to disease. After four years in the ocean, the females will return to within one metre of where they were hatched. After laying their eggs, they will die. Their bodies will be recycled to feed bears, eagles, and even the surrounding forest. In an evolutionary universe, ordeal is natural. The determination of the salmon to give themselves to a greater purpose is built into the fabric of our own being as well. We may call upon the fierce resolve of the salmon to face the journey we must now make as agents of planetary repair.

## The Prodigal Son
LUKE 15:11–32

The parable of the prodigal son centres around the youngest of two sons, who is anxious to take his share of his father's inheritance and see the world. He demands his share from the father, and then travels to a foreign country where he "squanders his property in dissolute living." He spends everything, and then to make matters worse a severe famine comes upon the land. He is forced to work for a Gentile, a source of great shame for a Jew. Things go from bad to worse as the job he lands involves feeding pigs, an unclean animal according to Judaism. The indignity is absolute.

Read through a cosmological lens, the younger son's insistence on receiving his inheritance immediately mirrors our adolescent stage of development as a species. We are young as planetary beings, relative to say, bacteria. We have not acquired the wisdom, nor steeped ourselves in the intelligence of the Spirit in all of creation. We are an impetuous bunch, demanding the inheritance freely given by 14 billion years of evolution, and squandering it. Like the younger son, we find ourselves wallowing in a poisonous atmosphere and in degraded biosystems. We have no one else to blame. Our dignity as an honoured species has been compromised. The food we eat is contaminated and genetically modified. If it were only our own dignity at stake, it would be bad enough. But we are taking other species down with us.

At a certain point, near starvation, the younger son finally "comes to himself" (Luke 15:17). He realizes his foolishness. We, on the other hand, have not yet "come to ourselves." In a sobering chapter he entitles "The Denial Industry," George Monbiot traces the money trail of global warming debunkers back to oil giant Exxon, and, surprisingly, to Philip Morris, the huge tobacco corporation. In fact, it was Philip Morris who first devised the strategy Exxon now employs. In short, Morris created the impression of a grassroots movement against "junk science," as a way of fighting back against a U.S. Environmental Agency report on the dangers of second-hand smoke. To divert attention from its specific agenda, Morris sought to link the "problem" of "junk science" to other areas of scientific concern, including global warming. Of course, it didn't take long for Exxon to recognize an opportunity, and to buy into the Morris strategy. Not surprisingly, Monbiot clearly shows that it is *their* science that is junk.[6]

Al Gore, former vice president of the United States, has tried for 20 years to get Congress to listen to his warnings about global warming. In response to Al Gore's powerful documentary, *An Inconvenient Truth*, a powerful oil lobby is funding a campaign to discredit it, a fact that David Suzuki points out in an article that appeared in *Common Ground*. In another effort to thwart the oil industry's attempts to spread misinformation, James Hoggan has created a website called desmogblog.com to debunk global warming critics. He names names, following the money trail back to big, U.S., conservative organizations and fossil fuel giants.[7] Not only are we not coming to our senses, there are forces actively committed to promoting denial. Our petulance is keeping us from coming to ourselves.

In the parable, the younger son experiences genuine remorse. He rehearses his apology before making the long and humbling journey back home to ask forgiveness from his father: "Father I have sinned against heaven and before you. I am no longer worthy to be called your son; treat me like one of your hired hands" (Luke 15:18–19). There is no cheap grace involved in this story. The son is willing to change his status, from privileged son to hired hand. Confession without repentance is what makes grace cheap. If our species is willing to relinquish our status as masters of the earth, and assume the role of servants of the Gaian ecology of life, our confession will have integrity. The way back home begins with confession.

With his speech well-rehearsed, the son sets off back home. "While he was still far off, his father saw him and was filled with compassion." The son doesn't even get halfway through his speech before his father throws his arms around him, lifts him off the ground, and plants a big, juicy kiss on his lips. Then he calls for a robe, a ring, and special sandals. It's a coronation ceremony for goodness sake! For a prodigal son, who blew the inheritance! Then the father throws a welcome home party.

It's a marvellous image for a cosmological homecoming. One needs to stretch the imagination a little to imagine Gaia calling together all the threatened species of the planet to welcome a humble and bedraggled species back into the family. They don't even mind handing us some royal robes, trusting that we intend to wear them with a new mind and a new heart. An elder brother, an Amazonian macaw perhaps, sits perched at a safe distance from the celebration. We might understand his resentment and caution, given that we've wiped out 99 percent of his family. He waits to see if we will back up our remorse with repentance. Are we are actually willing to "take up our cross," relinquish our identity as masters, and ask to be allowed as servants back into the kin-dom of God?

## The Great Banquet
Luke 14:7–24

At dinner one evening, Jesus notices men scrambling to assume the place of honour at the table. He gives them a little free advice. Their behaviour opens them to embarrassment, he says. The host could arrive and turf them into the cheap seats. Therefore, they should sit at the lowest place first, and then the host may elevate them to the seat of honour. Furthermore, when they are putting together the guest list, they shouldn't invite all their cronies, hoping to get invited back. Instead, they should invite those who cannot possibly repay their kindness: the poor, the crippled, the lame, and the blind. Their reward, Jesus assures them, will be assured in the "resurrection of the righteous" (Luke 14:7–14).

Jesus then tells a parable about a man who prepared a banquet and invited all his friends. His friends were full of excuses for why they could not attend. One had just purchased a piece of land and needed to inspect it. Another recently bought five new oxen, and was anxious to see them in action. The third was busy with marriage preparations. The man who prepared the banquet became angry and told his servant to go out into the streets and the lanes of the town, and bring in the poor, the crippled, the blind, and the lame. After the servant had done so, there was still room, so he went into the country roads, and "compelled" the social left-behinds to come. The intent of the host seems to be to make sure that there is absolutely no room left for those who were originally invited (Luke 14:24).

Read through a cosmological and planetary lens, one can't help but notice that *we* are the ones who have taken the seat of honour at the banquet of life. In both the prelude to the parable and the parable itself, the risk of a social reversal serves as a warning. Scramble for the seat of honour and you may find yourself in the cheap seats. Turn down the invitation to the banquet, and you may lose your seat permanently to the forgotten ones.

Recently, scientists have discovered ten to 100 times more bacteria than expected in the oceans. They took eight samples of water from the Atlantic and Pacific, and found 20,000 species of microbes. They expected to find fewer than 3000. Twenty percent of these species represented new discoveries. Mitchell Sogin, an evolutionary biologist, believes that these may be the genomic relatives of the earliest bacteria, the only life forms that existed for 80 percent of earth's history.[8] If this is true, these little creatures will have survived the various planetary cataclysms over the last five billion years. Furthermore, their capacity to survive periods of extinction, including ice ages, suggests that if conditions on earth change dramatically, they may re-emerge as the dominant life form.

Given the imminent danger global warming presents, and the degradation of our biosystems, we who have showed up late at the evolutionary party and yet have assumed the seat of honour, may indeed find ourselves displaced by lowly bacteria. Spirit is at work in every age warning us to be less concerned with dominating, and more concerned with joining the rest of creation. Either we assume a more humble place at the banquet of life, or Gaia, as self-regulator of earth's biosystems, will act to ensure that there is no room for us at the party. The survival of the planet takes precedence over human egos. Gaia will survive. New life forms will emerge from these hardy bacteria. God may act through bacteria to usher in a new creation should we destroy this one. The meek may indeed inherit the earth (Matthew 5:5).

We have been graciously invited to this incredible banquet of life. But, like the men in the parable, we are distracted by the affairs of our life. While the men in the parable offer their regrets, one intuits that they do not actually *feel* regret. They are busy with their affairs, and it's no accident that it is *business* affairs in the first two instances. "Getting and spending we lay waste our powers," writes Wordsworth. One of those powers, which have gone missing, is wisdom. We are so lost in the commerce of our lives that we do not know that the invitation we are turning down is to the banquet of life itself. Our fascination is fixed to material wealth, rather than to awe at the miracle of life. There is nothing inherently wrong with business. But when it blinds us to the reality that two-thirds of human beings suffer for lack of food and clean water, while we focus on accumulating more wealth, then something is indeed amiss. Similarly, while we go about our business mowing down forests, paving over peat bogs, and digging mines near watersheds, entire species disappear forever from the face of the planet. Our regret, at this point, is merely polite. We're worried about the colour of the linen and the script for our wedding invitations, while great white bears disappear from the planet.[9]

## Consider the Lily
### (Luke 12:27)

Janine M. Benyus, a biological science writer, coined the term *bio-mimicry* to suggest the future direction of business, food, and energy production; engineering, health services, and education.[10] It is time, she says, to apply the earth's wisdom to all these fields. We must learn to "consciously emulate life's genius." We have spent a few hundred years dominating nature, in an effort to extract her secrets. But rather than trying to improve on nature, it's time we began to learn from her. Those who undertake this discipline she calls "biomimics." The earth has been involved in 3.8 billion years of research and development. Doesn't it make sense to pay a little closer attention?

Jesus admonishes his disciples to "consider the lily" (Luke 12:27). The meaning of the Greek word translated as "consider" is actually closer to "study." On this particular occasion, Jesus uses the lily to teach a lesson about the futility of worry over what the disciples should wear. The lily, he reminds us, is more beautifully arrayed than King Solomon in his finest attire. The general principle underlying this lesson is that the grace of God is at work in and through natural processes. The earth and her creatures can teach us and convey wisdom.

Biologist Johann Wolfgang von Goethe considered not only lilies, but a vast array of plant species. His method involved studying plants with such intensity that an exact imprint of the plant was left in his mind. Then he would turn it over in his mind and look at it from every angle until he could see through the physical plant to the invisible spiritual form (archetype) from which it emerged. This is the living field of the plant, which gives it birth – what Rupert Sheldrake calls the morphogenetic field.[11]

This living field is itself a manifestation of what our tradition calls wisdom, personified in the Bible as the goddess Sophia (more on this in chapter 7).

William McDonough, an architectural engineer, and Michael Braungart, a chemist, base their industry consulting practice in the principles of biomimicry.[12] McDonough observed a simple equation at work in the natural world: *waste equals food.* In other words, nature produces zero waste that is not converted to food for the cycle of life. He then applied nature's equation to his work with multinational corporations. With Braungart, he was able to help an ecologically oriented textile company to use only non-toxic dyes in the manufacturing of their textiles. The water coming out of the plant at the end of the manufacturing process was cleaner than the water going in. Furthermore, the tailings left over from the textiles were all compostable.

## The Rich Man and Lazarus
### Luke 16:19–31

Jesus couldn't abide how the obsession over money blinded people to the suffering of others. And so he told a parable about a rich man who, every day on his way to and from work, steps over a hungry man covered with sores. The rich man dies and finds himself in hell. There, he cries for mercy, but Abraham tells him that the tables have been turned. An uncrossable chasm, as wide as the one separating the rich man and Lazarus in life, now exists between the rich man and eternal peace in the afterlife. His eyes now opened, the rich man asks that someone go and warn his relatives of the torment that awaits their oblivious souls, unless they repent. Abraham tells him it won't do any good. They already have the law and the prophets. The problem is that they're not *listening.* Even if someone went to visit them from the dead, they'd ignore the visitor, so caught up are they in their own affairs.

For years, environmental activists have been warning us of the dangers of pollution, deforestation, global warming, and species extinction. But the corporate lobby has cast them as quacks, alarmists, and eco-Nazis. The fiscal bottom line is still king. When it comes to making money, we're more than willing to step over the reality that the earth is suffering.

In truth, the cost to the earth is never included when calculating the cost of production. Extracting oil from the tar sands in northern Alberta, for example, requires millions of litres of fresh water daily. This water is taken out of the hydrological cycle forever. The oil companies don't pay for this water, and its loss is not reflected in the cost of gas at the pump. (Ironically, just south of the oil sands, Albertan farmers are facing a water shortage.)

Where is the cost of lost habitat for thousands of species accounted for? Or the fact that whales in the Arctic have become toxic waste dumps for the chemicals we use in manufacturing? Hard-nosed economists and accountants step right over the earth and her other-than-human creatures on the way to their desks to do their number-crunching. It is the parable of Lazarus, redux. The dire and irreversible consequences of ignoring ecological devastation will not be played out in hell in some afterlife, but rather right under our noses on the planet Earth.

## The Lord's Prayer
### Matthew 6:9–13

Our Father, which art in heaven, hallowed be thy name.
Thy kingdom come. Thy will be done on earth, as it is in heaven.
Give us this day our daily bread. And forgive us our debts,
as we forgive our debtors. And lead us not into temptation,
but deliver us from evil. For thine is the kingdom, and the power,
and the glory, for ever. Amen.

(KJV)

In the congregation I serve, we've been trying to use alternative versions of the Lord's Prayer in our worship service. To say the least, this has been traumatic for many members. Those who've been Christians all their life assume that King James himself was just holding the pen while the Holy Spirit moved his arm.

However, the King James translation doesn't really do full justice to the prayer Jesus taught his disciples. We know that Jesus' mother tongue was Aramaic. Neil Douglas-Klotz, an Aramaic scholar, has provided an invaluable service by offering us a fuller translation, one which captures the original meaning of Jesus' prayer more faithfully.[13] Aramaic is a language closely tied to the earth. The actual shape of the letters reflects the agricultural reality in which they were created. Many of them are meant to look like a person with a hoe, or someone bending over to plant seed.

*Our Father, which art in heaven, hallowed be thy name.*

Aramaic letters also have what Douglas-Klotz calls "sound-meaning." "Our Father," for example, doesn't capture the sound meaning of the word it is translating, *Abwoon*. Douglas-Klotz breaks the word down into four parts: "A" is the sound for Oneness and Unity; "bw" signifies a birthing of creation, or a flow of blessing; "oo" is the breath or the spirit which carries this blessing; "n" is vibration of the holy name, as it resonates and informs the material world.

Even if we went no further, we might appreciate how silly it is to insist that God is literally and exclusively our "Father." There's nothing wrong with using father as an image for God, of course, as long as we keep in mind that our intent is to convey that God is the Source of all creation, and that creation is a blessing that flows to us and through us continuously. We know God intimately as the Source of all creative activity.

*D'bwashmaya* is translated as "who art in heaven," which again suggests a cosmology that was foreign to Jesus' Aramaic culture. Heaven is not the metaphysical place beyond this universe, of Greek and, later, English imagination. *Shem* is Aramaic for light, sound, vibration, name, or word. The root *shm* means "that which rises and shines in space." *Aya* means that this shining is everywhere and in everything. The meaning of *shmaya*, therefore, is something closer to "whose radiant being shines out from the entire universe."

The next phrase invites us to "hallow" God's name. The word hallow means to make holy, that is, to set apart for a sacred purpose. We can already see that if we are hallowing "Our Father," who is "in heaven," it leads to a particular worldview. "*Our Father*" doesn't naturally extend to the other-than-human realm. It is an image custom-made for human beings. "Who art in heaven" conveys a distant God, which, when you think about it, contradicts the intimacy of the father image. An alternative translation of this opening line might be, "Loving Presence, luminous in all creation, hallowed be your name."

*Thy kingdom come. Thy will be done on earth, as it is in heaven.*

We have already looked in some detail at changing the word kingdom to kin-dom. The word translated as "kingdom" means sacred governance, as distinct from the governance of the world's leaders, who are interested in domination. "Will" should not be understood as willpower, but rather as "deep yearning," or "heart's desire." The heavenly bodies, following the governance of our Creator's deep intelligence, reflect a cosmic perfection. We have already looked at the precise calibrations required in the large-scale unfolding of universe for life to emerge on earth. Putting it together, we get something like, "May our heart's desire so align with the divine yearning, that the perfection of the heavens (large-scale cosmos) may be reflected in the way we live upon the earth and the way we govern ourselves." A possible translation could be, "Thy kin-dom come, may we reflect on earth, the yielding perfection of the heavens."

### Give us this day our daily bread.

Lachma, translated "bread," means *both* bread and wisdom, in Aramaic. Douglas-Klotz points out that the Aramaic root for bread, *HMA*, is used in *hochma*, Hebrew for holy wisdom. It is likely that Jesus intended a play on these two meanings. *Sunqanan*, translated as "daily," means "illumined measure." Here, Jesus picks up a common theme in his teachings. He was critical of the human propensity to "store up treasure," and to "build bigger barns" for excess grain. This was foolishness, as opposed to the wisdom of trusting the graciousness of the universe to provide for one's needs.

We live in an age when the developing nations hoard a disproportionate measure of the planet's natural resources, in order to perpetuate unsustainable lifestyles. We work to "grow the economy" year after year, without asking whether the earth can sustain such growth. We store up excess calories in our bodies, in the form of fat, to the point that we are now in the midst of an epidemic of obesity in our culture. And all of this in a world plagued by poverty and limited resources! When is enough enough? A possible translation of this line might be, "Help us to receive an illumined measure from the earth this day."

*Forgive us our debts, as we forgive our debtors.*

The word translated as "forgive," *washboqlan*, may also be translated "return to its original state," that is, prior to the offence, trespass, mistake, or sin. *Khaubayn*, which the King James Version translates as "debts," has alternative meanings, according to Douglas-Klotz. Another version of the Lord's Prayer uses "trespasses" rather than debts. This translation is also rich in meaning when looked at through an ecological lens. The fundamental trespass we're involved with, as human beings, is against the habitat of the other-than-human ones, who inhabit the planet with us. Having objectified and commodified the natural world, our trespass has been both spiritual and literal. Our refusal to limit population growth, our destruction of wildlife habitat and biosystems intended to serve Gaia as a whole, indicate that we have stepped over a line, as a species. This trespass is killing our planet. To ask forgiveness implies a willingness to retreat, to limit our growth, and to honour the wild ones and wilderness space as sacred. It is to return the land to its original state, and return to a way of living upon the earth that doesn't mortgage our children's future. Forgive us when we trespass against others, human and other-than-human, as we forgive others who trespass against us.

*And lead us not into temptation, but deliver us from evil.*

Douglas-Klotz says that this is the most mistranslated verse of the entire prayer. "No one, outside of us, leads us into temptation, least of all God. *Wela tahlan* could be translated 'don't let us enter,' or 'don't let us be seduced by the appearance of.'"[14] *Nesyuna* can be translated as "temptation," in the sense of something that leads us to vacillate, or be blown about in the wind, like a flag. Evil, *basha*, is a correct translation; but in the Aramaic evil, implies unripeness or inappropriate action. Basically, this line is a plea for help to keep our minds and hearts aligned with the wisdom of the cosmos. It's a plea to, "keep us on the path of wisdom, when we are tempted to take the selfish path."

*For thine is the kingdom, and the power, and the glory, for ever. Amen.*

Kingdom we have discussed as sacred governance. God's way of mutuality will prevail, not Caesar's rule of domination. Power, translated from *hayla*, is the life force or energy that produces and sustains. *Teshbukhta*, "glory," presents the image of a "generative fire that leads to astonishment." This is the radiance of the divine in all creation, reflecting the "love that fires the sun and keeps us burning," to quote a line from Bruce Cockburn's song, "Lord of the Starfields." The implication is that all other claims to divine rule, power, and glory are false. These things belong to God alone. "For ever" is much too abstract. In Aramaic, the meaning is closer to "until we meet again." This signals the importance of regular gatherings of the community of worshippers. At such gatherings, we are reminded and re-member. *Ameyn*, "amen," seals the deal.

A person's word sealed the agreement in Aramaic culture. The word itself carries the image of the ground from which the intended future will grow. A possible translation could be, "May it be your rule we follow, your power we exercise, and your radiance that allures us, until we meet again. This is the ground out of which your future will grow, until our next sacred gathering."

## An Alternative Lord's Prayer

Putting all this together, here's my version of the Lord's Prayer.

> Loving Presence, luminous in all creation,
> hallowed be your name.
> Thy kin-dom come.
> May we reflect on earth
> the yielding perfection of the heavens.
> Help us to receive an illumined measure from the
>     earth this day.
> Forgive us when we trespass against others,
> human and other-than-human,
> as we forgive others who trespass against us.
> Keep us on the path of wisdom
> when we are tempted to take the selfish path.
> May it be your rule we follow,
> your power we exercise,
> and your radiance that allures.
> May this be the truth that guides our lives,
> the ground from which our future will grow,
> until we meet again.

## Christ Is Not Jesus' Last Name

A popular misconception is that Christ is Jesus' last name. It's actually a title, which the early church gave to him. Usually it appears in the New Testament with the article "the" in front of it: Jesus, *the* Christ. The word translated as Christ is the same word for Messiah, which means, in Hebrew, "the anointed one." The first disciples believed that Jesus was the long-awaited Messiah. This didn't necessarily mean that he was God. In fact, in the Hebrew tradition, the Messiah was decidedly *not* God. Rather, this was a human being anointed by Spirit to restore Israel to national independence. He would also restore the Temple to its full glory. There was no implicit assumption that the Messiah would do this non-violently. If it required violence to overthrow the empire, then so be it.

Jesus didn't fit neatly into this scheme. For one thing, it's pretty clear that he eschewed violence in all forms. For another, it's not likely that he identified God's kingdom with a piece of land. This is not to say that he took kindly to the Roman occupation. He didn't. John Dominic Crossan believes that Jesus had a "sapiential eschatology." Eschatology means "end times." Sapiential is a fancy word for wisdom. In other words, Jesus believed that God would restore right relations on earth through spiritual wisdom, not violence. Jesus was anointed by Spirit to proclaim and enact this kind of divine rule. This fits much better with an evolutionary theology.

God doesn't unilaterally act to get God's own way. Rather, God acts in and through those who enter into a covenant to walk in the ways of wisdom. In the next chapter, I'll explore what this means.

# Chapter 7

## THE IRRESISTIBLE SOPHIA: WISDOM CHRISTOLOGY AND THE ECOLOGICAL IMPERATIVE

·Jesus Christ is the human being Sophia became.

ELIZABETH JOHNSON[1]

∽

God comes to you in whatever image you have been able
to form of God;
the wiser and broader and more gorgeous the image,
the more the grace and power can flow from the Throne
into your heart.
God is saying… "I am where My servant thinks of Me.
Every servant has an image of Me;
whatever image my Servant forms of Me, there I will be.
I am the servant of my servant's image of Me.
Be careful then, My servants,
and purify, attune, and expand your thoughts about Me,
for they are My House."

RUMI[2]

∽

There is in all visible things
an invisible fecundity,
a dimmed light,
a meek namelessness,
a hidden wholeness.
This mysterious Unity and Integrity
is Wisdom, the Mother of all...

THOMAS MERTON, "HAGIA SOPHIA"

What is the nature and character of the God who is immanent in creation?

How we conceive of God will define what matters most to us, who we think we are, and what in the world we think we're supposed to be doing. In this chapter, I present an alternative to the male God of scripture, Yahweh. Obviously, God is neither male nor female, in a literal sense. God is not literally personal, but neither is God less than what we mean by personal. God is personal plus.[3] The "plus" is about us creatures trying to describe what is beyond us to describe. God transcends all our categories and attempts to confine God to our images.

Nevertheless, our images and metaphors *do* concretize reality for us. Masculine images for God tend to dominate the scriptural witness. In and of itself this is not necessarily a bad thing. But these images tend to reflect, not surprisingly, the patriarchal culture out of which they emerged – that is, a culture of domination, male privilege, and explicit suppression of the feminine, which often endorses violence as a means of maintaining power.[4] *It is precisely this gestalt we need to deconstruct in an ecological age.*

# I. Meeting Sophia

The tradition of Sophia reflects the struggle within Judaism itself to transcend patriarchy and to present an image of the divine that rebalances the masculine with the feminine.

Sophia is a well-kept secret in church circles. She appears only rarely in the three-year-cycle of scripture readings called the lectionary. When she does show up, she is referred to as Wisdom, the English translation of the Greek Sophia. Sophia is more prominent in a part of the Bible that Protestants typically don't read: the Apocrypha. (The word *apocrypha* means "things that are hidden.") That's not to say that Sophia is not present at all in the Protestant Bible. But she comes on the scene rather unexpectedly as the presence of the divine feminine in an otherwise patriarchal library of books.

Just as the Jewish community's understanding of the nature and purposes of Yahweh God evolved and grew over time, so their understanding of Sophia evolved and grew more prominent over time. She first appears as a creation of God, one whom God discovers at work in creation; then as God's master worker; and eventually as God herself, "the fashioner of all things." Sophia delights in creation. She is a people-loving, friend-making, holy Presence, pervading all creation, calling people to feed at her table, and to turn from their foolish ways towards life. Sophia keeps popping up, like a recurrent dream, rebalancing the spiritual psyche of Judaism.

Scholars are virtually unanimous in their assessment that the final expression of the Sophia tradition was borrowed by the Jews from a non-biblical source. This "borrowing" would have happened as diaspora Jews, living outside Jerusalem, found themselves in cultures that worshipped other gods and goddesses. So, for example, one credible theory says that Sophia is the Jewish version of the Egyptian goddess Isis, since many of her characteristics are virtually identical to those of this goddess.[5] In Alexandria, Egypt, Isis would have represented a real temptation for Jews in the first century BCE. She was goddess of the quasi-official cult of the day. Worshipping in her cult would have made such pragmatic things as career advancement a whole lot easier.[6] Some Jewish scholars are convinced that Judaism dealt with this threat by transferring some of Isis' characteristics to Sophia. It wasn't *Isis* who gave life and redeemed humanity, it was *Sophia!* No need to chase after the goddesses of these other nations. We can match their goddesses with our own!

Elisabeth Schüssler Fiorenza, on the other hand, claims that Judaism didn't adopt Sophia out of fear of the goddess, but rather to present their own God in contemporary categories. "Divine Sophia is Israel's God in the language and gestalt of the goddess."[7] The introduction of Sophia allowed the Jews to retain God's transcendence, and yet have God be intimately involved in the affairs of creation. "Sophia renews all things while remaining in herself" (Wisdom of Solomon 7:27).

## A Biblical Tour

For those who haven't had the pleasure of meeting Sophia, gird up your loins for a quick journey through the Bible. (For this survey, I am indebted to the masterful work of Elizabeth Johnson.[8])

Sophia makes a cameo appearance in the book of Job. "Where shall Wisdom be found?" Well, miners can go deep into the earth and bring out gold, silver, and precious metals, but they won't find Wisdom. She is more precious than sapphires and jewels.

No amount of fine gold will buy her. Wisdom reveals herself only to those who stand in awe of God (Job 28). As Johnson says, "She is the personification of hidden treasure whose whereabouts are known only to God."[9] When God finally responds to Job, God asks, "Who has put wisdom in the inward parts?" (Job 38:36). This inner wisdom is present throughout all creation, as the latter chapters of the book of Job make abundantly clear.

In Proverbs 1:20–33, a feisty Wisdom stands at a busy crossroads in the city and thunders out a message of moral correction and promise. Refusing to listen to her brings calamity, but lending her an ear will bring safety and security. We are to "guard Sophia," for "she is your life" (4:13). One can't help but think about the recent tragedy in New Orleans, wrought ostensibly by hurricane Katrina, but actually caused in large part by human foolishness. The city itself is built below sea level, in a bioregion that was originally intended by Gaia to be a mangrove forest, well-suited to withstand these hurricanes. A levee built 30 years ago was known to be vulnerable, but nobody acted to reinforce it. Behind this unrepaired levee, America's poorest, predominantly black population awaited disaster. As we'll see later, Wisdom loves people – all people – and demands justice for the poor.

Sophia reappears in Proverbs 8. The text slips into the first person as she tells us about herself. She possesses all knowledge and truth. She hates arrogance and evil. She's the one who instituted just governance on earth: "By me kings reign, and rulers decree what is just" (verse 15). Then she presents her credentials:

> The Lord created me at the beginning of his work, the first of his acts of long ago… Ages ago I was set up, at the first, before the beginning of the earth; when there were no depths I was brought forth. When he established

the heavens, I was there, when he created everything, I was there like a master worker [or a little child]. I was daily his delight, rejoicing before him always, rejoicing in the inhabited world and delighting in the human race... (Proverbs 8:22–31)

This remarkable passage reflects some of the ambivalence of the tradition surrounding Sophia. Did God create her "at the beginning of his work," or was she already there, "when God established the heavens"? Previously, in Proverbs 3:19, the writer affirms that "the Lord, by Sophia, founded the earth." We shall see that at the pinnacle of the Sophia tradition, she is presented unambiguously as the creative agent herself. But in Proverbs 8:24, above, it's interesting that she is "brought forth," not created out of nothing. In other words, Sophia is already present in the divine milieu. She both delights God, and delights in creation and the human race (verses 30–31). To know her is to share in her delight (verse 34).

The Sophia tradition builds upon the creation-affirming theology present in Genesis, where God looks upon all that God has created and declares it to be "very good" (Genesis 1:31). What is unique to the Wisdom tradition, however, is that it presents Sophia as being more intimately involved in creation than Yahweh. This tradition balances the transcendent dimension of the Holy with divine immanence.

If our worship services are not characterized by delight, in God, in each other, and in creation, it's not likely Sophia's around. To find her is to find life. To miss her is to injure ourselves (verses 35–36).

In Proverbs 9, Sophia throws a party. She builds her house, slaughters the animals, mixes her wine, and sends out servant girls to invite "the simple" to the banquet. She tells them to invite those who are "without sense" to come and "eat of my bread and to drink of the wine I have mixed." They are to "lay aside immaturity and walk in the way of insight" (verses 1–9).

In Sirach 24, Wisdom says that she "came from the mouth of the Most High," and "covered the earth like a mist." She dwells "in the highest heaven" and her throne is a "pillar of cloud" (verses 3–4). Pacific Rim National Park, on the west coast of Vancouver Island, is one of those thin places where Spirit seems very near. At any time, even on rare sunny days, the mist can roll in an instant, and suddenly you feel like you're walking inside a cloud. The air quality changes. It feels as though the oxygen content increases. A feeling of purity pervades. When the mist descends, one feels as though one is in the presence of a profound mystery. It's not difficult to understand why the writer would associate Wisdom with mist and clouds.

Wisdom presents herself as cosmic in scope: "I compassed the vault of heaven, traversed the depths of the abyss; I held sway over the waves of the sea, over all the earth, and over every people and nation" (24:4–7). Then she receives a command from God to "pitch her tent" with a particular people, the Jews. After comparing herself in a very sensuous manner to the various fragrances of exotic flowers, and to the fruit of different plants, she issues an invitation: "Come to me, you who desire me, and eat your fill of my fruits... those who eat of me will hunger no more, and those who drink of me will thirst no more" (24:21–22). Ultimately, she identifies herself as Torah, the sacred scriptures of the Jews (verse 23).

Sophia reaches the peak of her development in the Wisdom of Solomon. This book was likely written in first-century Alexandria, in Egypt. Here, she is not exclusively identified with Israel, but rather takes on full divinity. She is a breath of the power of

God; a pure emanation of God's glory; a radiance of eternal light; a flawless mirror of the working of God; and an image of divine goodness (7:25–26).

She is "able to do all things"; she is the "fashioner all things"; she "orders all things well" (Wisdom of Solomon 8:1). Sophia knows all things, and therefore is able to teach in every field of knowledge. As Creator, she knows intimately "the structure of the world, and the activity of the elements; the beginning, end, and middle of times, the alternations of solstices, changes of seasons, cycles of the years, constellations of stars, natures of animals, the powers of spirits, varieties of plants, virtues of roots..." (7:17–22). All knowledge of science, mathematics, cosmology, and biology is revealed by her to those who seek her.

Sophia has 21 characteristics, three times the perfect number seven, indicating her identification with God.

> There is in her a spirit that is intelligent, holy, unique, manifold, subtle, mobile, clear, unpolluted, distinct, invulnerable, loving the good, keen, irresistible, beneficent, humane, steadfast, sure, free from anxiety, all-powerful, overseeing all, and penetrating through all spirits that are intelligent, pure, and subtle. (Wisdom of Solomon 7:22–23)

Remarkably, chapter 10 tells the story of Israel's salvation history as the activity of Sophia, rather than of Yahweh, the Lord. She redeems Adam from his sin, and gives him strength. Cain dies because, after his murder of Abel, he turns away from her. She saves the world from the fruits of his violence, steering Noah through the flood on a "paltry piece of wood." She is involved in the confusion of languages at Babel. She calls Abraham, and was with him when he was asked to sacrifice Isaac. She rescues Lot; she was with Jacob in his flight from his brother Esau, straightening Jacob out with wisdom, and showing him the "Kingdom of God." She stick-handled Joseph through his brothers' murderous plot, and made him great. Finally, it is Sophia who delivers the Hebrews from slavery in Egypt. Sophia plays the role of God in this passage!

The book of Baruch adds one more important detail: "She appeared on earth and lives with humankind" (3:37). Early Christian commentators regarded this as an allusion to the incarnation of Christ. Others connect this sentence to the following one in which the author affirms that "She is the book of the commandments of God" (3:38 – 4:1).

Johnson concludes, with other scholars, that for all intents and purposes, Sophia is a feminine personification of God's own being. Not merely the feminine *aspect* of God, she is rather Goddess. Her Spirit is God's Spirit. She creates, redeems, and possesses all knowledge. She is the principle of good order and government among all leaders and nations. She is the Torah. She is God.

## Wisdom in the Christian Tradition

If you're like me, at this point you will be wondering why the Christian tradition didn't pick up on Sophia. Well, it did, but in very subtle ways. She's present, as we shall see, throughout the New Testament. In fact, Elizabeth Johnson and other scholars are convinced that Jesus understood himself to have been anointed by Spirit-Sophia, in preparation for his mission. After Jesus' life and death, early Christians believed that he was actually God-in-the-flesh. But when they fished around in their own tradition for scriptural warrant, they found slim pickings. There was no way to bring Yahweh, the transcendent, ruling monarch, down to earth to dwell as a human being. Besides, the scriptural depiction of Yahweh as a stern cosmic judge, law-giver, ruler, and cosmic hammer, didn't quite fit their experience of Jesus. Furthermore, all existing metaphors in their scriptures – son of God, son of man, and messiah – didn't quite make the necessary ontological connection (the level of essential being) between God and Jesus. All of these titles referred to human figures. But there was one who *did* fit the bill – Sophia. After all, Sophia had already been portrayed as coming to a particular people, the Jews, in a particular location, Israel. Martin Hengel says that this was of "decisive significance" for the development of Christology.[10] It was a large, but not discontinuous, step from there to God/Sophia pitching her tent in a particular Jewish man (John 1).

## Jesus of Nazareth as Sophia's Child

The chart below indicates the remarkable connection between Sophia and Jesus in the New Testament. Patriarchy is undoubtedly responsible for a less-than-explicit connection between them. However, when one opens to the possibility that Jesus regarded himself as a child of Sophia (Matthew 11:19), and that the early church interpreted his life, death, and resurrection through the template of Sophia, the connection is hard to miss.

| SOPHIA | JESUS/CHRIST |
|---|---|
| She is a spotless mirror of the working of God (Wisdom of Solomon 7:26). | He is the image of the invisible God (Colossians 1:15). |
| Sophia is a reflection of eternal light (Wisdom of Solomon 7:26). She is more beautiful than the sun, brighter than any constellation of stars, superior to light (7:29). | He is the radiant light of God's glory (Hebrews 1:3). |
| She is brought forth from the depths, in the first act of creation (Proverbs 8:24). | He is the first-born of creation (Colossians 1:15). |
| She is the fashioner of all things (Wisdom of Solomon 7:22). | He is the one through whom all things were made (1 Corinthians 8:6, John 1). |
| She orders all things well (8:1). | He is the one who holds all things together (Colossians 1:17). |
| By her, kings reign and rulers decree what is just (Proverbs 8:15). | All rulers and principalities are subject to him (Colossians 1:16) |
| Sophia means wisdom. | The Christ is wisdom (1 Corinthians 1:24). |
| We are to guard Sophia, for she is our life (Proverbs 4:13). | In him is life and this life was the light of all people (John 1:4). |
| Wisdom passes into holy souls and makes them friends of God, and prophets (Wisdom 7:27). | Jesus calls his disciples friends, not servants (John 15:15). |
| Wisdom holds sway over the waves of the sea, over all the earth (Sirach 24:4–7). | Even the waves obey Jesus (Matthew 8:27). |

| | |
|---|---|
| She pitches her tent and dwells with humankind (Baruch 3:37). | The one who was in the beginning with God pitches his tent and dwells with human beings (John 1:14). |
| Sophia issues invitations to come to her banquet (Proverbs 9:1–5). | Jesus tells a parable of a man who issues invitations to come to his banquet (Luke 14:16). |
| Sophia prepares bread and wine for her guests (Proverbs 9:1–5). Those who eat of her fruits and who drink of her will hunger or thirst no more (Sirach 24:21–22). | Jesus makes arrangements for the last supper (Luke 22:8). Jesus identifies himself with the living bread; those who eat of it will live forever (John 6:51). |
| She is concealed from the eyes of the living. God alone knows her dwelling place (Job 28:23). | The ways of God are hidden from those who think they are wise, but revealed to "babes," those who "know the Son" (Matthew 11:25–27). |
| Sophia is Torah, the Law, or "yoke of God" (Baruch 3:38). | Jesus' "yoke" is easy. He is, like Sophia, the embodiment of the Law. In him, the weary will find rest (Matthew 11:29–30). |
| Only God knows the way to Wisdom (3:32). On the other hand, Wisdom is an initiate in the knowledge of God (Wisdom of Solomon 8:4). | Jesus and God enjoy mutual knowledge as "Son" and "Father." God's ways are revealed to those who seek the Son (Matthew 11:25–27). |
| Sophia cries out from the crossroads and the gates, uttering blessings and threats (Proverbs 8). | Jesus "cries out" in the Temple, uttering blessings and threats (John 7:28). |
| Sophia speaks in first person, "I am…" in long discourses (Proverbs 8 and Sirach 24). | Jesus speaks in first person, using a variety of "I am" statements (John 6:51, 10:14, 11:25). |

| Those who come to her will never hunger or thirst (Sirach 24:21). | Jesus is the bread of life, and those who drink of his waters will never thirst (John 4:7–15). |
|---|---|
| Sophia mixes wine for the banquet (Proverbs 9). | Jesus turns water into wine at the wedding feast at Cana (John 2:1–12). |
| Sophia rejoices in the inhabited world and delights in the human race (Proverbs 8:31). | God loves the world so much God sends the Son (John 3:16). Jesus came that his joy might be in the disciples, and that their joy might be full (John 15:11). |
| Sophia is hidden treasure (Job 28). | Jesus compares the kingdom of God to treasure hidden in a field (Matthew 13:44). In Christ is hidden all treasures of wisdom and knowledge (Colossians 2:3). |

The parallels are simply too numerous to list them all. Sophia, the wisdom of God, was the template the gospel writers used to tell the story of Jesus, particularly in Matthew and John's gospels. He was both teacher of Wisdom, child of Wisdom, and Wisdom incarnate. Listen to the conclusion of scholars.

"While the Jesus movement, like John, understood Jesus as the messenger and prophet of divine Sophia, the wisdom Christology of the early Christian missionary movement sees him as the divine Sophia herself."[11]

"Jesus is the exhaustive embodiment of divine wisdom."[12]

"[For Matthew] Jesus is Sophia incarnate."[13]

"In John, Jesus is personified Wisdom."[14]

The author of John's gospel changes Wisdom to Logos (the Word) in the opening of his gospel, possibly because it provided a valuable link to Greek culture, or possibly because, by this time, Gnostic sects had latched on to her. The Gnostics weren't a crowd the church wanted to run with. Listen to Philo, an influential Hellenistic Jew in the first century, tap dance around the awkwardness of presenting Jesus as an incarnation of the divine feminine.

> Pre-eminence always pertains to the masculine, and the feminine always comes short of it and is lesser than it. Let us then say that the daughter of God, Sophia, is not only masculine, but father, sowing and begetting in souls aptness to learn, discipline, knowledge, sound sense and laudable actions.[15]

Check. Sophia is masculine, father in fact, because, well, just because. God, as a male authority figure has had a good 10,000 years now to sort things out. Perhaps it's time we give Sophia a shot.

The Spirit of God is the Spirit of Sophia. She is the wind who swept over the face of the waters at creation. It is Sophia-Spirit who overshadows Mary at her conception (Luke 1:35). She is the dove who descends upon Jesus at his baptism in the Jordan, and it is she who drives him into the wilderness to test his resolve. Sophia is the Spirit who anoints him, as she anointed other prophets, to proclaim release to the captives, recovery of sight to the blind, and good news to the poor (Luke 4:14–19). In other words, Jesus is "the Christ," the anointed one, by virtue of having been anointed by Wisdom. In Paul's words, Christ is "the wisdom of God" (1 Corinthians 1:24).

As Jesus gathers his disciple-friends for a last meal, he presides as the very presence of Sophia, inviting his disciples to remember him in table fellowship, reminiscent of Sophia. As Sophia's child, he offers what she offers: bread and wine personally prepared for those who come to the banquet (Proverbs 9:5). In Aramaic, the word for bread, *lachma,* has the same root as the Hebrew word for wisdom, *hochma,* which was subsequently translated as Sophia in Greek. When Jesus teaches his friends to pray, "Give us this day our daily *bread,*" the word is a play on two meanings: food for the body; and food for the soul, or wisdom. This meal is an offer of his very being, his life anointed and animated by Sophia: "My body, broken for you. My blood, shed for you." When we participate in the sharing of this meal, we take Sophia-as-Jesus into our souls. To be nourished at this table is to be nourished by wisdom. This is the reason we gather at Jesus' table: to receive grace to give up our foolish ways, and enter the path of wisdom. This is the essence of a wisdom Christology (just in case you get seated beside a systematic theologian at your next dinner party).

## 2. Sophia, Quantum Physics, and Chaos Theory

By creating a dialogue between the Sophia tradition and the recent discoveries of science, new meanings emerge that may enrich both disciplines.

For example, this dialogue can offer new meaning and relevance to the doctrine of the Trinity. Many progressive Christians wish the doctrine of the Trinity would just disappear. It seems like an unnecessary complication – one in three, three in one. Why bother? Yet it is the historic experience of Christians that they experienced God in three distinct, yet related, modes. The classic version of the Trinity is Father, Son, and Holy Spirit. Using wisdom Christology, we would talk about Sophia-Mother,

Sophia-Jesus, and Sophia-Spirit, following Elizabeth Johnson. To use a natural metaphor, we can imagine God as the sun, God incarnate as a beam of that same light streaming to earth (Christ the sunbeam), and the Spirit as the point of light that actually arrives and infuses the earth with light and warmth: one light, three aspects.[16]

Interestingly, science is indeed confirming that ultimate reality is very much "Trinitarian," in the sense of being radically communal. God is not an individual being, but rather Being itself in mutual relation. This matters, because one's assumptions about the nature of God are reflected in one's assumptions about human nature. For example, until recently, all psychological models were based on individualistic assumptions about the nature of ultimate reality. They reflected a Newtonian cosmology, in which the universe is composed of isolated atoms, expending enormous energy just trying to stay connected with each other.

This made a whole lot of sense to men, who seem to exert greater amounts of energy trying to stay connected than women do. Men have spent decades going off to try to find their atomistic selves, so that they would then be able to hook up with a partner. Male psychologists even prescribed this cure for countless women, who were deemed to be too relational. Then came Carol Gilligan, who challenged the model of the isolated self.[17] She claimed that we are embedded in relationships from the moment we're born. It is only in the context of healthy relationships that our distinctive, healthy selves have a chance to emerge. We don't have to work at being in relationship. We're already there. We are made in the image of a relational God. Our sense of being discrete, isolated beings is an illusion.

# The Fit and Flow of Reality

The radical interconnectedness of the universe is implied by the doctrine of the Trinity. Ervin Laszlo calls this "coherence."[18] It means that everything fits and flows together seamlessly. You can't find a bit of stuff anywhere that is not connected to the rest. It's like a bowl full of fish hooks. Pick any single hook up, and you'll find that the rest of them are attached. Or to use an analogy from the human body, I was in the middle of stretching my neck in yoga class when my third toe on my left foot started to cramp! Every time I went into the stretch, my toe would involuntarily spasm. Just as our muscles and tendons form a single sheath, each part having a direct and immediate connection to every other part, so it is within the universe.

In an evolutionary universe, in which all emerging reality lays down the foundation for the successive levels of reality, we would expect this kind of interconnectedness. There are no sharp breaks between levels in this emergence. This is what prevented Darwin from publishing his book for 20 years: the differences *within* a species were on a continuum with the difference *between* species. There is no absolute break between bacteria and Beethoven. There's no line you can draw and say, "Okay, here's the place at which something of a completely different order, unrelated to anything that preceded it, comes into being." From bacteria to Beethoven, it's all a single procession of life. Of course, there is differentiation and diversity. But there is absolutely no disconnection, anywhere.

Coherence is what the author of John's gospel was on about when he put these words into Jesus' mouth: "On that day, you will know that I am in my Father, and you are in me, and I am in you" (John 14:20). Jesus also uses a natural metaphor to convey the same phenomenon: "I am the true vine, my Father is the vine grower, and every branch (the disciples) that bears fruit is pruned back to make it bear more fruit" (John 15:1). Extend this principle of unity-in-diversity to include the entire universe, and you arrive at the mystical understanding of the universe as a dance of radical coherence.

## The Dance of the Trinity: The Dance of the Cosmos

John Damascene, a fourth-century Greek theologian, came up with the word *perechoresis* to describe how the three persons of the Trinity are related. It means something like a revolution of a wheel, an encircling of each around the others. There's another Greek word *perichoreuo*, which means "to dance around." Imagine the Trinity in an ecstatic dance, encircling one another, responding in mutuality to the moves of the other. Think of the universe as the free-flowing dance of the Trinity. In truth, the large scale structures of the universe, such as galaxies, *do* spiral around each other endlessly. Our own solar system spirals around its mother galaxy, Virgo. The planets circle the sun as the sun itself follows the path of the galactic circle dance.

Matthew Fox began a workshop at the congregation I serve by teaching us a circle dance. We learned very simple steps, which enabled us to free our minds and *be* the dance. The experience was surprisingly powerful. I felt like I was engaged in an archetypal movement, synchronizing my movements with the movement of the universe itself. It was a dance of coherence, in which I gained a sense that I "fit in." The author of the Wisdom of Solomon says of Sophia that "She is more mobile than any motion" (9:24). Sophia, the great Cosmic Dancer!

## The Quantum Connection:
## Sophia Is "More Mobile Than Motion"

The writer might well have been describing the dance of particles at a quantum level. In fact, at this level, physicists agree that there is only the dance; the notion of discrete or individual particles bouncing off each other is false. Reality *is* relationship. As Fritjof Capra says, "Reality consists of dynamic patterns continually changing into one another – the continuous dance of energy."[19] These patterns are evoked into being, as though they were in hiding, waiting for some reason to appear. Put a couple of mesons into a bubble chamber, and, as they interact in this field, 12 different particles appear temporarily, out of nowhere, for no other reason than that they were invited to the dance.[20]

We still name these particles as though they were individuals – neutrons, electrons, etc. – but in truth they exist as "wave-packets"; sometimes they appear as waves and sometimes as particles. And here's the mysterious thing about them: they tend to oblige the observer by appearing in whatever form the scientist wants to observe them. You can measure the *position* of these wave-packets, or their *momentum*, but not both. They exist only as potentialities or tendencies. If you want to measure their position, all the potentialities "collapse" into measurable form. This phenomenon came to be known as Heisenberg's "uncertainty principle."

Edwin Schrödinger, reacting to the quantum reality, once said, "I don't like it and I'm sorry I ever had anything to do with it."[21] What he didn't like is that, at a quantum level, the universe is indeterminate. Quantum physics undermines the world of "things," of cause and effect, and replaces it with a relational universe in which everything is hitched to everything else. Whereas Newtonian physics offered classical ballet, quantum physics gives us ecstatic dance.

I once went to a play called *Copenhagen*, in which three famous physicists – Heisenberg, Bohr, and Einstein – meet to discuss how much responsibility they should each assume for the creation and detonation of the atomic bomb. The play is brilliant in the way it conveys Heisenberg's uncertainty principle in and through their very conversation. Each time one of the characters comes on stage to present his perspective, the stage revolves and you get a totally new take on the situation. Just when you thought one character was conveying reality definitively, the stage revolves and a new character, who tells the story from his perspective, enters. His view, like each of the others', is totally credible. Reality collapses down into that character's observations. Apparently, reality is not fixed. It bends, like quantum wave-packets, to the world we choose to draw forth.

## Constructing Reality

At the quantum level, we live in a radically participative universe. This means that awareness and choice are what bring reality into existence. The world exists only as potential before I become aware of it. The moment I make an interpretation, judgment, formulate a belief, or crystallize my take on reality, that is the reality that "collapses" into being.

The famous double-slit experiment still boggles physicists' minds. Take an electron and make a couple of slits in a barrier. Behind this barrier place a photographic plate. The pattern the electron leaves on the photographic plate depends on whether one slit is open, or both slits are open. If just one is open, the electron assumes its particle form. If both slits are open, it assumes its wave form, recorded as a wave pattern on the photographic plate. Incredibly, the electron seems to "know" what's being looked for by the experimenter. If you try to fool the electron by closing and opening the slits, it will appear as wave or particle based on whether one or both slits were open at the instant it passed through. Furthermore, it "knows" whether it's being watched. If it's not being watched, it remains as a probability wave. It only collapses into particle form when the experimenter observes it.[22] Weird.

I don't know about you, but this makes me want to be very careful about my ideas, beliefs, and judgments. "Whatever we call reality, it is revealed to us only through an active construction in which we participate."[23]

Foolishness brings forth one kind of world, wisdom another. Take forgiveness, for example. Jesus taught that the world of the wise is evoked by forgiving those who harm us, "not seven times, but seven times seven" (Matthew 18:21–22). In other words, forgiveness is a way of *being*, not merely a discrete act of forgiving someone who has hurt us. Of course, it is the latter, to be sure. But if we expand our understanding, forgiveness becomes the willingness to release my attachment to the world I brought forth yesterday through my judgments, interpretations, and beliefs. To let go of that world, knowing that it was a temporary take on reality, is a profound form of forgiveness. It releases my self and others from attachment to what is, in the end, always a partial perspective on reality.

Forgiveness is an act of creation in a participative universe. It means coming to terms with the truth that out of the vast sea of potential worlds available to me, I daily collapse it all down into the one world or perspective I call reality. Wouldn't it be a wonderful discipline to begin each day in a co-creative relationship with Sophia, asking oneself, what world do I wish to manifest this day? What kind of world would Wisdom delight in this day, if I let go of "yesterday's will of God," in order to create a Sophia day.

This quantum insight can also undergird our commitment to change the world we have collectively constructed. In truth, this reality is arbitrary. The core narratives that govern our lives collapse into reality, for good or ill. A narrative that privileges the earth and that reinforces an ethic of mutuality, instead of empire's ethic of domination, represents the path of wisdom.

On Sophia's path, all perspectives on reality are seen as partial. Paul Cezanne became known as the artist who introduced perspective. Once he got his subject all lined up, he developed a habit of tilting his head to one side or the other. This became known as "Cezanne's doubt," an intentional unwillingness to accept what is before the eye as the only way of seeing the world.[24] The trick is to stand before a person who is attacking me, tilt my head, and see a frustrated friend. No one said it would be easy.

This gives a whole new perspective on Jesus' statement that if the disciples had the faith of a mustard seed they could tell a mountain to go and jump in a lake, and it would obey (Mark 11:23). With enough faith, Peter could have walked on water. Perhaps this is hyperbole, as I learned in seminary. We don't *absolutely* create our reality. But we're responsible for more of it than we like to believe. The secret of Gandhi's success in bringing down the British Empire was his understanding of the participative nature of the universe. He told his followers that the only reason the empire existed was because they propped it up, and that the moment they withdrew their belief in it and their allegiance to it, it would come crumbling down. If it existed in their minds, it would exist in reality. In the same way, we can choose to deconstruct perspectives on reality that degrade our planet.

## The Quantum Leap and Non-Local Influence

Here's another thing about these "more-mobile-than-motion" wave-packets: the infamous "quantum leap" came into our vocabulary as a metaphor because physicists made the observation that electrons will sometimes jump ship and enter into another orbit without warning or apparent cause. These leaps are abrupt and discontinuous. What's even stranger is that electrons do this not by travelling across the dimension of time and space, the way we'd walk from our living room to our kitchen. Rather, they simply appear instantaneously in the other orbit, leaving no trace of their path; they are "more mobile than motion."[25]

Einstein didn't like this "spooky" stuff, so he conjured up a thought experiment to disprove the findings of his colleague Niels Bohr, who said that subatomic particles exhibited "non-local influence." In other words, Bohr theorized that one particle could be changed or influenced by another particle from vast distances, instantaneously. If this were true, it would undermine, among other things, Newtonian causality, which said that two objects had to bump into one another, like billiard balls, to influence each other.

To discredit Bohr's theory, Einstein created a thought experiment involving two electrons. Now, electrons have "spin" – either up, down, or sideways. So, for the purposes of the thought experiment, Einstein imagined two paired electrons, where if one electron spins up, the other must spin down; if one spins to the right, the other must spin to the left. Next, he imagined that these two electrons were separated by a vast distance, say several light years. Here's the problem. According to quantum theory, the electrons don't decide which axis they'll spin on until the experimenter decides which axis to measure. So, when an experimenter measures one of the electrons, thus establishing its spin, for the other electron to instantly match it by spinning in the opposite direction, the two electrons would have to 1) communicate at greater than light speed, and 2) have non-local influence, both of which violate the General Theory of Relativity.

In 1982, French physicist Alain Aspect was finally able to conduct an actual physical experiment to test Bohr's theory, though instead of using electrons he used photons, and instead of measuring spin he measured their polarity. The results were astounding. Bohr had been right. The photons were connected in a way that allowed them to influence each other instantly, and non-locally, that is, without touching.[26]

Physicists call this radical interrelatedness "entanglement," and it appears that it holds for all reality.[27] We're hopeless, marvellously, involved with each other – invisibly connected across time and space in a great cosmic dance.

## Non-Local Influence and Prayer

Every Sunday morning, the community of faith participates in the "prayers of the community." We hold the world and those we love in our prayers, believing that in some way these prayers make a difference. We address these prayers to God, as though God were "out there" somewhere. But what may actually be happening is that, in this vast field of entanglement, in which nothing and nobody is separate, we are enacting non-local influence. We're not beaming prayers off a satellite God in the sky, who then effects whatever it is we're praying for. Rather, anointed by Sophia to be the body of Christ, we act *as* Sophia in our impulse to pray. Because we exist in this fabric of interconnection, our prayers exert "non-local" influence instantly. Of course, in a universe as complex as ours, our prayers will not always "work" in terms of manifesting our desired outcome. But both our prayers and our actions, no matter how seemingly insignificant, can effect power-ful and lasting changes across vast distances.

In her brilliant synthesis of quantum science and leadership called *Leadership and the New Science*, Margaret Wheatley makes the point that, in a Newtonian universe, our actions and prayers can seem too small and insignificant to make a difference, in light of the intransigence of systems of oppression. If we see ourselves as individual units of consciousness trying to exert influence as external agents on massive systems, our efforts can seem piddly and hopeless. But in a quantum world, there is no "outside." We're already insiders, connected by a web-like medium. As Wheat-ley puts it, it's not about critical mass in this universe; it's about critical *connections*. Our local actions exert an immediate influ-ence that appears instantly on a global level, like the electron that makes a quantum leap into another orbit.[28]

## Wisdom Penetrates All Things

As the author of Wisdom of Solomon affirms, Wisdom "penetrates through all spirits that are intelligent, pure, and subtle" (Wisdom of Solomon 7:22–24). It's difficult to really appreciate the degree of interconnectedness in the universe. Most of us have been steeped in a Newtonian cosmology of "things," that move about only as other "things" bump into them. We walk around imagining that we are separate bags of skin and bones and grey matter, with our minds confined to the inside of our skulls. We have been taught to believe in an "out of sight – out of mind" universe. Yet our own experience contradicts this teaching.

Mothers wake up in the middle of the night knowing that a son or daughter is in danger or indeed has died. Dogs know when their owners have left work to come home. Parrots read the minds of their owners.[29] Jesus healed at a distance, as I learned to do when I was trained as a Reiki practitioner. Shamans enter into the consciousness of the plant world to receive information about which plant to use in healing rituals. Australian aboriginals tap into "song-lines," which connect them to their ancestors and to what is going on in their villages when they are away on a walkabout. We have a dream of an Egyptian hieroglyph we have never seen before – an example of tapping into what Carl Jung called the "collective unconscious," a psychic repository of the universe's experience from the beginning of time.

## Fields of Dreams
What's going on?

There seems to be a medium, or a fabric, to the cosmos, which connects all to each instantly across vast stretches of time and space. This medium acts mysteriously like Sophia, penetrating through all spirits and all physical reality. In the Newtonian universe, space was thought to be essentially empty; it was the "space" between "things." Things were real. Space was, well, just space. This led to an existentialist crisis characterized by immense loneliness in the modern worldview. Against the incomprehensible amount of space in the universe, the tiny speck of dust called earth was so insignificant as to be depressing. How could it have any meaning at all? In the Newtonian universe, the earth was deemed to be a lost ship in a vast cosmic sea, harbourless, travelling on a one-way ticket to oblivion. We were brave sailors, stoically facing the void, wringing meaning out of a meaningless universe.

How wrong that worldview turned out to be! Space is neither empty, nor inert. It is not the lifeless void of scientific materialism. We exist within invisible fields of connection. This all sounds pretty mysterious, but recall the last time you drove your car under electrical wires. The electromagnetic field created by those wires interfere with the radio waves that bring you your favourite tunes. All you get is static right at the moment your favourite song is playing!

These fields of connection are invisible, but there's plenty of evidence that they affect our lives. The other three fields – in addition to the electromagnetic field – are the strong and weak nuclear forces, and gravity. They shape all reality, literally. The dance between them is calibrated precisely in a way that allows life to exist on earth.

Rupert Sheldrake proposes that these four fundamental fields are just the beginning. There are fields within fields within fields. Just as levels of being – material, biological, mental, and spiritual – are nested within each other, atoms within molecules, cells within organs, and so on, so there are fields associated within each of these levels. There are quantum fields and galactic fields, and, in between, every species of every plant or animal both participates in and generates its own field of consciousness. These act primarily as fields of memory, or as intelligence banks, which new arrivals within a species tap into, in the process of growing into their unique identities.[30]

In other words, DNA is not the only source of an organism's memory. Each being also has the capacity to tap into its unique field. This explains evolutionary leaps. So, for example, a species of monkey on one side of the world learns to use its thumbs. This evolutionary advance "registers" in the monkey field. Once in the field, all monkeys have access to it. Soon, mysteriously, monkeys on the other side of the world, start using their thumbs. They don't actually have to learn the skill, so much as download it from the field. They resonate with their collective field. Sheldrake calls this *morphic resonance,* and the fields belonging to each being *morphogenetic fields.*

In a rather daring departure from pure science, Sheldrake engaged in a speculative conversation with theologian Matthew Fox about these fields. He wondered if each field is associated with its own particular angel who oversees its functioning.[31] One of the roles of angels in classical theology is to deliver messages. The message is always about helping the recipient to evolve spiritually, and to embrace the accompanying new mission. Angels, then, as the intelligent overseers of fields of consciousness associated with each level of being, play an evolutionary role. Another role of angels is to make connections; they are masterful mediators of divine intelligence. We might think of them as mediators of Sophia's wisdom, held within fecund angel-fields.

## Angelic Fields

Theologian Walter Wink notices that in the book of Revelation, the author writes not to the seven congregations, but to the *angels* of the seven congregations. The angel can be thought of as the "field" of consciousness distinct to each congregation. This field evolves over the years in relation to the congregation's historic culture and ethos, and to decisions made and not made, based in that culture. This speaks to the importance of congregations spending time determining their vision and mission, for in doing so they create the field into which worshippers and visitors unconsciously tap when they walk through the doors. We know, in fact, that people get a "vibe" from a congregation. As with morphogenetic fields, new people don't necessarily have to learn the ethos of the congregation; they can download it.

Now imagine congregations around the world creating "green fields," cultures of ecological sensibility. By signalling their ecological vision, they would activate a "green" angel-field. Newcomers would resonate with the "green angel" of the congregation. To be "in Christ" would be to resonate with the green angel of a congregation.

The mother of all fields may be the metaverse posited by Ervin Laszlo.[32] It is speculative to be sure, but it represents an imaginative extension of field theory. The metaverse is similar to what physicists call the "zero point energy field," or the realm of pure potential. Laszlo suggests that it is the source of our universe, and all the energy, information, and consciousness (I.C.E.) that ever existed or ever will exist. Our own universe, and perhaps many others, arose out of this field. It is primarily a field of cosmic memory, carrying the memories – and the code of life – of all previous universes. When our own universe came flaring forth, it came ready-made with the life code that had evolved through previous universes. Laszlo calls this field of memory the Akashic Field, or A-Field. He got name from Hindu philosophy, which posits an Akashic Record. Akasha means "cosmic sky," and it refers to something similar to the field-saturated space we've been discussing.[33]

## The Sophia Field: Are You Saved, Sister?

The Akashic Field gives a possible new meaning to the concept of salvation. Set aside, for a moment, traditional theology, in which only true believers are saved for eternal life, and think instead of the implications of field theory for this doctrine.

As a field of Sophia/Wisdom, nothing in all of creation is ever lost. It is "saved" in a more literal sense. Jesus' own mission to save what is lost is precisely directed toward those who have been left behind by society, those most vulnerable to being invisible or lost to the world. To whom do they matter? How do we know they matter? We know that what matters to victims of abuse, torture, and political oppression is that their story be heard. What is intolerable to the survivors of war or genocide is that their loved ones be forgotten and disappear from the annals of history. This is why the South African Truth and Reconciliation process so effectively de-escalated the violence during the transition from apartheid. People flock to Washington, DC, to view the wall of names and remember those who died in the Vietnam War. Every November 11, the congregation I serve reads out the names of those who died in World Wars I and II. Such remembering is itself an act of salvation.

Through his compassionate presence, Jesus conveyed the love of Sophia to those who had been forgotten. He gathered them up on her behalf to let them know that they have eternal value. They were "saved" by Jesus, in this earthly sense, by his validation of their presence, in contrast to the culture, which treated them as nobodies.

But this validation goes beyond earthly existence. Laszlo's Akashic Field can represent for us the science of eternity. It implies that there is eternal validation of our significance. Sophia-Jesus, as Sophia's child, acted in similar fashion on earth with those who had been left behind, as the Akashic Field functions in an eternal dimension – in other words, Jesus "saved" them from cultural oblivion, as the A-field "saves" all creation from eternal oblivion.

The "Sophia-field" gathers up each and every being and centre of consciousness from the 14-billion-year history of the universe and not only records them, like a cosmic hard drive, but *preserves* them as living entities, for eternity. Each and every being is "saved" from oblivion, and not merely for "eternal rest," but to serve the evolutionary purpose of future worlds.

This yearning for the salvation of all creation is found not just in the gospel accounts of Jesus' ministry, but also in Saint Paul's letter to the Romans, where he includes all of creation in the saving activity of God (Romans 8). Likewise, everything and everybody is "written in the book of life" (Revelation 1), to serve further evolutionary purposes.

This new understanding of salvation gives me hope. We are promised a future in which all creation will be renewed and restored (Romans 8). The impact of our ignorance, fear, and greed on all our relations, human and other-than-human, is not permanent in the realm of God's kin-dom. Even if we render our planet uninhabitable, the information, consciousness, and energy of all created beings since the great Flaring Forth is saved in the heart of Sophia-God, in order to serve the evolutionary purposes of a new creation.

Don't get me wrong. I have no time for the likes of evangelist James Bakker and his cohort, who passively acquiesce to the destruction of the planet because they think God is going to act to save us. We have already seen that this belief is contrary to an evolutionary faith. The destruction of species is unconscionable. We need to act urgently to stop the foolishness. Yet, in an ultimate sense, God non-coercively saves all beings in order that the fullness of God's dream of beauty and diversity may be realized.

Some progressive expressions of the Christian faith have jettisoned notions of eternal life, partly in reaction to the fundamentalist coupling of eternal life and correct belief. In their scheme, correct belief functions as the dogmatic hammer; believe this and gain eternal life; refuse and you're toast. But we can decouple the two and present a metaphysics of eternal life as simply being the way of Sophia. We have a deep spiritual need to know that we leave a lasting trace in the universe. The idea that our only legacy will be our family or the good work we've done over the course of our lifetime doesn't speak to our intuition that our lives have eternal significance. Our refusal to address this existential question in the liberal church has handed the souls of millions of people over to fundamentalist Christians. Nothing and nobody is ever lost in Sophia's field of eternal life.

## Chaos and Creativity:
## "While Remaining in Herself, She Renews All Things"

In most ancient creation myths prior to patriarchy, a goddess emerges out of chaos, to begin the creative process. There is no male God standing outside and over creation, imposing order on a threatening chaotic void. Chaos and cosmos (the ordered universe) are involved in a dance. They aren't enemies, nor are they opposites. They are inextricably involved as different aspects of a single dynamic involved in the creative process.

When the author of the Wisdom of Solomon affirms that Sophia "orders all things well," he was noticing what I've called the fit and flow of creation. The universe works, and works well. But it's not because an order is imposed from an outside, external agent. Form emerges as the hidden order within chaos itself. Sophia is both the divine pattern hidden in the chaos, and the chaos inherent in the order. The goal is evolution in all realms.

Chaos theory, as a scientific theory, is not so much about chaos as it is about the hidden patterns within chaotic structures. In the midst of the chaos, it is almost impossible to discern these patterns, but the patterns do indeed self-organize or emerge. David Ruelle and Floris Takens called these patterns "strange attractors."[34] Using supercomputers, it is possible to track chaotic systems. Each moment of the evolution of a chaotic system appears as a point of light on the screen. As the dots accumulate, the image first appears random and chaotic, but over time an exquisitely beautiful pattern emerges. The pattern is the strange attractor. Again, these patterns are not the shape of chaos. They are the shape of wholeness within apparent chaos.

Before this form emerges on the screen, it appears random and meaningless. To understand chaos theory is to develop a holistic consciousness. When we're in the midst of chaos in our personal lives, it is perhaps inevitable that we'll feel overwhelmed, as though life has no apparent meaning or pattern to it. We focus on the parts. Learning to trust in the dimension of life captured by the image of the strange attractor is a key spiritual discipline. The writer of the Wisdom of Solomon says that Sophia "orders all things well"; scientists are now helping us to understand how she accomplishes this feat.

These strange attractors start out as a "basin of attraction," the boundaries that define the limits of the fluctuation a system can endure and still remain itself.[35] This is the space within which a system will explore millions of possibilities of itself, trying on this and then that, as possible ways of manifesting itself. But there is a limit, a basin, which is gradually revealed *as* the strange attractor. God acts like a basin of attraction in the book of Job, when God asks Job, "Are you able to say to the sea, this far and no farther?" When Saint Paul calls the cosmic Christ "the one in whom all things hold together" (Colossians 1:17), he has expressed through spiritual intuition what science has now discovered. There are boundaries to chaos built into the universe.

There is a crucible of creativity, which incorporates chaos as a crucial component of creative evolution.

In 1995 I had a dream in which I was travelling in a bus filled with passengers. I looked out the window and saw a tornado coming right at us. There was no escape. The tornado picked the bus up, carrying it some distance. The bus landed and flipped three or four times. Miraculously, nobody was injured. I climbed out a window of the bus to survey the damage in the surrounding region. I was met by a man, who told me that I had been chosen to name a whole new species of tree. I knew nothing about trees, so I had no idea how I was supposed to carry out this task.

When God speaks to Job, it is no accident that it is from a whirlwind. The whirlwind is an archetypal symbol indicating that something new is about to happen. The spiral, in the form of a tornado, whirlwind, or vortex, is nature's harbinger of a new order emerging out of chaos. Many galaxies are spiral-shaped. Spirals are nature's expression of the state of balanced turbulence, the precondition of creative emergence. They embody the shape of old forms breaking down, in order to allow the new level of complexity to emerge. In my dream, the apparent destructiveness of the tornado is followed almost immediately by an invitation to participate in shaping a new creation, via the naming of a new species. The tornado in my dream was threatening and chaotic because it symbolized a state of transition. The dream was a premonition that new life was about to emerge in and through me.

## Chaos Trusted Becomes a Dancing Star

The New Testament often presents Jesus as having power over chaos. The story that best illustrates this power is the calming of the sea. In ancient myths, the seas and the waves represent chaos. When the waves obey Jesus' order to be still, the disciples are filled with awe: "Who is this, that even the wind and sea obey him?" (Mark 4:41). Jesus' ability to do this puts him in league with God's Spirit, who "swept over the face of the watery abyss" (Genesis 1:2), and with Sophia, "who holds sway over the waves of the sea" (Sirach 24:4–7). Jesus apparently did not think that these powers were confined to him, however. If Peter, for example, had enough faith, Jesus said that he could have walked on the stormy waters and not fallen in. Faith is the capacity to trust the hidden pattern, even in the midst of chaos.

When viewed in the context of chaos theory, Jesus is not simply the presence of order fighting against the dark forces of chaos. As the anointed presence of Sophia, he is the embodiment of the universal wisdom that recognizes chaos and order as implicit within each other, as two aspects of one creative force. He is, in this sense, the integral presence of both order and chaos. The Easter story affirms that Christ is the emergent order, even in the midst of a chaotic system. But, at other times, he is the chaos inherent in the ordered system of his day. Examples of Jesus as chaos include the overturning of tables in the Temple; his challenge to those who were about to throw rocks at the woman accused of adultery; his very upsetting question, in the presence of his family, about who exactly were his family, those who shared his genes or those who did the will of his Father; his criticism of the religiosity of narrow-minded priests and rabbis; and his teachings about the kingdom of God, which baffled the disciples. Jesus, as Sophia's child, is able to discern when to invoke chaos, and when to manifest God's hidden order within the chaos, in the service of the kin-dom of God.

## Demons in the New Testament

Jesus is portrayed in the gospels as casting out demons. In first-century Mediterranean culture, demons were believed to be the cause of disease and psychological illness. Today we might think of them as the mythological equivalent of hostile takeovers in the corporate world. They coercively possess what is not theirs to possess. Recall that in chaos theory the basin of attraction defines the limits within which a system can experiment with new forms and still remain itself. Demonic presences can be understood as influences that desire to change a person or an ecosystem into something they are not intended to be.

In Mark's gospel, for example, the demonic presence tells Jesus that its name is "Legion" (Mark 5:9). There is no question that the author of the gospel is referring to the Roman Legion, which, by its occupying force, has invaded both the nation and the souls of the conquered people. Rome's political and economic order goes beyond even chaos. It is demonic in the sense that Rome's influence threatens the very definition and identity of what it meant to be Jewish. "Legion," therefore, represents an influence needing to be cast out, not experimented with. This demon ends up in a herd of swine, an animal associated with gentile culture. That's where it belonged, not in Israel. This is also why every empire is eventually cast out. The current neo-imperialist regime of the U.S. administration will be forced to withdraw for the same reason. American culture and values cannot be forced upon other nations.

Chaos within systems is natural. Occupation by foreign powers is not. At this stage of history, human domination of the planet is demonic. Our name is Legion, as we possess and dominate the earth in a manner that is causing planetary degradation, and ultimately our own madness. Theodore Roszak, a pioneer in the field of eco-psychology, was one of the first to make the connection between planetary health and our own psychological health.[36] I remember having a nightmare about radium fallout, raining down around me. But everybody else thought it was ordinary rain and I almost went mad trying to convince them otherwise. Eco-psychologists warn us to explore these kinds of dreams more literally. Either we cease and desist from colonizing the planet for personal gain, or we may find ourselves cast out.


## The Mysterious Dance of Order and Chaos

The hidden order within chaos is without mass and without energy, but nevertheless it is *something* – a something that science can't really explain. John Haught, a Catholic theologian, calls this implicate order of the universe "information."[37] It is the mysterious power by which atoms organize themselves into molecules, which in turn leads to the emergence of biological life, with each form of life organizing itself over time into increasingly elegant and complex forms. It is disingenuous to simply say that a "selfish gene" is responsible for this ordering. What gives genetic material the intelligence to wind itself up into more complex forms? Why would mind emerge from mindless matter? From whence this mysterious dance between chaos and order, which results in conscious beings who can ask questions about it? What scientists call information, Christians call Sophia – information with loving intention, weaving her tapestry throughout the universe.

The following Zen poem captures the mystery of pre-existing intelligence at work in the universe.

Gaze at it; there is nothing to see.
It is called the formless.

Heed it; there is nothing to hear.
It is called the soundless.
Grasp it; there is nothing to hold on to.
It is called the immaterial.
Invisible, it cannot be called by any name.
It returns again to nothingness.[38]

Jesus thanks God that Wisdom is hidden from the eyes of those in the world who think they are wise, and revealed only to the humble. Humility is the path to Sophia. The word itself is derived from the word *humus*: to know oneself to be of the earth. Sophia is hidden from the eyes of those who would by force probe and dissect and exploit her for gain. But to the meek she is host and friend.

To heed Sophia's voice in the 21st century requires a cosmic re-enchantment with the world. The wisdom tradition affirms that the whole earth, the whole cosmos, is filled with the glory of God. It is infused with her divine mode of presence, a field of pervasive wisdom, active everywhere, infusing chaos with order and order with chaos, and all of it in the service of abundant life. This presence delights in creation and in human beings. She invites us to a banquet of abundant life; dinner will be followed by music and dancing. She loves justice, and speaks out fiercely against the foolishness of human arrogance. She is the "irresistible" presence of the divine, wooing us to her table where she can teach us her ways (Wisdom of Solomon 9). What we do to the earth, we do to ourselves and to Sophia's child: "What you have done unto the least of these, you have done unto me" (Matthew 25:40). It is no less than sacrilege to destroy the diversity of life on the planet. This is the cosmology and theology that needs to inform our ecological mission. It is to this mission that we now turn our attention.

## Evil: Natural and Human

A friend of mine witnessed two male mallard ducks fighting over a female for the right to mate with her. The victor aggressively held the female's head under water and had his way with her. It sickened my friend. He challenged me to tell him how God/Sophia was present in this "act of brutality."

Romanticism is indeed a temptation in regard to nature. Nature is both beautiful and brutal. One cannot deny that it is "red in tooth and claw." Furthermore, natural catastrophes such as earthquakes, tsunamis, fires, hurricanes, and disease cause enormous misery and loss of life.

In the realm of *human* nature, we see enormous capacity not just for compassion, but also for evil. Think Auschwitz, the Rwandan genocide, and the 160,000,000 million people who died in wars during the last century.[39]

This discussion is known as theodicy in theological circles. It's the attempt to understand God in light of physical and moral evil. Can God/Sophia really be thought of as immanent in the presence of so much innocent suffering?

I believe that God is present to us, even in the midst of evil and suffering, but it requires some theological updating to see how and where.

First, let go of omnipotence as a divine characteristic. God is not "up there," like a cosmic puppeteer, pulling all the strings. God is not all-powerful, at least not in the way we normally think of power. God's power is the non-coercive, alluring power of love. While some things are absolutely evil, evil is not ultimate. Evil needs to be set within the larger arc of the universe story and the gospel narrative. Both stories witness to an inexorable evolutionary movement, from simplicity to complexity, disorder to coherence, instinct to increasing levels of conscious awareness, selfishness to compassionate concern. This movement occurs through a love that orients all creation toward God's own heart, and enfolds even the worst atrocity into that same encompassing heart.

Second, remember Paul's insight that God's heart was on display in the "servanthood" of Jesus of Nazareth (Philippians 2). Specifically, the incarnation represents a "kenotic" or self-emptying process, whereby God continually makes room for others and for their evolutionary development. As a result, there is genuine freedom and novelty in creation. Genetic dead ends and natural disasters will occur, as all levels of creation find their own way. Empires, tyrants, and hearts filled with hate express one cost of the divine gift of freedom. As the Holy One makes room, we may choose to fill up the space with unbridled greed and lust for power. God doesn't unilaterally intervene on these occasions because it is not in God's nature to do so. On the other hand, God is always present, offering love to hearts that are closed.

Third, the theology of the cross affirms that God was present *on* the cross. This was considered foolishness by the religions of the day. A God who suffers and dies! Get serious! But it's only preposterous if we insist on clinging to a God who exercises coercive power. The God of the gospels deals with suffering by entering into it. The presence of the divine in suffering is not limited to the occasion of the crucifixion. It extends throughout the entire 14-billion-year story of creation. For Christians, this pan-cosmic, suffering presence of the divine is symbolized by the crucifixion.

Finally, remember that nothing is ever lost in this universe. Quantum physics teaches us that energy changes form but can never be destroyed. Similarly, human and other-than-human victims of brutality, disease, and natural disaster are gathered into God's heart. At the point of death, everything is transformed in the twinkling of an eye, as Saint Paul affirms (1 Corinthians 15:51–52). Paul's experience of the Resurrection convinced him that death itself was defeated by Christ. Suffering and death are set within the more comprehensive context of eternal life, God's own heart.

The temptation for Christians is to either minimize evil or to give it ultimate status. Rather, we are called, with Christ, to enter into the suffering of all creation, trusting in God's redeeming power, known in and through the presence of noncoercive love.

# Chapter 8

## WISING UP:
## SPIRITUALITY AND PRAXIS FOR
## PLANETARY CHRISTIANS

Love all Creation,
The whole of it and every grain of sand
Love every leaf
Every ray of God's light
Love the animals
Love the plants
Love everything
If you love everything
You will perceive
The divine mystery in things
And once you have perceived it
You will begin to comprehend it ceaselessly
More and more every day
And you will at last come to love the whole world
With an abiding universal love

FYODOR DOSTOYEVSKY

❧

From the perspective of the Sophia tradition, two paths stretch out before us: the path of foolishness and the path of wisdom. The path of foolishness, from a biblical perspective, involves entering into covenants that are not sacred. They lead to death and destruction. These covenants are implicit in the profane cultural narratives that compete with another narrative, another covenant, for our allegiance – that is, our sacred covenant with the living God, known for Christians in Jesus of Nazareth, child of wisdom.

The cultural stories we currently tell ourselves to help us find our way are inadequate for the immensity of the ecological crisis we face.

Consumerism may be the most obvious of these stories. In the West, we are initiated, from a very early age, into a narrative of consumerism. As consumerist adults ourselves, when it comes to teaching our children, we no longer light a fire and sit them down to tell them, face to face, the story of who they are and where they fit in the larger community of life. Instead, we press the "on" button of the remote control and relinquish our sacred responsibility to multimedia conglomerates, who are only too happy to initiate our children into the values of consumerist culture.

Advertising tells us – children and adults alike – another story. This is a story of insufficiency, in which we learn not only that we do not *have* enough, but that we *ourselves* are not enough – our bodies are not thin enough, we are not beautiful enough, and the purpose of our lives is to figure out how to get more. In a culture of insufficiency, we lose both the capacity to see the wonder of what lies before our eyes and our ability to be grateful.[1] We see only what we do not yet have and presume we need in order to be complete. Anxiety due to a chronic sense of insufficiency replaces gratitude for life itself.

Recently, a group of children were asked what they wanted to be when they grew up. An alarming number of them said, "famous." The cult of celebrity, a third story, is an attempt to inculcate awe, but both the awe it generates and its subject are superficial. It focuses on qualities of glamour, fame, and wealth. In the movie *Notting Hill*, Julia Roberts plays the role of a successful American film star. At one point in the film, she stands before the man she loves and says, "I'm just a girl, standing before a boy, asking him to love me." The irony is that it is her authentic humanity, not her cult status, that makes her irresistible. Many celebrities know this, and are using their status to try to make a positive difference in the world. But in a culture devoid of a spiritual narrative, they become the gods and goddesses of the masses, icons of unattainable beauty and wealth who reinforce the myth of insufficiency.

We are, then, living in a culture of consumerism, insufficiency, and celebrity. These are profane narratives, not sacred ones. They promise security while deepening our collective exile. More critically, these cultural narratives distract us from taking up what Thomas Berry calls the "Great Work," the vocation of repairing our planet.

## The Imperial Story

David Korten identifies three other stories, which emerge out of the worldview of empire as opposed to earth community.[2] These stories, embedded in the evening news and implicit in all advertising, keep us disoriented and living out of the value system of the dominant culture. They also represent the path of foolishness. While Korten writes from within the context of American culture, the values and messages the stories contain are present and embodied throughout the Western world.

- **The Imperial Prosperity Story:** This story tells us that economics is the ultimate driver of human life. We must continue to grow the economy, and wealthy people do this best by creating jobs for the rest of us. Therefore, it is imperative that we get out of their way. We must remove all impediments to perpetual economic growth. Corporate taxes must be kept low, businesses must be free to set up shop anywhere in the world, and environmental restrictions must be kept to a minimum. The wealthy do the sacred work of growing the economy.

- **The Imperial Security Story:** There are terrorists and criminals lurking behind every nook and cranny, at home and abroad. These evildoers are the problem. The solution is to hunt them down, imprison, and/or execute them. This story necessitates the diversion of vast amounts of money away from education, health, and the environment, toward the army and the penal system.

- **The Imperial Meaning Story:** God is on our side. "He" rewards the good guys and punishes the bad guys. Therefore, God supports our efforts to divide the world up into evildoers (them), and good guys (us).

Taken together, these stories/myths constitute conventional "wisdom," the path of foolishness. Most of us are not conscious of having ever "bought into" these narratives. They are simply the medium in which we live and move and have our being, like water to fish. We absorb them by osmosis. One day, our three-year-old granddaughter asked her mother how God gave people words so we could talk to each other. The actual question she asked was, "How did *He* do it?" Her mother was much more interested in how a three-year-old, who had never attended church, learned that God was a "He"? She tried gently to help her daughter understand that God isn't a he *or* a she. Our granddaughter responded, "You're wrong, Mom. God is a boy's name!" These stories are *caught*, not just taught.

# Breaking the Spell

The *Matrix* is a film about a society in which the citizens go about their lives oblivious to the fact that they're all subjects in a computer program. Their lives seem real enough as they carry on their private dramas. But it's a matrix of illusion. The protagonist, Neo, intuits that something is wrong, but not until he is approached by a group of people who know the *true* story of what's happening is he given the opportunity to exit that world. He is presented with two pills: one red and one blue. If he takes the red pill, he exits the Matrix, the world of illusion, and takes up the cause of the resistance; if he takes the blue pill, he remains in the Matrix and life carries on as usual. The choice to exit is a choice for authentic suffering, rather than the bliss of unconsciousness. Neo chooses to leave the Matrix and join the resistance. Thus begins his long and arduous initiation into the real world. Re-entering reality is a painful ordeal, because it involves hearing a story so foreign to the one he's been told all his life.

The profane cultural narratives described above have us collectively and individually in their spell. Combined, they initiate us into a world of individualism, competition, and ultimately disenchantment. To underestimate their power is foolishness itself.

Breaking this spell requires strong medicine, in the form of a spiritual discipline or practice. During the 1700 years of Christendom, particularly in the West, such discipline has been in short supply. When one can be a Christian simply by virtue of being a citizen of a Christian culture, the *practice* of faith gets lost. The secularization of culture, particularly in my country, provides us with an opportunity to return to the discipline of faithful living. The practices I recommend include meditation, sacred ritual, and Sabbath-keeping. Each of these represents an ancient practice within the Christian tradition. They are the roots from which a contemporary cosmological practice can flower.

## Meditation: Making Space for Wisdom

Many people associate meditation with escapism, and it certainly *can* be that. When not practised in the service of breaking the spell of conventional wisdom, it can contribute to a passive acquiescence to the status quo. However, every religious tradition advocates one form of meditation or another, and for good reason. Meditation is, in fact, a very useful tool that can help us deconstruct the myths that lead to foolishness. The meditation I recommend involves gently emptying the mind of all thoughts and images, until one arrives at a quality of consciousness that is at once both still and alert. Nothing is more needed today than the ability to distinguish between the chattering ego and the call of Sophia.

Most of the thoughts, images, and worries that preoccupy our mind do so outside of our conscious awareness. We only become aware of how busy our minds are when we attempt to quiet the activity of the brain. The vast majority of this activity is nothing more than brain chemistry, neurons firing habitually as our egos gnaw away at the high drama we confuse with our lives. When we are living out of the dominant myths of our culture, we will invariably be concerned with issues related, in one way or another, to fear and insecurity. Do we have enough? Are we enough? Does she like me? How did I perform? What kind of impression did I make? How can I get what I want? Why am I such an idiot? All of this is simply brain chatter, but it's powerful in the way it keeps us distracted from "the way, the truth, and the life," as Jesus put it in John's gospel.

Meditation is the practice of intentionally quieting the chatter in order to detach from it, to see what else constitutes this centre of consciousness I call "me." A curious thing happens when we begin to notice the chatter. Who is the "me" noticing all this brain activity, which I've been confusing with myself? What might happen if I chose to identify with this witnessing consciousness, rather than with the chatter?

The deep stillness of a quiet mind can be frightening at first. But over time you learn to love it. Our soul (as opposed to our active mind) migrates naturally toward imageless stillness. The soul feasts on silence. It is God's first language. Silence is not simply the absence of noise. It is a presence unto itself. This kind of stillness is the font of all creativity, the womb of creation itself. As we enter this deep stillness, we access a divine mode of consciousness. My meditation teacher once compared meditation to the art of dying cloth. You dip the cloth repeatedly into the desired colour. The more times you dip it in, the closer it gets to the pure colour of the dye. As we dip our consciousness into this vat of cosmic consciousness, our own minds begin to more closely take on the quality of Consciousness itself. This is the same consciousness that gave rise to the universe. Or to use a scientific metaphor coined by physicist David Bohm, when we attain this stillness, we access the "hidden wholeness" of the universe. This is Wisdom's home. She welcomes all guests.

I have learned to set aside two 20-minute periods for meditation, once in the morning and once in mid-afternoon. It's not easy setting aside this time. We can come up with a thousand excuses for not doing it. Our ego is quite attached to the version of reality it has helped us construct. The trick, if you can call it that, is not to be too earnest about it all. The capacity to notice ourselves noticing ourselves is one of the most evolved expressions of this

14-billion-year-old universe. We have not been given this capacity for no reason. It is a spell-buster without parallel.

Silence reminds us that we are not separate and isolated. To enter silence is to enter a field of interconnectedness and share in the consciousness and intelligence that animates all of life. Far from withdrawing from reality, we connect back into hidden wholeness that pervades the universe. Each time we take a dip in this refreshing pool of being, we emerge with a little more wisdom, and are a little more liberated from the cultural myths that separate and disenchant.

## Sacred Ritual

For Christians, the name for sacred ritual is liturgy. *Liturgy* is the English translation for a Greek word that means "the work of the people." Now, I realize that the typical church service looks like anything but the work of the people. The opening and closing prayers are prepared and often delivered by a professional. The minister or priest offers a sermon. Even the "prayers of the people" are often prepared by the minister or a trained layperson.

What would our sacred rituals look like if we trusted Shug's wisdom in *The Color Purple*? Remember Shug? She said that everything she ever knew about God she brought *with* her into church.

Ritual should properly be like the banks of a river, which contain and direct the flow of water. But the flow itself should come from the people, who bring their experiences of awe, heartbreak, inspiration, and commitment with them to the worship service. Each person is like a tributary, joining up with all the other streams of energy, flowing to the Great Ocean.

The congregation I serve has designated six weeks each spring as the liturgical "season of creation." During these weeks, our prayers, readings, and sermons are planetary and cosmological in scope. Below, I talk about five aspects central to cosmological ritual: awe, lament, embodiment, hearing our sacred narrative, and Communion or the Eucharist.

## Awe

People need permission to bring with them into church their experiences of awe, for awe is the beginning of wisdom.

As an acronym, A.W.E. can mean Awakening to Wonder Everywhere. Matthew Fox has developed a sacred ritual he calls the Cosmic Mass. This Mass begins with a prolonged period during which participants experience and express awe through images, music, and movement. Fox is right. Ritual needs to begin with people sharing awe and wonder. It is the way of the child who recognizes each and every creature as "a mirror of God that glistens and glitters" (Hildegard of Bingen). Fox says that we should fall in love at least three times each day with something like a galaxy, a tree, our cat, or a song.

To open ourselves to awe, to wonder at the sheer beauty of this world and of this life we've been given, is to enter into the mystery of creation. The ancient Chinese philosopher Lao Tsu said, "Where there is an absence of awe, there is destruction." It's impossible to dump raw sewage into river or an ocean if the river or the ocean is a source of wonder and inspiration for us.

When people gather for sacred ritual, they need to experience a re-enchanted cosmos. Wonder doesn't have a chance when stories and images of violence saturate the evening news, when the pressure to produce at work is relentless, and when people are too exhausted to notice their lives. Yet given some space to re-collect, we all carry inside of us sacred moments, intimations of the sacred mystery we're involved in.

Imagine people gathering for worship, as the leader solicits such experiences. At first, there will be awkward silences. We have unwittingly nurtured passivity. It will take time. But with a little encouragement, the images and experiences will flow. One person shares about the way an old fence, lit up by the sun, was so beautiful; another speaks of how a view from a mountaintop put things in perspective; the resident mystic shares how a bird's morning song, unfiltered by waking consciousness, was unquestionably a song of praise to the Creator. These are everyday experiences, but unless we provide a sacred space for them to be honoured, they get lost in the routine of life. As we reclaim and honour them, our hearts fall back in love with the life we've been given, praise flows, and our souls expand to fill the cosmos.

## Lament

It was William Blake who said that joy and sorrow are woven fine. To open our hearts to wonder is to simultaneously allow the grief of what we're doing to each other and to the planet surface. Why, when we've been given so much, do we destroy? Why do we hurt each other? Why would we take the sacred trust of creation and enact a reign of terror on the other-than-human ones who share it with us? The traditional name for these actions is sin, and if there's not a place in our sacred ritual to face into it, we're not involved in reality. Awe opens us not only to the beauty and wonder of life, but to that which is *not-life*.

We need to do more than face sin, however. We need to *feel* it. Please understand: this is not about a formulaic prayer of confession, followed by a statement of pardon. It's not a ritualistic cleansing from "original sin." We're not born into the world as sinners.

But we are born into a sinful world. The cultures we inhabit, our families, neighbourhoods, nations, and political systems, are shot through with histories of violence, with belief systems that justify that violence, and with a "conventional wisdom" (described above) that leads to death. We internalize these attitudes, beliefs, and norms before we ever consciously choose them. Through lament, we face our complicity in these systems, with as much honesty as possible. We choose to notice the terrible cost of not living in right relationship with God, self, neighbour, and the earth.

Joanna Macy has written about the high cost of psychic numbing, a term coined first by Robert Lifton in his study of Hiroshima victims.[3] This is the defence mechanism that kicks in when we are overwhelmed by pain. It is natural. But over time it shuts out not only pain, but joy and awe as well. In the context of the good news of the Christ, we are given permission to open our hearts once again to the scope of planetary suffering, both human and other-than-human. Authentic worship involves expressions of deep sadness. This means leaving enough time in our rituals for lament to surface. Margaret Atwood once wrote that the world is seen clearly only through tears.

Once, at a sacred ritual we called Earth Revival,[4] we handed out cards to participants, with images of animals threatened with extinction, and their associated characteristics. During a section of the ritual called *Via Negativa*, we invited people to be the voice of their animal.[5] In the darkened silence of the sacred space, we gave voice to the tiger, the antelope, the turtle, the frogs, the spotted owl, and the prairie birds, to name just a few. The grief was palpable. We broke through the psychic numbing. In the 21st century, this lament for the other-than-human ones belongs right beside our lament for the human victims of injustice.

## Embodiment

It is time to bring our bodies back to sacred ritual in the church. Percussion was actually banned in the church because the deep rhythms, mimicking the pulse of the heart, awakened the second chakra, the seat of our sexuality. Organ music is beautiful, and I wouldn't ever want to lose it. But wouldn't our hymns benefit from the backbeat of a *jambe*, a drum of the Pacific islands? Our hips would want to get involved, and God forbid, strange feelings may stir within, in a church of all places! Our feet would naturally do what feet do when they hear a compelling beat, namely move! Our legs would be activated by an ancient memory of our tribal peoples, and would want to spring into action. Arms would make like tree branches and sway to the rhythm.

The whole cosmos is involved in an intricate, ecstatic dance. Ask your body if it wants to sit on a hard pew, your nose buried in a hymnbook, your arms close to your sides. To bring our bodies back into worship is to open our hearts to Sophia, who is "more mobile than motion." Jesus said that unless we become like children, we won't enter the kin-dom of God. Ever noticed that children are in constant motion?

## Listening for Sophia in Scripture and Sermon

Broken open by awe and lament, and bodies in motion, we are now ready to hear the unconventional wisdom of the gospel of the Christ. Most worship services don't open us up sufficiently in preparation for the gospel. In my hot yoga class, we're not allowed to get into the deeper postures until we've sweated buckets and our minds have gained sufficient focus. In worship, once we're softened up, we're ready to hear from Jesus, child of Sophia. For Christians, he is Sophia incarnate. He is the one who has broken the spell himself, and has power to wake us up.

John Dominic Crossan points out how different literary forms serve different functions.[6] The role of myth as a literary form is to create the world. Myths are the narratives of conventional wisdom. Parables, on the other hand, subvert myth. It's no accident that Jesus used parables to pull the rug out from under the dominant myths of both the Roman Empire and his own religious tradition. Parables work by drawing listeners in through a routine situation they can relate to. Once the listener has entered the scene in her or his imagination, there is an unexpected and often shocking twist to the story that explodes the very substructure of the listener's take on reality. The father *forgives* the ungrateful son! After the son squandered his inheritance, and ended up eating pig food?!

Sacred wisdom at this point has an opening. Jesus takes every one of the myths we live by, and sets the TNT of unconventional wisdom under them. Unbridled consumption, we learn, is a spiritual malaise, not a civic responsibility. Are we lacking? Nonsense. God gives us everything we need and more. The lily doesn't strive to be anything more than what it is, and look at its beauty. Why look to kings and queens, or, in more modern times, celebrities, to find radiance? The divine radiance shines out everywhere, for those with eyes to see, including each one of us. Is excess wealth really a sign of wisdom? In fact, it is the *foolish* man who builds bigger barns. Give away your wealth, Jesus counsels, rather than hoard it! The way to peace? It's not bigger armies; violence begets violence. Lasting security emerges when we share our wealth with the poor. Rather than propping up empire, God non-violently subverts it. Righteousness, alignment with wisdom, is its own reward; unrighteousness, living in fear and greed, is punishment enough. To really listen to Jesus is to walk the path of the banana peel, never knowing when we are going to lose our footing on his subversive wisdom.

## Communion

Once a month our congregation serves Communion. We re-enact Jesus' last meal with his disciples, sharing symbols of bread and wine. If you were to ask a hundred different people what they think we're doing, I'm sure you'd get a hundred different answers. I am grateful to Crossan for pointing out that Jesus used table fellowship as an intentional strategy for enacting the kingdom of God.[7] He invited people who didn't belong together, according to the norms of the culture, to a common table: men and women, pure and "impure," poor and rich, marginalized and mainstream. Communion is a re-enactment of Jesus' open-table strategy, a symbolic proclamation of radical inclusivity. It's not about believing "the right things," or about being a member of the church; it's about enacting the cosmological imperative of discovering unity in diversity.

As host of these meals, Jesus acted as Sophia's child. Jesus as Sophia incarnate prepared and presided at these meals, inviting people from the highways and byways of life to feast upon a subversive wisdom. When we partake of the "body" and "blood" of Christ, we are not re-enacting a blood sacrifice. We are taking the wisdom of Sophia's child into our very lives – his very life, flesh, and blood, broken open and poured out that we might receive grace to walk the costly path of wisdom; grace to exit the path of foolishness and take wisdom's narrow road. The radically inclusive nature of the meal extends to more than just the human race. To be "one in Christ" is to be one with *all* our kin. For this reason, our Communion prayers need to be cosmological in scope, situating us within the unfolding story of the universe, and within the entire community of life on earth, the "kin-dom" of God.

# Sabbath

Six days a week we seek to dominate the world;
on the seventh we try to dominate the self.

Many of us have negative associations with Sabbath. Some grew
up associating Sabbath with not being able to eat ice cream, dance,
or have any fun. The Puritan tradition within Protestantism did
a great disservice to the wisdom of this ancient Jewish practice.
When Ann and I visited Jerusalem, we stayed in a conservative
Jewish neighbourhood. On Friday night, traffic came to a complete stop. Families, dressed in brightly coloured clothes, poured
into the streets. Music and laughter filled the air. Jewish couples,
we discovered, are obliged to make love during Sabbath. Our Puritan ancestors missed the point.

Sabbath is a 24-hour period during which the faithful are
strictly forbidden to engage in any activity that might be con-
strued as an attempt to improve upon creation, including oneself,
in any manner. We cease and desist from all of our clever projects, in order to simply notice what God has done, and is doing,
in all of creation. We rest in God. We re-order our lives by remembering that it's all gift from a God who loves us and who delights
in creation. We don't have to do anything, except show up. The
predominant sentiment, the faithful mood associated with Sabbath, is joy!

The families we saw in Jerusalem welcomed the Sabbath by
personifying her as Queen Sabbath. They acted as hosts for a divine mode of consciousness. They prepared food fit for a queen,
dressed for royalty, and behaved toward each other as though
they were in her presence, with great love and respect. Imagine

beginning Sabbath with a ritual to welcome Sophia as Queen of Wisdom into our homes. For 24 hours we would immerse ourselves in her ways, treating each other and the earth according to her wisdom. We would make a special effort to walk lightly upon the earth, to connect with creation, and to cultivate awe and wonder.

The ancient practice of Sabbath applied to creation itself. Beasts of burden were given the day off, and fields were allowed to rest and renew. Creation participated in this ritual of renewal and celebration. Sabbath gives us the opportunity to practice a different way of being. We can ride bikes instead of automatically jumping in the car, or cook a vegetarian meal and get together with other families committed to the restoration of creation. By taking a day off from the culture of "getting and spending," we create some distance between ourselves and the dominant culture in order to remember who we are and whose we are.

Honouring a Sabbath day is a powerful witness to a world gone mad in its allegiance to increasing productivity and efficiency. We stop to enjoy what *God* has made of creation, breaking our fascination with what *we* have made of the world. When the Romans came up against the Jewish refusal to work on the Sabbath, they reacted with contempt. They knew it would subvert their projects of domination and empire building. The Jews stopped and clearly signalled that they worshipped another God, not Caesar, and that this God was Lord of creation.

These three disciplines, then – meditation, sacred ritual, and Sabbath practice – help to break the spell of conventional wisdom. They open a door in our heart through which wisdom may enter.

# Practicing an Ecological Faith: Greening the Church

"Faith without works is dead," offered James, writing to a community that may have been feeling very spiritual, but in practice was enacting the myth of the surrounding culture (James 2:17). They were catering to the rich in their midst, giving them the seats of honour, while giving the poor among them the cheap seats. They told the poor to go, eat their fill, and be happy, but forgot to actually feed them.

We need to be involved not only in the practice of gaining the mind and the heart of the Christ, but in translating this renewed consciousness into concrete actions to change the world. The following are some ideas for a mission agenda of a green church, which come out of an ecological Christianity.

The congregation I serve has just been visited by a team of professional ecological auditors, who assessed the imprint of our property and buildings. This initiative was driven by an ecological ministry team. They looked at our heating and lighting systems, the toxicity of cleaning products we use, the fertilizers we use for our garden, as well as at our paper use and recycling practices. Before the church can be a voice for the earth, we need to clean up our own act.

## Families for Earth: A Dream

I can imagine a congregation setting a target to reduce carbon emissions, not only in relation to church operations, as described above, but also extending outward to the families within the church. It's my experience that families need a transcendent purpose in order to thrive. Imagine a local congregation starting a program called Families for Earth. The goal would be to set a target for cumulative carbon reduction of a congregation. It is now easy to go online (davidsuzuki.org/carboneutral) to calculate the carbon footprint of a family. Factors such as car usage, plane trips, and heating and lighting are calculated as measures of carbon output. A dollar figure is then associated with that figure. This is the true cost of our lifestyles. After determining that figure, the family would then make a charitable donation of this amount to the designated Eco-Fund of the congregation. The money from this fund would then be used to pay for the implementation of the recommendations of the ecological audit team: testing for the viability of geothermal heating, upgrading the furnace, changing to greener light bulbs, installing solar panels in the church roof, or covering the cost of changing to recycled paper.

The participating families would be encouraged to share the story of their reduced footprint with other families, encouraging these families to do the same. There are green funds currently set up outside the church, which families who don't participate in church life may choose to support. This is a kind of evangelism, which progressive Christians could get behind. It would represent a persuasive invitation to participate in the greening of the planet, rather than a coercive attempt to get others to believe what we believe.

I imagine family representatives of participating congregations visiting neighbouring congregations to tell their story and to provide support for them to start their own Families for Earth team. There would be a nationwide, loose affiliation of participating families, who would perhaps come together for an annual conference. These conferences would be opened and closed by sacred ritual, which would incorporate prayers, songs, and reflections, all grounded in a new cosmology.

## Stream-Keepers

In Vancouver, the municipal and provincial governments support a program to reclaim ancient salmon streams. At one time there were 50 such streams, but these were polluted, paved over, or diverted into storm drains, until only one remained. Musqueam Creek is being restored under the leadership of Nicholas Scapillati and Terry Point. The Coho salmon are slowly beginning to return. There are now organizations called Stream-Keepers, who train volunteers how to "daylight" streams that were covered over. Up and down the Burrard Inlet, in Vancouver, stream-keepers are daylighting these streams. The salmon are returning. Imagine a Sunday school class taking workshops in stream-keeping. The children would learn that this kind of work is a sacred vocation.

## Bless the Caulking Gun

Will Braun asks, "What if the cracks around our church windows are letting the holy spirit out as they let the wintry cold in?"[8] He wonders if the text for next Sunday's sermon should be the monthly heating bill. Mr. Braun imagines blessing the caulking gun at a worship service before it's deployed. He points out that if all houses of worship in the U.S. cut back on energy use by 25 percent, they would save $500 million and prevent five million tons of carbon from being released into the atmosphere. Church revival in the 21st century involves ecological revival.

## Conscious Consumerism

The average head of lettuce in North America travels 2000 kilometres to get to your kitchen. The planetary cost of the carbon emissions associated with transporting it to your home, especially if you drive to the grocery store, far exceeds the cost of the lettuce. An organization called BALLE (Business Alliance for Local Living Economies, www.balle.ca) promotes conscious consumerism. We need to buy our produce locally.

Alisa Smith and J. B. McKinnon, a couple from Vancouver, began the 100-mile diet. For a full year, they dedicated themselves to the task of only eating food that could be purchased from within a 100-mile radius of their home. (They literally took out a map and drew a circle.) It wasn't easy. Their story can be found in their book *The 100-Mile Diet: A Year of Local Eating.*

Pesticides and fertilizers are leaching away into our rivers, lakes, and oceans, ending up eventually in our bodies. As well as buying locally, we need to promote organic farming by paying the extra cost this entails. If enough people do this, we'll reach a tipping point where the demand for organics is high enough to drop the prices.

*Natural Capitalism,* by Amory Lovins, L. H. Lovins, and Paul Hawken, is a wonderful book that promotes a greener capitalism. It is filled with good-news stories of companies who have gone green. Enlightened companies are realizing that by mimicking the processes of nature, they can not only save the planet, but also reduce their own costs. Photocopy companies are leading the way in a shift toward taking responsibility for their products from "cradle-to-grave." The practice of leasing may be the way forward. Companies who lease their products take older models back to the factory and refit them, so that they can be leased out at more reasonable rates. Literally all the parts are recyclable. Businesses should be responsible for taking their products back when the consumer is finished with them. The cost of dumping a product at a landfill site should increase dramatically, forcing consumers and businesses to become like my father. He would hang a paper towel up to dry after using it, until it literally fell apart. I used to laugh at him. Today, I honour his instincts.

In *The Ecology of Commerce*, Paul Hawken holds the business world's feet to the fire. One of the stories he tells concerns Ray Anderson, the owner and CEO of one of the largest commercial carpet manufacturers in the world. Ray woke up one day, convicted of the sin of plundering the earth for personal and corporate gain. He made it his mission to go and address those whom he affectionately called "fellow plunderers," CEOs and presidents of companies who operate out of a single, bottom-line mentality. Mr. Anderson is moving consciously towards a zero-footprint goal. This is not a pipe dream. Companies all over the world are waking up to the true cost of doing business in the traditional paradigm. As consumers, we need to seek out responsible companies and buy from them. Many websites lay out the best and worst companies related to the environment. *Corporate Knights* is a Canadian magazine that holds the corporate world accountable (corporateknights.ca). Learning to be conscious consumers is an act of Christian discipleship in the 21st century.

## The Power of Subtle Influence

Edward Lorenz, a meteorologist, was working on a project designed to better predict weather patterns on a global level. This involved feeding mathematical equations, representing as many variables in weather patterns as he could imagine, into a supercomputer. The computer then went to work. One day, to save some time, he decided to shave a few decimal points off a numerical value, an infinitesimally small difference. He went for a coffee, and when he returned he was flabbergasted by what he found. This minute change had made an enormous difference. This led him to ask his now famous question: "If a butterfly flaps its wings in Mexico, does it cause a hurricane in Texas?"

What he had stumbled onto was the power of subtle influence. In a radically interconnected universe, the smallest difference can lead to enormous change. We literally cannot tell what difference our smallest act will make. Our smallest gestures, for good or ill, set off a cycle of interactions through a feedback loop. This leads to exponential change beyond anything we can imagine. Vicious cycles can be transformed into virtuous cycles. Combine this insight with the phenomena of non-local influence, discussed earlier, and we have a scientific basis for hope. Or to use theological language, all Sophia needs (she who "penetrates all things" and is "more-mobile-than-motion") is the smallest gesture of good will in order to reap a harvest of transformation.

To illustrate, during the time it has taken to write this book, climate change has surpassed health care as the number one issue on the Canadian public's list of concerns. The minority government is being forced by public opinion to make it their top priority. We have reached a tipping point.

Environmental journalist Martin Mittelstaedt has called this "the equivalent of a public-opinion earthquake."[9] Suddenly and unexpectedly the environment is on everybody's minds. Even Exxon Mobil Corporation has withdrawn funding from the denial industry, acknowledging, in the words of Kenneth Cohen, vice president for public affairs, that the issue has "evolved."[10]

We have no reason be discouraged about our capacity to make a difference, and every reason to hope.

# Epilogue

## EARTH AS CHRIST CRUCIFIED AND RISEN

John Vaillant's Governor-General award-winning book, *The Golden Spruce*, tells the story of Grant Hadwin, a logger who became disillusioned with the forestry industry.[1] As an act of protest, Hadwin travelled to Haida Gwai, an island off the west coast of British Columbia, and, under cover of night, cut down a very special spruce tree. Because of a rare gene, this Sitka spruce was a radiant gold. By rights it should not have been able to thrive because it lacked the chlorophyll molecules necessary to convert sunlight into food. But it had. The tree was considered a sacred being by the Haida people, who believed it possessed the spirit of a departed chief. The loss of the tree devastated the native people of the island.

No one knows why Hadwin did it. Perhaps he was frustrated by the attention this one tree received, while old-growth forests throughout British Columbia continued to be decimated. He may have wanted the world to recognize the intrinsic radiance of all forests, not just this one protected tree. Or perhaps he was emotionally unstable. We'll never know. Hadwin disappeared after his act of eco-terrorism, and is believed to be dead.

Ruth Jones, a Vancouver artist, captured the sacrilege implicit in the destruction of the golden spruce in an exquisite tapestry. It depicts a crucified Christ hanging from the golden spruce. We displayed her work during the lament section of a worship service. The impact was visceral and immediate. Her artistic sensibility was surely accurate. The Christ suffers the pain of all creation.

Start with the crucified Christ hanging from the golden spruce, but then extend this image to the entire planet. Imagine photographs of our planet taken from outer space with the figure of the crucified Christ superimposed over it. The desecration of our planet is a crucifixion of Wisdom's child.

## The Future: The Risen Christ as Planet Restored

This is not, however, the end of the story. Cuttings from the golden spruce have spread around the planet. Vaillant points out that it is a testament to the intelligence of this splendid tree that it "harnessed the same species that killed it, and made it a vehicle for its own success."[2] He celebrates that "the golden spruce has become the most widely dispersed Sitka spruce on earth." So far, only dwarf versions of the tree survive, but they are alive and well, and who knows, in this unpredictable universe full of novelty and surprise, one may yet reach up to attain the full glory of its mother.

The story of Easter is an affirmation that Jesus' death, while tragic, was not final. In the crucifixion, the heart of Jesus burst open, like a Sitka spruce cone, to seed the cosmos with a new heart and a new mind suited for a new creation. The seeds that the Christ scattered – humility, compassion, kinship, and justice for all beings – fall into the soil of willing hearts. Those who open their hearts to the Christ are seedlings of a new creation, ushered in by the Christ. As Meister Eckhart put it, we are anointed by Sophia to become "little Christs."

Sophia calls us from the busiest street corners to gather at her table and be nourished for the work of fashioning God's preferred future. She calls not just from "up above," but also from out ahead of us, from that very future which is her dream for a renewed creation. She is, after all, the one who "renews all things." Her dream is for the evolutionary path of the universe to continue in and through the cooperation of humanity.

## Grace under Pressure

My yoga instructor encourages us to attain the meditative state of "grace under pressure." This is an apt description of the Christian journey. Grace, in a cosmological context, is the gift of arriving on the planet with the dynamics of a 14-billion-year-old universe built into our DNA, into our hearts and minds, and into the very fabric of an enchanted cosmos. This new cosmological model called the human being comes equipped with the creative power of a supernova, the radiance of a golden spruce, the resiliency of our bacterial cousins, the determination of a spawning Coho salmon, and the heart-wisdom of Sophia. In the "fullness of time," Jesus emerges, a perfect reflection of the light of God, who along with the whole procession of cosmological beings takes up residence in open hearts. Through his subversive, divine wisdom, we participate in creating the new thing the Holy One is doing on earth.

This grace doesn't come cheap. Those who open to it feel the pressure of an evolutionary universe, the push and pull of Sophia moving through us to reflect the divine. This pressure bears down upon us and within us to choose the path of conscious evolution. To lay waste these powers is to betray the promise that animated all our ancestors – geological, biological, and human. To allow these dynamics to animate our lives is to join in the sacred dance of the cosmos.

Saint Paul foresees that creation itself will be set free to obtain "the glorious freedom of the children of God" (Romans 8:21). On December 11, 2006, a 50-foot female humpback whale became entangled in crab nets near the Farallon Islands. A rescue team of local divers saw the huge mammal and set out to rescue her. She was having trouble staying afloat, as the ropes dug into her blubber and the weights pulled her down. According to Peter Fimrite, the journalist who covered the story, the whale remained perfectly still as the divers cut through the ropes. When she was freed, witnesses said that she swam out 100 yards to sea, and then returned to her rescuers, gently nudging each of them one by one. The divers said that it felt "amazing and unforgettable, as though she was saying thank you."[3] Grace under pressure.

All creation, Paul writes, "waits with eager longing for the revealing of the children of God" (8:19). These rescuers revealed themselves to be children of God. Creation is waiting for all of us to show up, ready and willing by the grace of Sophia, to set creation free.

# ENDNOTES

## Prologue

[1] Brian Handwerk, "Frog Extinctions Linked to Global Warming," for *National Geographic News*, Jan. 12, 2006, at http://news.nationalgeographic.com/news/2006/01/0112_060112_frog_climate.html

[2] Ibid.

[3] Tina and Rhett Butler, "Kihansi Spray Toad Faces Extinction," June 7, 2005, at http://news.mongabay.com/2005/0606-Kihansi_Spray_Toad.html

## Introduction

[1] Scott Simpson, "Global Meltdown Feared, UN Report," *The Globe and Mail*, September 25, 2006.

[2] Terry Glavin, *Waiting for the Macaws and Other Stories from the Age of Extinctions* (Toronto: Penguin, 2006).

[3] Dan Joling, "Polar Bear Turning to Cannibalism: Global Warming the Cause," *The Globe and Mail*, June 13, 2006.

## Chapter 1

[1] Jere Pramuk, in *Wellness Workbook: How to Achieve Enduring Health and Vitality*, by John W. Travis and Regina Sara Ryan (Berkeley, CA: Celestial Arts, 2004).

[2] Walt Whitman, *Leaves of Grass* (Philadelphia: David McKay, c. 1900).

[3] John Gribbin and Martin Rees, *Cos-mic Coincidences: Dark Matter, Mankind, and Anthropic Cosmology* (New York: Bantam Books, 1989), 27.

[4] Richard C. Foltz, *Worldviews, Religion, and the Environment: A Global Anthology* (Toronto: Thomson/Wadsworth Learning, 2003), 526.

[5] Marcus Borg, *The Heart of Christianity: Rediscovering a Life of Faith* (San Francisco: HarperSanFrancisco, 2003), 6-20.

[6] Bruce Lipton, *The Biology of Belief: Unleashing the Power of Consciousness, Matter, & Miracles* (Santa Rosa: Mountain of Love/Elite Books, 2005), 75-94.

[7] Ibid.

[8] Matthew Fox, *Original Blessing: A Primer in Creation Spirituality* (Santa Fe, Bear and Co., 1983). Matthew must be regarded as one of the first theologians responsible for helping Christians set their faith in a cosmological context. We owe him a debt of immense gratitude. This book was pivotal in helping me shift from a redemption-centered to a creation-centred faith.

[9] James W. Fowler, *Weaving the New Creation: Stages of Faith and the Public Church* (Eugene, OR: Wipf and Stock Publishers, 2001), 19.

[10] Janine M. Benyus, *Biomimicry: Innovation Inspired by Nature* (New York: Harper, 1997), 59-94.

[11] Jeremy Narby, *Intelligence in Nature: An Inquiry into Knowledge* (New York: Jeremy P. Tarcher/Penguin, 2006), 9.

[12] John D. Ebert, *Twilight of the Clockwork God: Conversations on Science and Spirituality at the End of an Age* (Tulsa: Council Oak Books, 1999), 5–7.

[13] Ralph Abraham, *Chaos, Gaia, Eros: A Chaos Pioneer Uncovers the Three Great Streams of History* (San Francisco: HarperSanFrancisco, 1994).

**Chapter 2**

[1] Richard Tarnas, *Cosmos and Psyche: Intimations of a New World View* (New York: Viking, 2006), 16–36.

[2] Ibid., 4.

[3] Ibid.

[4] Ibid., 7.

[5] Ken Wilber, *Integral Psychology: Consciousness, Spirit, Psychology, Therapy* (Boston: Shambhala, 2000), 60–61, 190–192.

[6] Ibid.

[7] Martin Mittelstaedt, "Risk of 4000 Everyday Chemicals," *The Globe and Mail,* September 14, 2006, A17.

[8] Martin Mittelstaedt, "Are Plastics Coated in Peril?" *The Globe and Mail,* May 3, 2006, A3.

[9] E. O. Wilson, *Creation: An Appeal To Save Life On Earth* (New York: W. W. Norton and Co., 2006), 78.

[10] Tarnas, *Cosmos and Psyche,* 18.

[11] Ibid., see chapter 2, "Synchronicity and Its Implication," for a fuller discussion.

[12] Ibid., 55.

[13] Ibid., 23.

[14] Ken Wilber, *Sex, Ecology, Spirituality: The Spirit of Evolution* (Boston: Shambhala, 1995), 382.

[15] This tendency to identify mind with the brain is widespread. But consciousness research is clear that the brain is the physical organ associated with consciousness, not the cause of consciousness. The brain is a highly evolved medium of consciousness, but is not to be confused with consciousness itself. In other words, consciousness doesn't come out of a brain; rather, the brain is a vehicle for a pre-existing consciousness.

[16] Wilber, *Integral Psychology,* 162–163.

[17] From Tarnas, *Cosmos and Pyche,* 34.

[18] Ibid., 23.

[19] Ibid., 24.

[20] Susan Sachs, "An Ursine Battle Brews in the Pyrenees," *The Globe and Mail,* October 5, 2006, A12.

[21] Denis Edwards, *The God of Evolution* (New York: Paulist Press, 1999), 12.

**Chapter 3**

[1] For much of what follows in this chapter, I am indebted to the groundbreaking work of Brian Swimme and Thomas Berry found in *The Universe Story from the Primordial Flaring Forth to the Ecozoic Era: A Celebration of the Unfolding of the Cosmos* (San Francisco: HarperSanFrancisco, 1992).

[2] Sri Aurobindo, *The Life Divine* (Pondicherry, India: Sri Aurobindo Ashram Trust, 1990), 34.

3 Kabir, *The Enlightenment Heart: An Anthology of Secret Poetry*, Stephen Mitchell, ed., Robert Bly, trans. (New York: HarperCollins, 1989).

4 Sally McFague, *The Body of God: An Ecological Theology* (Minneapolis: Fortress Press, 1993), 159–196.

5 Aurobindo, *The Life Divine*, 10.

6 See article at www.time.com/time/time100/scientist/profile/hubble.html

7 Swimme and Berry, *The Universe Story*, 29.

8 Barbara Brown Taylor, *The Luminous Web: Essays on Science and Religion* (Cambridge: Cowley Publications, 2000), 38.

9 Swimme and Berry, *The Universe Story*, 74.

10 Ibid., 73–79.

11 Ibid., 81–111.

12 Ibid., 100.

13 Randy Boswell, "Researchers Find Remains of Our Ultimate Ancestors," *The Globe and Mail*, June 3, 2006.

14 Lynn Margulis cited in Ebert, John D., *Twilight of the Clockwork God: Conversations on Science and Spirituality at the End of an Age* (Tulsa: Council Oak Books, 1999), 68–87.

15 George Johnson, *Fire in the Mind: Science, Faith, and The Search for Order* (New York: Vintage Books, 1995), 222.

16 Susan McCaslin, "I Was Fashioned in Times Past," *Locutions* (Victoria, B.C.: Ekstasis Editions Canada Ltd, 1995), 14.

17 Pat Milton, "Art from Space Gets Sky-High Prices," *New York Times* News Service, April 13, 2006, R4.

18 See John David Ebert's interview of Brian Swimme in Ebert, *Twilight of the Clockwork God*, 30–31.

**Chapter 4**

1 Darwin's Journal, Summer 1842–1844.

2 For the content of much of this chapter, I am grateful to David Quammen and his highly readable account of Darwin's life, *The Reluctant Mr. Darwin: An Intimate Portrait of Charles Darwin and the Making of His Theory of Evolution* (New York: Atlas Books, W.W. Norton and Company, 2006).

3 Erasmus Darwin, *Zoonomia: Or the Laws of Organic Life*, 2nd American ed. (Boston: Thomas and Andrews, 1803), 392.

4 For an expanded discussion of this, see Quamman, *The Reluctant Mr. Darwin*, 224–228.

5 Brian Goodwin, *How the Leopard Changed Its Spots* (New York: Simon and Schuster, 1996), 29–30.

6 From a radio interview with Charles Birch, found at *The New Believers: Charles Birch, Scientist and Theologian*, interviewed by Rachel Kohn, Sunday, April 7, 2002, Radio National, www.abc.net.au/rn/relig/spirit/stories.

7 See article at www.ratical.org/LifeWeb/Articles/AfterDarwin.html. Also Elisabet Sahtouris, *Earth Dance: Living Systems in Evolution* (Lincoln, NE: iUniverse, 2000).

[8] Lynn Margulis, "The Real Evolution Debate," *What Is Enlightenment? Magazine*, Issue 35, January–March 2007, 91.

[9] Robert Sapolsky, "A Natural History of Peace," *Harper's Magazine*, April, 2006, 15–22.

[10] Ibid.

[11] Ibid., 72.

[12] Jablonka and Lamb cited in Bruce Lipton, *The Biology of Belief: Unleashing the Power of Consciousness, Matter, & Miracles* (Santa Rosa: Mountain of Love/Elite Books, 2005).

[13] Margulis, *What Is Enlightenment?*, 90.

[14] Swimme and Berry, *The Universe Story*, 245.

[15] Ervin Laszlo, *Evolution: The Grand Synthesis* (Boston: Shambhala Press, 1972), 9.

[16] For the most comprehensive listing of these models and the associated theorists, see Ken Wilber, *Integral Psychology: Consciousness, Spirit, Psychology, Therapy* (Boston: Shambhala Press, 2000), 197–217.

[17] Ken Wilber, *The Essential Ken Wilber: An Introductory Reader* (Boston: Shambhala, 1998), 49–54.

[18] For a succinct summary of hierarchies and holarchies, see Ken Wilber, *A Theory of Everything* (Boston: Shambhala Press, 2000), 36–42.

[19] In a speech called "Confrontation of Cosmological Theories," Krakow symposium, 1973.

[20] John F. Haught, *God after Darwin: A Theology of Evolution* (Boulder: Westview Press, 2000), 126–132.

[21] Alfred North Whitehead, *Adventures of Ideas* (New York: The Free Press, 1967), 265.

[22] Haught, *God after Darwin*, 131.

[23] Quammen, *The Reluctant Mr. Darwin*, 117–121.

## Chapter 5

[1] Marcus J. Borg, *Reading the Bible Again for the First Time* (San Francisco: HarperSanFrancisco, 2001), 40.

[2] Maurice Bridge and Darah Hansen, "Migratory Bird Nest Seen on Eagleridge Bluffs, North Vancouver," *The Vancouver Sun*, May 31, 2006.

[3] Borg, *Reading the Bible Again*.

[4] Daniel Quinn, *Ishmael: An Adventure of the Mind and Spirit* (New York: Bantam/Turner, 1995).

[5] Rod Mickleburgh, "'Fort Knox' Bear Pen No Match for Boo," *The Globe and Mail*, June 27, 2006, S1.

[6] E. O. Wilson, *The Creation: An Appeal to Save Life On Earth* (New York: W. W. Norton and Company, 2006), 5.

[7] Ibid., 75.

[8] Umarah Jamali, "India's Vanishing Tiger," *The Globe and Mail*, n.d.

[9] Terry Glavin, *Waiting for the Macaws and Other Stories from the Age of Extinctions* (Toronto: Penguin, 2006), 72.

[10] Alex Dobrota, "Fish Stocks Face Collapse within Our Lifetime," *The Globe and Mail*, November 3, 2006, A9.

[11] Peter Cheney, "Planes, Cranes, and Automobiles," *The Globe and Mail*, September 16, 2006.

[12] René Girard, *Things Hidden Since the Foundation of the World*, Stephen Bann and Michael Metteer, trans. (Stanford: Stanford University Press, 1987).

[13] For a succinct presentation of these ideas see Gil Baillie, *Violence Unveiled: Humanity at the Crossroads* (New York: Crossroad Publishing Company, 1996), 149–152.

[14] John Dominic Crossan, *Who Killed Jesus?* (San Francisco: HarperSanFrancisco, 1995), 64–65.

[15] Girard, *Things Hidden*, 234.

[16] Richard Dawkins, *The God Delusion* (Boston: Houghton Mifflin, 2006)

[17] David C. Korten, *The Great Turning: From Empire to Earth Community* (San Francisco: Berrett-Koehler, 2006).

[18] From Brian Swimme's video, *The Powers of the Universe*. See lecture on allurement. Available at www.brianswimme.org.

[19] For a complete discussion of stages and states see Ken Wilber, *Integral Psychology: Consciousness, Spirit, Psychology, Therapy* (Boston: Shambhala Presss, 2000), 196–217.

## Chapter 6

[1] Matthew Fox and Rupert Sheldrake, *Natural Grace: Dialogues on Creation, Darkness, and the Soul in Spirituality and Science* (New York: Doubleday, 1996), 53–55.

[2] John D. Crossan, *In Parables: The Challenge of the Historical Jesus*, 1st ed. (New York: Harper & Row Publishers, 1973), 265–302.

[3] James Lovelock, *The Revenge of Gaia: Why the Earth Is Fighting Back – and How We Can Still Save Humanity* (London: Allen Lane, 2006), 7.

[4] Janine M. Benyus, *Biomimicry: Innovation Inspired by Nature* (New York: HarperCollins Publishers, 1997), 18.

[5] Barbara Brown Taylor, *Leaving Church: A Memoir of Faith* (San Francisco: HarperSanFrancisco, 2006).

[6] George Monbiot, *Heat: How to Stop the Planet From Burning* (Toronto: Doubleday Canada, 2006), 20–42.

[7] "Hired Guns Aim to Confuse," *Common Ground*, August 2006, 20.

[8] Anne McIlroy, "New Underwater Bacteria Leaves Scientists Shocked," *The Globe and Mail*, August 1, 2006, A2.

[9] Norbert Rosing, *The World of the Polar Bear* (Richmond Hill, ON: Firefly Press, 2006).

[10] Benyus, *Biomimicry*, 2.

[11] Mathew Fox and Rupert Sheldrake, *The Physics of Angels: Exploring the Realm where Science and Spirit Meet* (San Francisco: HarperSanFrancisco, 1996), 101. See also Rupert Sheldrake, *The Sense of Being Stared At: And Other Unexplained Powers of the Human Mind* (New York: Crown Publishers, 2003), 275–279.

[12] William McDonough and Michael Braungart, *The Next Industrial Revolution: The Birth of the Sustainable Economy*, DVD.

[13] Neil Douglas-Klotz, trans., *Prayers of the Cosmos: Meditations on the Aramaic Words of Jesus* (San Francisco, Harper & Row Publishers, 1990).

[14] Ibid., 35.

## Chapter 7

1. Elizabeth A. Johnson, *She Who Is: The Mystery of God in Feminist Theological Discourse* (New York: The Crossroad Publishing Company, 1992).

2. Andrew Harvey, trans., *Light upon Light: Inspirations from Rumi* (New York: Jeremy P. Tarcher/Penguin, 1996), 131.

3. I am indebted to Ken Wilber for this insight.

4. It should be noted that Jesus' own habit of addressing God as Abba, best translated as "Daddy," can be understood as an intentional attempt to subvert the dominant tradition of Yahweh. Jesus was in no way free to choose a feminine image, but he did the next best thing.

5. Johnson, *She Who Is*, 92–93.

6. C. Larcher, *Le livre de la sagesse* (Paris: J. Gabalda, 1969), 402–414.

7. Elisabeth Schüssler Fiorenza, *In Memory of Her: A Feminist Theological Reconstruction of Christian Origins* (New York: The Crossroad Publishing Company, 1983), 133.

8. Johnson, *She Who Is*.

9. Ibid., 87.

10. Martin Hengel, *Judaism and Hellenism: Studies in the Encounter in Palestine during the Early Hellenistic Period*, John Bowden, trans. (London: SCM Press, 1974), 157–162.

11. Schüssler Fiorenza, *In Memory of Her*, 189.

12. James D. G. Dunn, *Christology in the Making: A New Testament Inquiry into the Origins of the Doctrine of the Incarnation*, 2nd ed. (Grand Rapids: W. B. Eerdmans Publishing, 1996), 195.

13. M. Jack Suggs, *Wisdom, Christology, and Law in Matthew's Gospel* (Cambridge: Harvard University Press, 1970), 58.

14. Raymond Brown, *The Gospel According to John 1-12* (Garden City, N.Y.: Doubleday, 1966), cxxv.

15. Quote by Johnson, *She Who Is*, 97, who in turn references Richard Baer, *Philo's Use of the Categories of Male and Female* (Leiden: Brill, 1970).

16. Johnson, *She Who Is*, 127.

17. Carol Gilligan, *In a Different Voice: Psychological Theory and Women's Development* (Cambridge: Harvard University Press, 1982).

18. Ervin Laszlo, *Science and the Akashic Field: An Integral Theory of Everything* (Rochester, VT: Inner Traditions, 2004), 24–27.

19. Fritjof Capra, *The Turning Point: Science, Society, and the Rising Culture* (New York: Bantam Books, 1983), 91.

20. Margaret Wheatley, *Leadership and the New Science: Discovering Order in a Chaotic World* (San Francisco: Berrett-Koehler Publishers, 1999), 35.

21. John R. Gribben, *In Search of Schrödinger's Cat: Quantum Physics and Reality* (New York: Bantam Books, 1984), 5.

22. Ibid., 169–174.

[23] Ilya Prigogine and Isabelle Stengers, *Order Out of Chaos* (New York: Bantam, 1984), 293, and Margaret Wheatley, *Leadership*, 65.

[24] Joyce Medina, *Cezanne and Modernism: The Poetics of Painting* (Albany: State University of New York Press, 1995).

[25] Mathew Fox and Rupert Sheldrake, *The Physics of Angels: Exploring the Realm where Science and Spirit Meet* (San Francisco: HarperSanFrancisco, 1996), 105–107.

[26] See http://www.ahisee.com/content/epressay.html

[27] Laszlo, *Science and the Akashic Field*, 33–34, 46, 72, 82.

[28] Wheatley, *Leadership*, 45.

[29] Rupert Sheldrake, *The Sense of Being Stared At: And Other Unexplained Powers of the Human Mind* (New York: Crown Publishers, 2003), 80–81, 83–88.

[30] Ibid., 16, 275, 276, 278, 280.

[31] Fox and Sheldrake, *The Physics of Angels*, 42–43.

[32] Laszlo, *Science and the Akashic Field*, 65–69.

[33] Ibid., 57–105.

[34] James Gleick, *Making a New Science* (New York: Viking, 1987), 131.

[35] Wheatley, *Leadership*, 118.

[36] Theodore Roszak, *The Voice of the Earth: An Exploration of Ecopsychology* (New York: Simon & Schuster, 1992).

[37] John F. Haught, *God after Darwin: A Theology of Evolution* (Boulder, Colorado: Westview Press, 2000), 77–80.

[38] *Tao: A New Way of Thinking – A Translation of the Tao Te Ching*, Chang Chung-yuan, trans. (New York: Harper & Row, 1975), ch 11, 35.

[39] See front page headline, *The Vancouver Sun*, November 11, 2006.

## Chapter 8

[1] Mary Jo Leddy, *Radical Gratitude* (Maryknoll: Orbis Books, 2002), 14–36.

[2] David C. Korten, *The Great Turning: From Empire to Earth Community* (San Francisco: Berrett-Koehler, 2006), 237–250.

[3] See Joanna Macy and Molly Young Brown, *Coming Back to Life: Practice to Reconnect Our Lives, Our Worlds* (Gabriola Island, B.C. and Stony Creek, CN: New Society Publishers, 1998), 34.

[4] Maureen Jack-Lacroix is the founder and director of Earth Revival, a multi-faith movement dedicated to the healing of the planet, by acting as a catalyst toward a revolution in human consciousness, based in our radical interconnectedness.

[5] Matthew Fox bases his sacred liturgy in four ancient movements: *Positiva, Negativa, Creativa and Transformativa*. As far as I know, he is the originator of these terms.

[6] John Dominic Crossan, *In Parables: The Challenge of the Historical Jesus* (New York: Harper & Row, 1973).

[7] John Dominic Crossan, *The Historical Jesus: The Life of a Mediterranean Jewish Peasant* (San Francisco: HarperCollins, 1992), 340–343.

[8] Will Braun, "High Efficiency Worship," *Geez Magazine* (Summer 2006), 41.

[9] Martin Mittelstaedt, "Why It's Peak Time to Hit the Brakes," *The Globe and Mail*, January 27, 2007, A6.

[10] Mitchell Anderson, "Trust Us, We're the Media," *Georgia Straight*, January 25, 2007.

## Epilogue

[1] John Vaillant *The Golden Spruce: A True Story of Myth, Madness, and Greed* (Toronto: Alfred A. Knopf, 2005).

[2] Ibid., 236.

[3] Peter Fimrite, "Peta Honors Rescuers of Whale Trapped in Crab Pot Lines," *San Francisco Chronicle*, February 1, 2006.

# BIBLIOGRAPHY

Aurobindo, Sri. *The Life Divine*. Pondicherry, India: Sri Aurobindo Ashram Trust, 1990.

Benyus, Janine M. *Biomimicry: Innovation Inspired by Nature*. New York: HarperCollins Publishers, 1997.

Birch, Charles, et al. *Liberating Life: Contemporary Approaches to Ecological Theology*. Maryknoll: Orbis Books, 1990.

Briggs, John, and F. David Peat. *Seven Life Lessons of Chaos: Spiritual Wisdom from the Science of Change*. New York: HarperCollins Publishers, 1999.

Borg, Marcus J. *The Heart of Christianity: Rediscovering a Life of Faith*. San Francisco: HarperSanFrancisco, 2003.

*Meeting Jesus Again for the First Time: The Historical Jesus & the Heart of Contemporary Faith*. San Francisco: HarperSanFrancisco, 1994.

*Reading the Bible Again for the First Time*. San Francisco: HarperSanFrancisco, 2001.

Brown, Raymond. *The Gospel According to John 1–12*. Garden City, N.Y.: Doubleday, 1966.

Capra, Fritjof. *The Hidden Connections: A Science for Sustainable Living*. New York: Anchor Books, 2002.

*The Turning Point: Science, Society, and the Rising Culture*. New York: Bantam Books, 1983.

Capra, Fritjof, and David Steindle-Rast, with Thomas Matas. *Belonging to the Universe: Explorations on the Frontiers of Science and Spirituality*. New York: HarperCollins Publishers, 1991.

Chung-yuan, Chang. trans. *Tao: A New Way of Thinking – A Translation of the Tao Te Ching*. New York: Harper & Row, 1975.

Crossan, John Dominic. *The Historical Jesus: The Life of a Mediterranean Jewish Peasant*. New York: HarperCollins Publishers, 1991.

*In Parables: The Challenge of the Historical Jesus*. 1st ed. New York: Harper & Row Publishers, 1973.

*Jesus: A Revolutionary Biography*. San Francisco: HarperSanFrancisco, 1994.

Crossan, John Dominic, and Jonathan L. Reed. *In Search of Paul: How Jesus' Apostle Opposed Rome's Empire with God's Kingdom*. New York: HarperCollins Publishers, 2004.

Davies, Paul. *God and the New Physics*. New York: Simon & Schuster, 1984.

Douglas-Klotz, Neil, trans. *Prayers of the Cosmos: Meditations on the Aramaic Words of Jesus*. San Francisco, Harper & Row Publishers, 1990.

Dunn, James D. G. *Christology in the Making: A New Testament Inquiry into the Origins of the Doctrine of the Incarnation, 2nd ed.* Grand Rapids: W. B. Eerdmans Publishing, 1996.

Ebert, John D. *Twilight of the Clockwork God: Conversations on Science and Spirituality at the End of an Age.* Tulsa: Council Oak Books, 1999.

Edwards, Denis. *The God of Evolution.* New York: Paulist Press, 1999.

*Jesus and the Cosmos.* Eugene: Wipf & Stock Publishers, 2004.

Fabel, Arthur, and Donald St. John, eds. *Teilhard in the 21st Century: The Emerging Spirit of Earth.* Maryknoll: Orbis Books, 2003.

Flannery, Tim. *The Weather Makers: How We Are Changing the Climate and What It Means for Life on Earth.* Toronto: HarperCollins Publishers, 2006.

Foltz, Richard C. *Worldviews, Religion, and the Environment: A Global Anthology.* Toronto: Thomson/Wadsworth Learning, 2003.

Fowler, James. W. *Weaving the New Creation: Stages of Faith and the Public Church.* Eugene: Wipf and Stock Publishers, 2001.

Fox, Matthew. *The Coming of the Cosmic Christ.* San Francisco: Harper & Row Publishers, 1988.

*Meditations with Meister Eckhart.* Rochester, VT: Bear & Company, 1983.

*Original Blessing: A Primer in Creation Spirituality.* Sante Fe: Bear and Co., 1983.

*One River, Many Wells: Wisdom Springing from Global Faiths.* New York: Jeremy P. Tarcher/Penguin, 2004.

Fox, Matthew, and Rupert Sheldrake. *Natural Grace: Dialogues on Creation, Darkness, and the Soul in Spirituality and Science.* New York: Doubleday, 1996.

*The Physics of Angels: Where Science and Spirit Meet.* San Francisco: HarperSanFrancisco, 1996.

Gilligan, Carol. *In A Different Voice: Psychological Theory and Women's Development.* Cambridge: Harvard University Press, 1982.

Girard, René. *Things Hidden Since the Foundation of the World.* Bann, Stephen, and Michael Metteer, trans. Stanford: Stanford University Press, 1987.

Glavin, Terry. *Waiting for the Macaws and Other Stories from the Age of Extinctions.* Toronto: Penguin, 2006.

Gribben, John R. *In Search of Schrödinger's Cat: Quantum Physics and Reality.* New York: Bantam Books.

Gribbin, John, and Martin Rees. *Cosmic Coincidences: Dark Matter, Mankind, and Anthropic Cosmology.* New York: Bantam Books, 1989.

Habel, Norman C. *Seven Songs of Creation: Liturgies for Celebrating and Healing Earth.* London: Sheffield Academic Press, 2004.

Habel, Norman C., and Vicky Balabanski, eds. *The Earth Story in the New Testament.* London: Sheffield Academic Press, 2002.

Habel, Norman C., and Shirley Wurst, eds. *The Earth Story in Genesis*. Sheffield: Sheffield Academic Press, 2000.

Harvey, Andrew. *Light upon Light: Inspirations from Rumi*. New York: Jeremy P. Tarcher/Penguin, 2004.

Haught, John F. *God after Darwin: A Theology of Evolution*. Boulder: Westview Press, 2000.

Hawken, Paul. *The Ecology of Commerce: A Declaration of Sustainability*. New York: HarperCollins, 1993.

Heintzman, Andrew, and Evan Solomon, eds. *Fueling the Future*. Toronto: House of Anansi Press, 2003.

Hengel, Martin. *Judaism and Hellenism: Studies in the Encounter in Palestine during the Early Hellenistic Period*, Bowden, John, trans. London: SCM Press, 1974.

Heschel, Abraham J. *The Sabbath: Its Meaning for Modern Man*. New York: Farrar, Straus and Young, 1951.

Johnson, Elizabeth A. *She Who Is: The Mystery of God in Feminist Theological Discourse*. New York: The Crossroad Publishing Company, 1992.

Knudtson, Peter, and David Suzuki. *Wisdom of the Elders: Native and Scientific Ways of Knowing about Nature*. Vancouver: Greystone Books, 1992.

Korten, David C. *The Great Turning: From Empire to Earth Community*. San Francisco: Berrett-Koehler, 2006.

Larcher, C. *Le livre de la sagesse*. Paris: J. Gabalda, 1969.

Laszlo, Ervin. *Evolution: The Grand Synthesis*. Boston: Shambhala Press, 1972.

*Science and the Akashic Field: An Integral Theory of Everything*. Rochester, VT: Inner Traditions, 2004.

*Science and the Reenchantment of the Cosmos: The Rise of the Integral Vision of Reality*. Rochester, VT: Inner Traditions, 2006.

Leddy, Mary Jo. *Radical Gratitude*. Maryknoll: Orbis Books, 2002.

Liebes, Sidney, et al. *A Walk through Time: From Stardust to Us*. New York: John Wiley & Sons, 1998.

Lipton, Bruce. *The Biology of Belief: Unleashing the Power of Consciousness, Matter, and Miracles*. Santa Rosa: Mountain of Love/Elite Books, 2005.

Lovelock, James. *The Revenge of Gaia: Why the Earth Is Fighting Back – and How We Can Still Save Humanity*. London: Allen Lane, 2006.

McFague, Sally. *The Body of God: An Ecological Theology*. Minneapolis: Fortress Press, 1993.

*Life Abundant: Rethinking Theology and Economy for a Planet in Peril*. Minneapolis: Fortress Press, 2001.

*Models of God: Theology for an Ecological, Nuclear Age*. Philadelphia: Fortress Press, 1987.

Monbiot, George. *Heat: How to Stop the Planet from Burning.* Toronto: Doubleday Canada, 2006.

Narby, Jeremy. *Intelligence in Nature: An Inquiry into Knowledge.* New York: Jeremy P. Tarcher/Penguin, 2006.

O'Murchu, Diarmuid. *Evolutionary Faith: Rediscovering God in Our Great Story.* Maryknoll: Orbis Books, 2004.

Prigogine, Ilya, and Isabelle Stengers. *Order Out of Chaos.* New York: Bantam, 1984.

Quammen, David. *The Reluctant Mr. Darwin: An Intimate Portrait of Charles Darwin and the Making of His Theory of Evolution.* New York: W. W. Norton & Company, 2006.

Quinn, Daniel. *Ishmael: An Adventure of the Mind and Spirit.* New York: Bantam/Turner, 1995.

Reagan, Michael, ed. *The Hand of God: Thoughts and Images Reflecting the Spirit of the Universe.* Philadelphia: Templeton Foundation Press, 1999.

Reese, Erik. *Lost Mountain: A Year in the Vanishing Wilderness: Radical Strip Mining and the Devastation of Appalachia.* New York: Riverhead Books, 2006.

Rosing, Norbert. *The World of the Polar Bear.* Richmond Hill, ON: Firefly Press, 2006.

Roszak, Theodore. *The Voice of the Earth: An Exploration of Ecopsychology.* New York: Simon & Schuster, 1992.

Schwartzentruber, Michael, ed. *The Emerging Christian Way: Thoughts, Stories, and Wisdom for a Faith of Transformation.* Kelowna: CopperHouse, 2006.

Senge, Peter, et al. *Presence: An Exploration of Profound Change in People, Organizations, and Society.* New York: Doubleday, 2005.

Sheldrake, Rupert. *The Sense of Being Stared At: And Other Unexplained Powers of the Human Mind.* New York: Crown Publishers, 2003.

Smith, Huston. *The Soul of Christianity: Restoring the Great Tradition.* San Francisco: HarperSanFrancisco, 2005.

Soelle, Dorothée. *The Silent Cry: Mysticism and Resistance.* Rumscheidt, Barbara and Martin, trans. Minneapolis: Fortress Press, 2001.

Suggs, M. Jack. *Wisdom, Christology, and Law in Matthew's Gospel.* Cambridge: Harvard University Press, 1970.

Suzuki, David. *Inventing the Future: Reflections on Science, Technology and Nature.* Toronto: Stoddart, 1989.

Suzuki, David, and Holly Dressel. *Good News for a Change: How Everyday People Are Helping the Planet.* Vancouver: Greystone Books, 2003.

Swimme, Brian. *The Hidden Heart of the Cosmos: Humanity and the New Story.* Maryknoll: Orbis Books, 1996. *The Universe Is a Green Dragon: A Cosmic Creation Story.* Santa Fe: Bear & Company, 1984.

**Swimme, Brian, and Thomas Berry.** *The Universe Story from the Primordial Flaring Forth to the Ecozoic Era: A Celebration of the Unfolding of the Cosmos.* San Francisco: HarperSanFrancisco, 1992.

**Tarnas, Richard.** *Cosmos and Psyche: Intimations of a New World View.* New York: Viking, 2006.

*The Passion of the Western Mind: Understanding the Ideas That Have Shaped Our World View.* New York: Ballantine Books, 1991.

**Taylor, Barbara Brown.** *Leaving Church: A Memoir of Faith.* San Francisco: HarperSanFrancisco, 2006.

*The Luminous Web: Essays on Science and Religion.* Cambridge: Cowley Publications, 2000.

**Teilhard de Chardin, Pierre.** *Le Milieu Divin: An Essay on the Interior Life.* London: Collins, 1960.

**Tucker, Mary Evelyn, and John A. Grim, eds.** *Worldviews and Ecology: Religion, Philosophy, and the Environment.* Maryknoll: Orbis Books, 1994.

**Vaillant, John.** *The Golden Spruce: A True Story of Myth, Madness and Greed.* Toronto: Alfred A. Knopf Canada, 2005.

**Wheatley, Margaret J.** *Leadership and the New Science: Discovering Order in a Chaotic World.* 2nd ed. San Francisco: Berrett-Koehler Publishers, 1999.

**Wilber, Ken.** *The Essential Ken Wilber: An Introductory Reader.* Boston: Shambhala, 1998.

*Integral Psychology: Consciousness, Spirit, Psychology, Therapy.* Boston: Shambhala, 2000.

*Sex, Ecology, Spirituality: The Spirit of Evolution.* Boston: Shambhala, 1995.

*A Sociable God: Toward a New Understanding of Religion.* Boston: Shambhala, 2005.

*A Theory of Everything: An Integral Vision for Business, Politics, Science and Spirituality.* Boston: Shambala, 2001.

ed. *Quantum Questions: Mystical Writings of the World's Greatest Physicists.* Boston: Shambhala, 2001.

**Wilson, E. O.** *Creation: An Appeal To Save Life on Earth.* New York: W. W. Norton and Co., 2006.

# INDEX

# C

# D

## M

## N

## O

## P